LIBRARY
SOUTH BEND CAMPUS
INDIANA UNIVERSITY

THE DOCTRINES OF THE
GREAT EDUCATORS

By the same author

*

AN OUTLINE OF EXPERIMENTAL EDUCATION

THE DOCTRINES
OF THE
GREAT EDUCATORS

BY

ROBERT R. RUSK

REVISED AND ENLARGED
THIRD EDITION

MACMILLAN
Melbourne · London · Toronto

ST MARTIN'S PRESS
New York
1965

Copyright © R. R. Rusk 1965

—

First Edition *1918*
Reprinted *1922, 1924, 1926, 1930, 1937, 1941, 1948, 1952*
Second Edition *June 1954*
Reprinted *1955, 1956, 1957, 1962*
Third Edition *1965*

LA 13
R85
1965
COPY 2

MACMILLAN AND COMPANY LIMITED
Little Essex Street London WC2
also Bombay Calcutta Madras Melbourne

THE MACMILLAN COMPANY OF CANADA LIMITED
70 Bond Street Toronto 2

ST MARTIN'S PRESS INC
175 Fifth Avenue New York 10010 NY

INDIANA
UNIVERSITY
LIBRARY

SOUTH BEND

PRINTED IN GREAT BRITAIN

CONTENTS

CONTENTS

v

PREFACE

A HISTORY OF EDUCATION should explain how educational doctrines are related to the intellectual and social tendencies of the times in which they originated, should expound these doctrines and should indicate how they affect educational practice. This work does not profess to be a history of education; it confines itself to an exposition of the doctrines of a limited number of representative educators. The chapters are designed to give readers a general idea of the doctrines of the great educators without recourse to the works of the original authors.

For the present edition some chapters have been almost entirely reconstructed, the references throughout have been brought more up to date, and an effort has been made to increase the readability of the work.

CHAPTER I

PLATO [1]

IT is to Greek thought that we first turn when we wish to consider any of the problems of ethics, education or politics, for in Greece we find the beginnings of Western culture. Although every day is disclosing that the Mycenaean, Minoan and Egyptian civilisations have all contributed to Greek development, yet the boast of Plato was not an empty one that whatever the Greeks acquired from foreigners they subsequently developed into something nobler.[2]

Greek thought has, in addition to its originality, a surprising universality, not a mere municipal fitness. The principles of logic, ethics and politics which Plato and Aristotle enunciated are generally regarded as universally valid; the writings of the Greek poets are still read; the Greek tragedies are acted before modern audiences; and the surviving works of Greek art are appreciated by the untutored.

Greek thought has likewise a simplicity which enables us to image the problems involved more easily than under modern complex conditions. It is accordingly both

[1] Born about May in the year 427 B.C., died in 347 B.C. See R. S. Bluck, *Plato's Life and Thought* (London: Routledge & Kegan Paul, 1949). Or A. E. Taylor, *Plato: The Man and his Work* (London: Methuen: University Paperbacks, 1960).

[2] *The Epinomis of Plato*, translated by J. Harward (Oxford University Press, 1928), § 487. On the assumption that the *Epinomis* can be ascribed to Plato, see A. E. Taylor, *Plato*, pp. 497–8.

All the succeeding quotations from Plato's writings are from Jowett's translation (Oxford University Press, 1875), and the references are to the marginal page numbers of that work.

natural and necessary to begin our study of the doctrines
of the great educators with a consideration of the Greek
thinkers.[1]

About the fourth or the third century before the
Christian era, at a time of intellectual unrest in Greece, a
new school of teaching came into being. The enlargement
of the intellectual horizon resulting from the unrest that
ensued demanded a class of men who could impart quickly
every kind of knowledge; and to satisfy this demand all
sorts and conditions were pressed into the service of education and classed under the general title 'Sophist'. 'Is
not a sophist one who deals wholesale or retail in the food
of the soul?' it is asked in the *Protagoras*.[2] Fencing
masters like Euthydemus and his brother Dionysodorus,[3]
Prodicus with his stock of philological subtleties,[4] and
Protagoras 'the wisest of all living men'[5] declared themselves 'the only professors of moral improvement'.[6]

The teaching of the sophists was unsystematic; it was
also limited to the few who could pay for it,[7] and we find

---

[1] For Greek education see Werner Jaeger, *Paideia: The Ideals of Greek
Culture*, translated by G. Highet (Oxford: Basil Blackwell, vol. i, 1939;
ii, 1944; iii, 1945). H. I. Marrou, *A History of Education in Antiquity*,
translated by G. Lamb (London: Sheed & Ward, 1956). W. Barclay,
Educational Ideals in the Ancient World (London: Collins, 1959).

[2] § 313.

[3] Plato's testimonial to them reads as follows (*Euthydemus*, § 282). 'They
are capital at fighting in armour, and will teach the art to anyone who
pays them; and also they are most skilful in legal warfare; they will
plead themselves and teach others to speak and to compose speeches which
will have an effect upon the courts. And this was only the beginning of
their wisdom, but they have carried out the pancratiastic art to the very
end, and have mastered the only mode of fighting which had been hitherto
neglected by them; and now no one dares to look at them; such is their
skill in the war of words that they can refute any proposition whether true
or false.'

[4] *Protagoras*, § 340. Cf. *Euthydemus*, § 277.

[5] *Protagoras*, § 309.   [6] *Laches*, § 186.

[7] Protagoras was the first to accept payment (*Protagoras*, § 348): 'You
proclaim in the face of Hellas that you are a Sophist or teacher of virtue
or education and are the first that demanded pay in return.'

His method of exacting payment — a form of payment by results —
was as follows (*Protagoras*, § 328): 'When a man has been my pupil, if he

Socrates, for example, saying : 'As for myself, I am the first to confess that I have never had a teacher ; although I have always from my earliest youth desired to have one. But I am too poor to give money to the sophists, who are the only professors of moral improvement.'[1] The fact that they accepted payment for their services created a certain prejudice against the sophists, for this enabled those who could afford their instruction to acquire a definite superiority over their fellow-citizens. The popular attitude towards them may be inferred from the violent outburst of indignation with which Anytus received the suggestion of Socrates that Meno should go to the sophists for his education. 'The young men', says Anytus,[2] 'who gave their money to them [the sophists] were out of their minds, and their relations and guardians who entrusted them to their care were still more out of their minds, and most of all the cities who allowed them to come in and did not drive them out, citizen or stranger alike. . . . Neither I nor any of my belongings has ever had, nor would I suffer them to have, anything to do with them.'

The prejudice against the sophists was intensified by the fact that they degraded knowledge by making its aim direct utility. Education was with the Greeks a training for leisure, not for a livelihood. In the *Protagoras*,[3] for example, it is asked : 'Why may you not learn of him in the same way that you learned the arts of the grammarian or musician or trainer, not with the view of making any of them a profession, but only as a part of education and because a private gentleman ought to know them?'

likes he pays my price, but there is no compulsion ; and if he does not like, he has only to go into a temple and take an oath of the value of the instructions, and he pays no more than he declares to be their value.'

The result was, as reported by Socrates in the *Meno*, § 91 : 'I know of a single man, Protagoras, who made more out of his craft than the illustrious Pheidias, who created such noble works, or any ten other statuaries.'

The sophists have been designated the founders of educational science : W. Jaeger, *Paideia*, vol. i, p. 295.

[1] *Laches*, § 186.   [2] *Meno*, § 92.   [3] § 312.

Socrates recognised the unscientific nature of the methods of the sophists, and his own method, although superficially resembling theirs, was essentially systematic and founded on general principles.[1] 'There are', according to Aristotle,[2] 'two things which we may fairly attribute to Socrates, his inductive discourses and his universal definitions.' Inductive reasoning was his method of arriving at a definition. The result attained by his method could not in many instances be regarded as satisfying the requirements of scientific exactness, but this did not disturb Socrates, for he himself continually and emphatically disclaimed the possession of any knowledge, except perhaps the knowledge of his own limitations. 'He knows nothing', the intoxicated Alcibiades says of him in the *Symposium*,[3] 'and is ignorant of all things — such is the appearance which he puts on.' Although not possessing knowledge himself, Socrates claimed to have the gift of discerning its presence in others, and of having the power to assist them to bring it to light.[4]

His first task was to arouse men from that false self-satisfaction which was by him believed to be the cause of their misery, and to lead them to self-examination and self-criticism. 'Herein', he says,[5] 'is the evil of ignorance, that he who is neither good nor wise is nevertheless satisfied with himself: he has no desire for that of which he feels no want.' The mission which Socrates conceived himself as charged to fulfil was to make men feel this want, to teach others what the utterance of the Delphic oracle had taught him — his own ignorance; to imbue them with a divine discontent; to make them feel, as Alcibiades puts it,[6] 'the serpent's sting', 'the pang of

---

[1] See A. E. Taylor, *Socrates* (London: Peter Davies, 1933), and R. W. Livingstone, *Portrait of Socrates* (Oxford University Press, 1938).

[2] *Metaphysics*, § 1078, b.   [3] § 216.

[4] Cf. metaphor of midwife in *Theaetetus*, § 150; also *Symposium*, § 209. Cf. W. Jaeger, vol. ii, p. 27: ' He [Socrates] is the greatest teacher in European history.'   [5] *Symposium*, § 204.   [6] Ibid., § 217.

philosophy'. And in his defence Socrates neither disowned his mission nor his method: 'I am that gadfly', he tells his judges,[1] 'which God has attached to the state, and all day long and in all places am always fastening upon you, arousing and persuading and reproaching you.'

A characteristic of the method of Socrates was the necessity for having a companion in the pursuit of truth. Anyone sufficed for this purpose, and Socrates had many devices for luring men into this search, though not infrequently they were unwilling companions who soon discovered that for the onlookers 'there is amusement in it'.[2] In the *Protagoras* Socrates is represented as saying: 'When anyone apprehends alone, he immediately goes about and searches for someone to whom he may communicate it and with whom he may establish it.'[3] The principle implied is that if one other can be convinced, then all others can likewise be persuaded, and consequently the belief in question is universally valid. Carlyle expresses the same idea when he cites the statement: 'It is certain my conviction gains infinitely, the moment another soul will believe in it.' The dialogue is thus a necessary and essential feature of the method of Socrates.

In the Socratic discourses three stages can generally be distinguished; first, the stage called by Plato 'opinion', in which the individual is unable to give valid reasons for his knowledge or assumed knowledge; second, the destructive or analytic stage, in which the individual is brought to realise that he does not know what he assumed he knew, and which leads to contradiction and a mental condition of doubt or perplexity; third, a synthetic stage for the results of which Plato would reserve the term 'knowledge'. When this last stage is attained, the

---

[1] *Apology*, § 31.   [2] Ibid., § 33.   [3] § 348.

individual's experience is critically reconstructed and he can justify his beliefs by giving the reasons for them.[1]

The possibility of applying a method similar to that of Socrates in the teaching of school pupils has frequently been questioned and sometimes even denied. Pestalozzi is probably the most vigorous opponent of what he terms 'Socratizing'. In one passage[2] he says: 'Socratizing is essentially impossible for children, since they want both a background of preliminary knowledge and the outward means of expression — language.' If, however, the teacher adequately recognises the limits of his pupils' experience and adapts his terminology to their vocabulary, the method can be applied quite successfully.[3]

Education was a subject to which Plato attached the greatest importance.[4] In the *Republic*[5] he reckons it with war, the conduct of campaigns and the administration of states as amongst 'the grandest and most beautiful' subjects, and in the *Laws*[6] he repeats that it is 'the first and fairest thing that the best of men can ever have'. In the *Laches*,[7] which is professedly a treatise on education, he asks: 'Is this a slight thing about which you and Lysimachus are deliberating? Are you not risking the greatest of your possessions? For children are your riches; and upon their turning out well or ill depends the whole order of their father's house.' Again in the *Crito*[8] he says: 'No man should bring children into the world who is unwilling to persevere to the end in their nurture and education.' The extent and elaborateness of

[1] Cf. *Theaetetus*, § 201 : 'Knowledge is true opinion accompanied by a reason.'

[2] *How Gertrude teaches her Children*, English translation (London : Swan Sonnenschein & Co., 1907), p. 46. Cf. p. 57.

[3] Cf. for successful examples, J. Adams, *Primer on Teaching* (Edinburgh : T. & T. Clark, 1903), pp. 90–108 ; also *Exposition and Illustration* (London : Macmillan & Co., 1909), pp. 80–82.

[4] See R. C. Lodge, *Plato's Theory of Education* (London : Routledge & Kegan Paul, 1947).

[5] § 599.   [6] § 644.   [7] § 185.   [8] § 45.

the treatment of education in the *Republic* and in the
Laws likewise testify to the importance of the subject in
Plato's mind.

The difficulties which arose from the educational
methods of the sophists deeply perplexed Plato. His early
dialogues everywhere bear the mark of this perplexity, a
perplexity which, it seems, was common to the foremost
minds of Greece at that time. The *Laches* records the
concern of Lysimachus and Melesius as to the education
of their children and their eagerness to accept guidance
from any quarter; the *Euthydemus* ends with an appeal to
Socrates by Crito concerning the education of Critobulus,
his son.

The type of education which was then current in Greece
we can gather from several references in the dialogues. In
the *Crito*[1] it is asked : 'Were not the laws which have the
charge of education right in commanding your father to
train you in music and gymnastic?' and the answer of
Socrates is : 'Right, I should reply'. In the *Protagoras*[2]
it is stated : 'I am of opinion that skill in poetry was the
principal part in education and this I conceive to be the
power of knowing what compositions of the poets are
correct, and what are not, and how they are to be distinguished and of explaining, when asked, the reason of
the difference.' In the *Timaeus*[3] there is a reference
which gives us an interesting side-light on ancient Greek
education. Critias there says : 'Now the day was that
day of the Apaturia which is called the registration of
youth, at which, according to custom, our parents gave
prizes for recitations, and the poems of several poets were
recited by us boys, and many of us sang the poems of
Solon, which at that time had not gone out of fashion.'

An idealised education of a Greek youth is sketched in
the *Protagoras* :[4] 'Education and admonition commence
in the first years of childhood, and last to the very end of

[1] § 50.   [2] § 339.   [3] § 21.   [4] §§ 325–6.

life. Mother and nurse and father and tutor are quarrel-ling about the improvement of the child as soon as ever he is able to understand them; he cannot say or do anything without their setting forth to him that this is just and that is unjust; this is honourable, that is dis-honourable; this is holy, that is unholy; do this and abstain from that. And if he obeys, well and good; if not, he is straightened by threats and blows, like a piece of warped wood. At a later stage they send him to teachers, and enjoin them to see to his manners even more than to his reading and music; and the teachers do as they are desired. And when the boy has learned his letters and is beginning to understand what is written, as before he understood only what was spoken, they put into his hands the works of great poets, which he reads at school; in these are contained many admonitions, and many tales and praises, and encomia of ancient famous men, which he is required to learn by heart, in order that he may imitate or emulate them and desire to become like them. Then, again, the teachers of the lyre take similar care that their young disciple is temperate and gets into no mischief; and when they have taught him the use of the lyre, they introduce him to the poems of other excellent poets, who are the lyric poets; and these they set to music, and make their harmonies and rhythms quite familiar to the children's souls, in order that they may learn to be more gentle and harmonious, and rhythmical, and so more fitted for speech and action; for the life of man in every part has need of harmony and rhythm. Then they send them to the master of gymnastic, in order that their bodies may better minister to the virtuous mind, and that they may not be compelled through bodily weakness to play the coward in war or any other occasion. This is what is done by those who have the means, and those who have the means are the rich; their children begin education soonest and leave off

latest. When they have done with masters, the state
again compels them to learn the laws, and live after the
pattern which they furnish, and not after their own fancies ;
and just as in learning to write, the writing-master first
draws lines with a style for the use of the young beginner,
and gives him the tablet and makes him follow the lines,
so the city draws the laws, which were the invention of
good law-givers who were of old time ; these are given
to a young man, in order to guide him in his conduct
whether as ruler or ruled ; and he who transgresses them
is to be corrected, or, in other words, called to account,
which is a term used not only in your country, but also
in many others.'[1]

Xenophon's *The Economist*[2] furnishes the complementary
education of the Greek maiden. 'Ah, Ischomachus, that
is just what I [Socrates] should like particularly to learn
from you. Did you yourself educate your wife to be all
that a wife should be, or when you received her from
her father and mother was she already a proficient well
skilled to discharge the duties appropriate to a wife? Well
skilled ! (he replied). What proficiency was she likely to
bring with her, when she was not quite fifteen at the time
she wedded me, and during the whole prior period of her
life had been most carefully brought up to see and hear
as little as possible, and to ask the fewest questions? Or
do you not think one should be satisfied, if at marriage
her whole experience consisted in knowing how to take
the wool and make a dress, and seeing how her mother's
handmaidens had their daily spinning-tasks assigned
them? For (he added) as regards control of appetite and
self-indulgence [in reference to culinary matters], she had
received the soundest education, and that I take to be

[1] For a reconstruction of Plato's own upbringing see Graham Wallas,
The Art of Thought (London : Jonathan Cape, 1926), p. 230.
[2] *The Works of Xenophon*, translated by H. G. Dakyns (London : Macmillan & Co., 1897), vol. iii, pt I, pp. 226–7 and note. See also W. Jaeger,
Paideia, vol. iii, pp. 175–7.

the most important matter in the bringing up of man or woman.'

It is in the *Republic*, however, that Plato's chief treatment of education is to be found.[1] Rousseau has said :[2] 'If you wish to know what is meant by public education, read Plato's *Republic*. Those who merely judge books by their titles take this for a treatise on Politics, but it is the finest treatise on Education ever written.' Edward Caird has likewise affirmed of the *Republic* that 'perhaps it might best be described as a treatise on Education, regarded as the one great business of life from the beginning to the end of it'.[3]

The *Republic* is professedly an inquiry into the nature of justice, that is, morality or righteousness.[4] But justice is essentially a social virtue ;[5] consequently to determine the nature of justice Plato is driven to construct in thought an ideal state wherein he hopes to find justice 'writ large'.[6]

Because of the multiplicity of human wants and of the insufficiency of any one individual to satisfy these by his own efforts, the state, in Plato's view,[7] is necessary. It is likewise advantageous, since by reason of the diversity in the natural endowment of the individuals constituting the state the greatest efficiency can only be attained by

[1] W. Boyd, *Plato's Republic for Today* (London : Heinemann, 1962).

[2] *Émile* (Everyman edition), p. 8.

[3] *Evolution of Theology in the Greek Philosophers* (Glasgow : J. MacLehose & Sons, 1904), i. 140.

[4] Cf. W. Jaeger, *Paideia*, vol. i, pp. 102–4. 'All virtues are summed up in righteousness.' Also ii, p. 202.

[5] Cf. Aristotle, *Politics*, iii. 13 : 'Justice has been acknowledged by us to be a social virtue.'

[6] Cf. Rousseau, *Émile*, p. 202 : 'It is true . . . that we have a very imperfect knowledge of the human heart if we do not also examine it in crowds ; but it is none the less true that to judge of men we must study the individual man, and that he who had a perfect knowledge of the inclinations of each individual might foresee all their combined effects in the body of the nation.' Also Jaeger, vol. ii, p. 366 : 'He [Plato] is founding politics upon ethics. . . . For Plato the perfect state is only the ideal frame of a good life.'   [7] *Republic*, § 369.

the application of the principle of the division of labour
and by co-operative effort.[1]   These two principles are
implied in the oft-quoted statement of Aristotle :[2] 'The
state comes into existence originating in the bare needs
of life, and continuing in existence for the sake of a good
life.'

The application of the principle of the division of
labour results in the separation of the citizens of the state
into two classes — the industrial or artisan and the
guardian class, the duty of the former being to provide
the necessaries of life,[3] the duty of the latter being to
enlarge the boundaries of the state[4] — a proceeding
which involves war — that luxuries may be available for
the citizens and the state be something more than 'a
community of swine'.[5]   The guardian class Plato further
subdivides into the military and governing classes, representing respectively the executive and deliberative
function of government.

After the division of the citizens into the three classes —
the industrial, the military and the ruling — has been
established, the state assumes the nature of a permanent
structure, and this has caused Plato's constitution to be
designated 'a system of caste'.[6]   To give sanction to the
divisions in the state thus constituted Plato would bring
into play 'a seasonable falsehood', and the myth which
he suggests is as follows : he would tell the people[7] —
'You are brothers, yet God has framed you differently.
Some of you have the power of command, and in the
composition of these he has mingled gold, wherefore also
they have the greatest honour; others he has made of
silver, to be auxiliaries; others again who are to be

---

[1] Note that Plato presupposes an initial inequality.   Cf. Aristotle,
Politics, ii : 'Similars do not constitute a state.'
[2] *Politics*, i. 2.   [3] *Republic*, §§ 369–72.   [4] Ibid., § 373.
[5] § 372.
[6] Lewis Campbell, *Plato's Republic* (London : John Murray, 1902), p. 54.
[7] *Republic*, § 415.

husbandmen and craftsmen he has composed of brass and iron.' The barriers between the classes are not, however, absolute, nor is the hereditary principle in legislation regarded as infallible, for Plato immediately adds : 'But as all are of the same original stock, a golden parent will sometimes have a silver son, or a silver parent a golden son. And God proclaims as a first principle to the rulers, and above all else, that there is nothing which they should so anxiously guard, or of which they are to be such good guardians, as of the purity of the race. They should observe what elements mingle in their off-spring ; for if the son of a golden or silver parent has an admixture of brass and iron, then nature orders a trans-position of ranks, and the eye of the ruler must not be pitiful towards the child because he has to descend in the scale and become a husbandman or artisan, just as there may be sons of artisans who having an admixture of gold or silver in them are raised to honour, and become guardians or auxiliaries. For an oracle says that when a man of brass or iron guards the state, it will be destroyed.'[1]

For each of the three classes of the community — the producing, the military and the governing — Plato ought to have provided, we should imagine, an appropriate form of training ; but although the education of the soldier and that of the ruler or philosopher are treated at considerable length, no mention is made in the *Republic* of the education of the industrial class.[2] The education of the members of this class, had Plato dealt with it, would doubtless have been of a strictly vocational nature, not, however, a state scheme of vocational training but something resembling rather 'the constitution of apprenticeship as it once existed in Modern Europe'.[3] There would be no specific

[1] *Republic*, § 423.
[2] Cf. Aristotle, *Politics*, ii. 5, 23 : 'What will be the education, form of government, laws of the lower class Socrates has nowher determined.' Cf., however, *Republic*, § 467.
[3] Lewis Campbell, *Plato's Republic*, p. 65.

training in citizenship, for these members of the community have no voice in the government of the state;
their characteristic virtue is obedience, technically 'temperance' — to know their place and to keep it.[1]

The fact that this large element in the community is
denied the benefits and privileges of citizenship, the communistic scheme being confined to the guardian class,
must be regarded as a serious defect in Plato's ideal state.
It has been attributed to Plato's aristocratic prejudices,
and to the Greek contempt for the mechanical arts.[1]
Aristotle regards the artisans as of even less account than
the slaves, and maintains[2] that they can only attain excellence as they become slaves, that is, come under the
direction of a master. If, however, the constitution is to
be stable, or be 'a unity', as Plato phrased it, all must
share in the government.[3] Contrasting the Greek with the
modern ideal of virtue, T. H. Green says :[4] 'It is not the
sense of duty to a neighbour, but the practical answer to
the question Who is my neighbour? that has varied.' This
explains the defect in Plato's scheme, and helps us to
appreciate the increased difficulty of our present-day
ethical, social and educational problems.

Plato's first treatment of education,[5] the training of
the guardians including the military and ruling classes, is
a general education governed mainly by the principle of
imitation. Its two main divisions are the current forms
of Greek education, namely, music[6] and gymnastic, but
as Plato again warns us :[7] 'Neither are the two arts of

---

[1] Ibid., p. 54. Plato refers to the workers as 'those whose natural talents
were defective from the first, and whose souls have since been so grievously
marred and enervated by their life of drudgery as their bodies have been
disfigured by their crafts and trades'. *Republic*, § 495.

[2] *Politics*, i. 3.

[3] Cf. *Protagoras*, § 322 : 'For cities cannot exist, if a few only share in the
virtues as in the arts.' Also Aristotle, *Politics*, iii. 15, and ii. 2.

[4] *Prolegomena to Ethics* (Oxford University Press, 1899), § 207.

[5] *Republic*, §§ 376–412.

[6] Almost equivalent to the term Arts in a university curriculum.

[7] *Republic*, § 410. Cf. passage from *Protagoras* quoted above.

music and gymnastic really designed, as is often supposed, the one for the training of the soul, the other for
the training of the body. I believe that the teachers
of both have in view chiefly the improvement of the
soul.'

Remembering this, and likewise mindful of Plato's
general idealistic position, we are not surprised when at
the outset of his treatment of education he asserts that we
should begin education with music and proceed thereafter
to gymnastic;[1] mental is thus to precede physical education. The mothers and nurses are to tell their children
the authorised tales only: 'Let them fashion the mind
with such tales, even more fondly than they mould the
body with their hands.'

Education for Plato cannot begin too early; he
recognises the importance of first impressions. 'The
beginning', he says,[2] 'is the most important part of any
work, especially in the case of a young and tender thing.'
Consequently consideration of the tales to be told to
infants he does not assume to be beneath the dignity of a
philosopher.[3]

Music includes narratives, and these are of two kinds,
the true and the fictitious.[4] Somewhat paradoxically
Plato maintains that the young should be trained in both,
and that we should begin with the false; fables, he implies,
are best suited to the child mind. He thus recognises the
truth of art as well as the truth of fact. But not all fables
should, according to Plato,[5] be taught, 'for a young person
cannot judge what is allegorical and what is literal; anything that he receives into his mind at that age is likely to
become indelible and unalterable; and therefore it is

---

[1] *Republic*, § 376: Cf. and contrast Aristotle, *Politics*, vii. 15. 'The care
of the body ought to precede that of the soul, and the training of the
appetitive part should follow: none the less the care of it must be for the
sake of the reason, and our care of the body for the sake of the soul.'

[2] *Republic*, § 377.   [3] Cf. Aristotle, *Politics*, vii, 17.

[4] *Republic*, § 376.   [5] Ibid., § 378.

most important that the tales which the young first hear should be models of virtuous thoughts.'

Here we have formulated Plato's guiding principle — that nothing must be admitted in education which does not conduce to the promotion of virtue. For 'true and false' he substitutes the standard 'good and evil'. Plato declines to take upon himself the task of composing fables suitable for children, but using as a criterion the principle just enunciated, he assumes a moral censorship over the tales then current. 'The narrative of Hephaestus binding Hera his mother, and how on another occasion Zeus sent him flying for taking her part when she was being beaten, and all the battles of the gods in Homer — these tales must not be admitted into our state, whether they are supposed to have an allegorical meaning or not.'[1]

Plato proceeds to pass in review the stories about the gods and formulates the following theological canons : (1) 'God is not the author of all things, but of good only' — and the poet is not to be permitted to say that those who are punished are miserable and that God is the author of their misery.[2] (2) 'The gods are not magicians who transform themselves, neither do they deceive mankind in any way.'[3] The tales to be told to children must conform to these principles, and others are not to be told to the children from their youth upwards, if they are to honour the gods and their parents, and to value friendship.[4]

After having considered the fables dealing with the gods, Plato proceeds to consider those relating to heroes and the souls of the departed. To make the citizens free men who should fear slavery more than death, the other world must not be reviled in fables but rather commended. All weepings and wailings of heroes must be expunged from fables ; likewise all descriptions of violent laughter, for a fit of laughter which has been indulged to excess

[1] § 378. [2] § 380. [3] § 383. [4] § 386.

almost always produces a violent reaction.[1]

In the tales to be recited to children a high value is to be set upon truth; 'if anyone at all is to have the privilege of lying, the rulers of the state should be the persons; and they, in their dealings either with their enemies or with their own citizens, may be allowed to lie for the public good. But nobody else should meddle with anything of the kind.'[2] Temperance, implying obedience to commanders and self-control in sensual pleasures, is to be commended, while covetousness is to be condemned. The fables concerning heroes and others must accordingly be amended to agree with these principles.

The use is likewise to be forbidden of such language as implies that wicked men are often happy, and the good miserable; and that injustice is profitable when undetected, justice being a man's own loss and another's gain.[3]

Having thus discussed the matter of the narratives to be used in education, Plato addresses himself to a consideration of their form.[4] In compositions he distinguishes between direct speech, which he calls 'imitation', and indirect speech, which he calls 'simple narration'. 'Imitation' is only to be allowed of the speech and action of the virtuous man: the speeches of others are to be delivered and their actions described in the form of narration. The reason Plato gives is that 'imitation beginning in early youth and continuing far into life, at length grows into habits and becomes a second nature, affecting body, voice and mind'.[5]

In respect to music in its limited and modern sense, Plato maintains that all harmonies which are effeminate and convivial are to be discarded and only such retained as will make the citizens temperate and courageous. The

---

[1] *Republic*, §§ 386–8.
[2] § 389.   Cf. the international morality in More's *Utopia*.
[3] *Republic*, § 392.   [4] Ibid., §§ 392–403.   [5] § 395.

rhythm is to be determined by the nature of the words, just as the style of words is determined by the moral disposition of the soul.

So must it be with the other arts and crafts, and not only the poets, but the professors of every other craft as well must impress on their productions the image of the good.[1] Here we have the origin of the old quarrel between poetry and philosophy, or between art and morality. Plato will not entertain the idea of 'art for art's sake'; the only criterion he will recognise is the ethical.

The reason of Plato's solicitude for a good and simple environment for the children who are to be the future guardians of the state is his belief in the efficacy of unconscious assimilation or imitation in the formation of character. As evidence of this we may cite the following:[2] 'We would not have our guardians grow up amid images of moral deformity, as in some noxious pasture, and there browse and feed upon many a baneful herb and flower, day by day, little by little, until they silently gather a festering mass of corruption in their own soul. Let our artists rather be those who are gifted to discern the true nature of the beautiful and graceful; then will our youth dwell in a land of health, amid fair sights and sounds, and receive the good in everything; and beauty, the effluence of fair works, shall flow into the eye and ear, like a health-giving breeze from a purer region, and insensibly draw the soul from earliest years into likeness and sympathy with the beauty of reason.'

'And therefore', Plato continues, 'musical training is a more potent instrument than any other, because rhythm and harmony find their way into the inward places of the soul, on which they mightily fasten, imparting grace,

---

[1] § 401.

[2] § 401. Cf. Aristotle, *Politics*, vii. 17: 'All that is mean and low should be banished from their sight.' Also B. Bosanquet, *The Education of the Young in the Republic of Plato* (Cambridge University Press, 1904), p. 102, footnote.

LIBRARY
SOUTH BEND CAMPUS
INDIANA UNIVERSITY

and making the soul of him who is rightly educated graceful, or of him who is ill-educated ungraceful.' That the result of a musical education should be the production of harmony and grace in the individual is repeated in the introduction to Plato's treatment of higher education or the education of the philosopher. There,[1] he says, 'music was the counterpart of gymnastic, and trained the guardians by the influence of habit, by harmony making them harmonious, by rhythm rhythmical.' The end throughout was the Greek ideal of manhood, a life which in itself was a work of art.

Plato's treatment of gymnastic in the *Republic* is decidedly brief;[2] he contents himself with indicating no more than the general principles. 'Gymnastic as well as music should begin in early years; the training in it should be careful and should continue through life', he says, adding, however, 'Now my belief is, not that the good body by any bodily excellence improves the soul, but, on the contrary, that the good soul, by her own excellence, improves the body as far as this may be possible.'

Plato prescribes a simple moderate system such as would be productive of health and the utmost keenness of both eye and ear.[3] Of the habit of body cultivated by professional gymnasts he disapproves as unsuitable for men who have to undergo privations in war and variations in food when on a campaign. Abstinence from delicacies is also enjoined. The whole life, however, is not to be given up to gymnastics, for everyone who does nothing else ends by becoming uncivilised — 'he is like a wild beast, all violence and fierceness, and knows no other way of dealing; and he lives in all ignorance and evil conditions, and has no sense of propriety and grace'.[4]

---

[1] *Republic*, § 522. [2] Ibid., §§ 403–12.
[3] § 404. [4] § 411.

Such then is, in outline, Plato's scheme of early education with its training in music and gymnastic. The dances
which will be in vogue, the hunting and field exercises
and the sports of the gymnasium and the race-course, he
adds,[1] must correspond with the foregoing outlines.

There is one omission from this early education to
which attention ought to be directed, for the omission
is intentional on Plato's part; it is the absence of any
reference to a training in the manual arts. The reason
for the omission is incidentally disclosed by Plato in a
later section of the *Republic* :[2] 'All the useful arts were
reckoned mean.'

There are other omissions evidently unintentional. The
subjects of the higher education, Plato later recognises,
must be begun in youth, hence in dealing with the education of the ruler or philosopher we find him stating :[3]
'Calculation and geometry and all the other elements of
instruction, which are a preparation for dialectic, should
be presented to the mind in childhood; not, however,
under any notion of forcing our system of education.'

The principle of teaching method here implied he
elaborates by adding : 'Bodily exercise, when compulsory,
does no harm to the body; but knowledge which is
acquired under compulsion obtains no hold on the
mind. . . . Then do not use compulsion, but let early
education be a sort of amusement; you will then be
better able to find out the natural bent.' In the *Laws* the
positive significance of play in education is emphasised.
Thus, as has frequently been pointed out, we do not
have to come to modern times, to Herbart, Froebel or
Montessori, to find the child's interest or his play taken
as a guiding principle in education : it is formulated in
Plato.

Those who are to undergo the early education and
become guardians of the state are to unite in themselves

[1] § 412.   [2] § 522.   [3] § 536.

'philosophy and spirit and swiftness and strength'.[1] Throughout their education they are to be watched carefully and tested and tried in various ways;[2] and those who, after being proved, come forth victorious and pure are to be appointed rulers and guardians of the state, the others remaining auxiliaries or soldiers.

The qualities required for the higher education[3] or for the philosophic character Plato frequently enumerates. Preference is to be given to 'the surest and the bravest, and, if possible, to the fairest; and, having noble and generous tempers, they should also have the natural gifts which will facilitate their education'.[4] Another account runs:[5] 'A good memory and quick to learn, noble, gracious, the friend of truth, justice, courage, temperance'; again,[6] 'Courage, magnificence, apprehension, memory'.

The aim of the higher education is not a mere extension of knowledge; it is, in Plato's phrase,[7] 'the conversion of a soul from study of the sensible world to contemplation of real existence'. 'Then, if I am right,' he explains,[8] 'certain professors of education must be wrong when they say that they can put a knowledge into the soul which was not there before, like sight into blind eyes. Whereas, our argument shows that the power and capacity of learning exist in the soul already; and that just as the eye was unable to turn from darkness to light without the whole body, so too the instrument of knowledge can only by the movement of the whole soul be turned from the world of becoming into that of being, and learn by degrees to endure the sight of being, and of the brightest and best of being, or in other words, of the good.'

[1] *Republic*, § 376. Here we have the beginnings of vocational selection and of Selection Board procedures.
[2] § 413. Not quite 'an education through perfect circumstances', as Lewis Campbell supposed, *Plato's Republic*, p. 73.
[3] *Republic*, §§ 521–41.
[4] Ibid., § 535.   [5] § 487.   [6] § 490.   [7] § 521.   [8] § 518.

Such is the aim of the higher education, the education of the philosopher or ruler.[1] Plato, having determined the aim, next proceeds to consider the scope of higher education. It includes number or arithmetic, plane and solid geometry, astronomy, theory of music or harmonics, all preparatory to the highest of the sciences, namely, dialectic. 'Through mathematics to metaphysics' might be said to sum up Plato's scheme of higher education.

The principles that decide the selection of the studies of the higher education are that they must lead to reflection rather than deal with the things of sense ;[2] they must likewise be of universal application.[3] The first subject that satisfies these requirements is number, hence Plato concludes :[4] 'This is a kind of knowledge which legislation may fitly prescribe; and we must endeavour to persuade those who are to be the principal men of our state to go and learn arithmetic, not as amateurs, but they must carry on the study until they see the nature of numbers with the mind only; nor again, like merchants or retail traders, with a view to buying or selling, but for the sake of their military use, and of the soul herself; and because this will be the easiest way for her to pass from becoming to truth and being.' The main function of number is thus to afford a training in abstraction.

The value which Plato assigns to number, as a subject in the training preparatory to philosophy, strikes the modern mind as somewhat exaggerated. This can be explained, however, by the fact that philosophers had then only begun the search for universal or conceptual notions, and the science of number presented itself as satisfying their requirements in a remarkable degree. The Pythagoreans had indeed maintained that number was the rational principle or essence of things, and it is generally agreed that Plato was for some time under

[1] See Jaeger, vol. ii, pp. 267–8 for description of Plato's philosopher
[2] *Republic*, § 523.   [3] § 522.   [4] § 525.

Pythagorean influences; in fact, by some it is maintained that by 'Ideas' he understood at one stage in the development of that doctrine nothing other than numbers themselves. At the time of writing the *Republic*, however, he had outgrown the naïve identification of numbers with things themselves, for we find him asserting:[1] 'Yet anybody who has the least acquaintance with geometry will not deny that such a conception of the science is in flat contradiction to the ordinary language of geometricians. They have in view practice only, and are always speaking, in a narrow and ridiculous manner, of squaring and extending and applying and the like — they confuse the necessities of geometry with those of daily life; whereas knowledge is the real object of the whole science.' If the Greeks, as is implied in Plato's statement, were at times in danger of ignoring the purely conceptual nature of number, we of the present day are in danger of disregarding the practical needs which brought the science into existence and the concrete bases in which numbers were first exemplified.

In insisting on the value of number as a means of training in abstraction Plato gives expression to a statement which implies the doctrine of formal discipline or transfer of training, that is, that a training in one function results in a general improvement of the mind, which in turn favourably influences other functions. Thus he asks: 'Have you further observed, that those who have a natural talent for calculation are generally quick at every other kind of knowledge; and even the dull, if they have had an arithmetical training, although they may derive no other advantage from it, always become much quicker than they would otherwise have been?'[2] When in the

[1] *Republic*, § 527.
[2] Ibid., § 526. This argument is repeated in almost identical terms in the *Laws*, § 747: 'Arithmetic stirs up him who is by nature sleepy and dull, and makes him quick to learn, retentive, shrewd, and aided by art divine he makes progress quite beyond his natural powers.'

same section he adds: 'and indeed, you will not easily find a more difficult subject, and not many as difficult', he approximates to the doctrine that the more trouble a subject causes the better training it affords, the fallacy of which is evident in its enunciation by a modern paradoxical philosopher, namely, it matters not what you teach a pupil provided he does not want to learn it.

In dealing with geometry[1] Plato also remarks that 'in all departments of knowledge, as experience proves, any one who has studied geometry is infinitely quicker of apprehension than one who has not.'

These views must nevertheless be qualified by the statement[2] occurring in the discussion of the relation between mathematics and dialectic. 'For you surely would not regard the skilled mathematician as a dialectician? Assuredly not, he said; I have hardly ever known a mathematician who was capable of reasoning.' This qualification, it has been contended,[3] acquits Plato of the responsibility of initiating the doctrine of formal training, but if it does so, it is only at the cost of consistency. In his defence, however, it may be said, that in Plato's day little was known of, although much was hoped from, the science of number; and no objection could have been urged against him had he said that a knowledge of number 'broadened' rather than 'quickened' the mind. Number, like language, affords us an invaluable means of mastering and controlling experience, and does not require to be defended on the ground of some hypothetical influence on the mind in general.

As number is the first subject, so geometry is the second, selected for inclusion in the curriculum of the

[1] Ibid., § 752.   [2] § 531.
[3] E. C. Moore, *What is Education?* (Boston and London: Ginn & Co., 1915), ch. iii. It must be put to Plato's credit that in interpreting a faculty as a function (*Republic*, § 477) he avoided the 'faculty' doctrine which long retarded the development of psychology.

higher education.   Its bearing on strategy is acknowledged, but what Plato is concerned about is whether it
tends in any degree to make easier the vision of the idea
of good.[1] This, he believes, geometry does accomplish;
'geometry will draw the soul towards truth, and create
the spirit of philosophy',[2] consequently those who are to
be the rulers of the ideal state must be directed to apply
themselves to the study of geometry.

The study of solid geometry, or the investigation of
space of three dimensions, should, Plato admits,[3] logically
follow plane geometry and in turn precede astronomy, or
the study of solid bodies in motion, but the unsatisfactory
condition of the subject at the time causes him to dismiss
it briefly.

Astronomy is the next of the instrumental subjects of
the higher training, and in enumerating its practical
advantages to the agriculturist and navigator Plato remarks :[4] 'I am amused at your fear of the world, which
makes you guard against the appearance of insisting upon
useless studies ; and I quite admit the difficulty of believ-
ing that in every man there is an eye of the soul which,
when by other pursuits lost and dimmed, is by these
purified and re-illumined ; and is more precious far than
ten thousand bodily eyes, for by it alone is truth seen.'
'Then in astronomy, as in geometry, we should employ
problems, and let the heavens alone if we would approach
the subject in the right way and so make the natural gift
of reason to be of any real use.'[5]

The last of the studies preparatory to dialectic is music,

[1] *Republic*, § 526. The idea of good, or 'the Form of the Good', is the
ultimate principle in Plato's philosophy, at once the source of all being
and of all knowledge. Cf. ibid., § 509.   [2] § 527.

[3] § 528 — designated by Jaeger, vol. ii, p. 305, 'stereometry'.

[4] § 527.

[5] § 530. In accordance with this principle the calculation of Neptune
into existence by Adams and Leverrier would have been commended
by Plato ; the verification of its existence by actual observation would have
merited his contempt.

not, however, music as an art as dealt with in the early education, but the theory of music, harmonics, the mathematical relations existing between notes, chords, etc., or what we should now probably term the physical bases of music[1] — 'a thing', Plato affirms,[2] 'which I would call useful; that is, if sought after with a view to the beautiful and good; but if pursued in any other spirit, useless'.

If a common basis for the mathematical studies just enumerated could be discovered, Plato believes that it would advance the end in view, namely, preparation for the science of dialectic.

Dialectic is, for Plato, the highest study of all. It is as far removed from the mathematical sciences as they are from the practical arts. The sciences assume certain hypotheses, or make certain assumptions; geometry, for example, assumes the existence of space and does not inquire whether it is a perceptual datum, a conceptual construction or, as Kant maintained, an *a priori Anschauung*. Philosophy, or dialectic as Plato calls it, tries to proceed without presuppositions or, at least, seeks critically to examine their validity and to determine the extent of their application.

'I must remind you', says Plato,[3] 'that the power of dialectic can alone reveal this (absolute truth), and only to one who is a disciple of the previous sciences.' 'And assuredly', he continues, 'no one will argue that there is any other method of comprehending by any regular process all true existence or of ascertaining what each

[1] Marrou, p. 371, translates music here by 'acoustics' — 'the science of mathematics introduced by Pythagoras, the study of the numerical structure of intervals and rhythms'.

[2] *Republic*, § 531.

[3] Ibid., § 533. In the *Cratylus* Plato defined the dialectician as 'he who knows how to ask questions and how to answer them'. In the *Phaedrus* he identifies dialectic with the process of division and generalisation, and he adds, *Republic*, § 537, 'For according as a man can survey a subject as a whole or not, he is or is not a dialectician.'

B

thing is in its own nature; for the arts in general are concerned with the desires and opinions of men, or are cultivated with a view to production and construction, or for the preservation of such productions and constructions; and as to the mathematical sciences which, as we were saying, have some apprehension of true being — geometry and the like — they only dream about being, but never can they behold the waking reality so long as they leave the hypotheses which they use unexamined, and are unable to give an account of them. For when a man knows not his own first principle, and when the conclusion and intermediate steps are also constructed out of he knows not what, how can he imagine that such a fabric of convention can ever become science?'

'Then dialectic, and dialectic alone, goes directly to the first principle and is the only science which does away with hypotheses in order to make her ground secure; the eye of the soul, which is literally buried in an outlandish slough, is by her gentle aid lifted upwards; and she uses as handmaids and helpers in the work of conversion, the sciences which we have been discussing.'

Dialectic then is the coping-stone of the sciences;[1] no other science can be placed higher; it completes the series. All who would be magistrates in the ideal state must consequently address themselves to such studies as will enable them to use the weapons of the dialectician most scientifically.

Having determined the subjects which the philosopher or ruler must study, Plato proceeds to consider the distribution of these studies.[2] For three years after the completion of the early education, that is, from seventeen to twenty years of age, the youths are to serve as cadets, being brought into the field of battle, and, 'like young hounds, have a taste of blood given them'.

During these years of bodily exercises there is to be no

---

[1] *Republic*, § 534.   [2] Ibid., §§ 537–41.

intellectual study, 'for sleep and exercise are unpropitious to learning'.

At the age of twenty the choice characters are to be selected to undergo the mathematical training preparatory to dialectic. This training is to continue for ten years, and at the age of thirty a further selection is to be made, and those who are chosen are to begin the study of dialectic.[1] Plato deliberately withholds the study of dialectic to this late age, giving as his reason that 'youngsters, when they first get the taste in their mouths, argue for amusement, and are always contradicting and refuting others in imitation of those who refute them; like puppy-dogs, they rejoice in pulling and tearing at all who come near them'.[2] This study is to be prosecuted for five years, every other pursuit being resigned for it. For the next fifteen years, that is, from thirty-five to fifty years of age, the philosophers or rulers are to return to practical life, take the command in war and hold such offices of state as befit 'young men'. After the age of fifty the lives of the rulers are to be spent in contemplation of 'the Good', so that when they are called upon to regulate the affairs of the state, their knowledge of this will serve as a pattern according to which they are to order the state and the lives of individuals, and the remainder of their own lives also; 'making philosophy their chief pursuit, but when their turn comes, toiling also at politics and ruling for the public good, not as though they were performing some heroic action, but simply as a matter of duty; and when they have brought up in each generation others like themselves, they will depart to the Islands of the Blest and dwell there'.[3]

Such is Plato's scheme of education as set forth in the

---

[1] § 536. The tests for philosophers include intelligence tests. The tests for the guardians are mainly temperament tests.

[2] § 539. Cf. Aristotle, *Ethics*, i. 3 : 'The young man is not a fit student of Politics.'

[3] *Republic*, § 540.

Republic, and he warns us in conclusion that it is an education for women as well as for men ; they are to have the same training and education, a training in music and gymnastic, and in the art of war, which they must practise like men, 'for you must not suppose', he adds,[1] 'that what I have been saying applies to men only and not to women as far as their natures can go'.

Plato dismisses as irrelevant the ridicule which would be excited by his proposal that women should share with men the exercises of the gymnasia, maintaining that the question should be decided on principle. The principle, he argues, which applies in this case is that each member of the state should undertake the work for which he is best fitted by nature, and while admitting that physically the woman is weaker than the man, he nevertheless maintains that in respect to political or governing ability the woman is the equal of the man. Had he affirmed that in respect to intellectual ability the woman is *on the average* the equal of the man, he would have anticipated the conclusions of modern research.

His coeducational proposal arouses distrust, not so much on its own account but because the second 'wave', the community of wives and children, results from it.[2] To secure and preserve the unity of the state Plato was forced to destroy the family as the social unit ; the family with its bonds of kinship and ties of natural affection was the only institution which he feared might challenge the supremacy, or lead to the disruption, of the state, and the pains he displays to eliminate every trace of family influence are witness to its power. Plato can only secure the unity of the state at the cost of sacrificing all differ-

[1] *Republic,* § 540. Cf. ibid., §§ 451–7.
[2] Ibid., § 457. The great waves or paradoxes in the construction of Plato's ideal state are : (*i*) the community of goods and of pursuits ; (*ii*) the community of wives and children ; (*iii*) summarised in the statement — 'Until kings are philosophers or philosophers are kings, cities will never cease from ill.'

ences ; he makes a wilderness and calls it peace. This is
the great defect of his ideal state, and on this ground
his communistic scheme has been effectively criticised
by Aristotle.[1] A similar criticism has been applied by
Rousseau,[2] who says : 'I am quite aware that Plato, in
the *Republic*, assigns the same gymnastics to women and
men. Having got rid of the family, there is no place for
women in his system of government, so he is forced to
turn them into men. That great genius has worked out
his plans in detail and has provided for every contingency ;
he has even provided against a difficulty which in all
likelihood no one would ever have raised ; but he has
not succeeded in meeting the real difficulty. I am not
speaking of the alleged community of wives which has
often been laid to his charge ; . . . I refer to that sub-
version of all the tenderest of our natural feelings, which
he sacrificed to an artificial sentiment which can only
exist by their aid. Will the bonds of convention hold
firm without some foundation in nature? Can devotion
to the state exist apart from the love of those near and dear
to us? Can patriotism thrive except in the soil of that
miniature fatherland, the home? Is it not the good son,
the good husband, the good father, who makes the good
citizen?'

In the *Laws*, the work of his old age, Plato readdresses
himself to the subject of education. The dialogue com-
mencing with a consideration of the laws of Minos drifts
into a consideration of the perfect citizen-ruler and how
to train him — into a discussion on education, in short.
Disillusioned by the experiences of life, Plato in the *Laws*,
so some interpreters maintain, recants the idealistic
schemes which he projected in the *Republic* ; in the later
work he does not, however, really abandon his earlier
principles, but rather seeks to illustrate their application
in practice ; he describes, if not the ideal city, the pattern

[1] *Politics*, ii. 3.   [2] *Émile*, p. 326.

of which is laid up in heaven, at least 'the second best', which might be realisable 'in present circumstances'.[1]

The treatment of education in the *Laws* supplements that in the *Republic*, emphasising the practical aspects and thus approximating to Aristotle's treatment of education in the *Politics*. The aim of education nevertheless remains the same, for as Plato says in the *Laws*:[2] 'At present when we speak in terms of praise or blame about the bringing-up of each person, we call one man educated and another uneducated, although the uneducated man may be sometimes very well educated for the calling of a retail trader, or of a captain of a ship, and the like. For we are not speaking of education in this narrower sense, but of that other education in virtue from youth upwards, which makes a man eagerly pursue the ideal perfection of citizenship, and teaches him how rightly to rule and how to obey. This is the only education which, upon our view, deserves the name; that other sort of training, which aims at the acquisition of wealth or bodily strength, or mere cleverness apart from intelligence and justice, is mean and illiberal, and is not worthy to be called education at all. But let us not quarrel with one another about a word, provided that the proposition which has just been granted holds good: to wit, that those who are rightly educated generally become good men. Neither must we cast a slight upon education, which is the first and fairest thing that the best of men can ever have, and which, though liable to take a wrong direction, is capable of reformation, and this business of reformation is the great business of every man while he lives.'

Education in the *Laws* is to be universal, not restricted as in the *Republic* to the guardian class, and is to be compulsory; 'the children shall come [to the schools] not only if their parents please, but if they do not please; there

[1] *Laws*, §§ 739, 753.   [2] Ibid., §§ 643-4.

shall be compulsory education, as the saying is, of all and
sundry, as far as this is possible; and the pupils shall be
regarded as belonging to the state rather than to their
parents. My law shall apply to females as well as males;
they shall both go through the same exercises.'[1] To the
coeducational principle and the communistic scheme on
which it is based Plato frequently alludes in the *Laws*,[2]
thus indicating that the proposal in the *Republic* was regarded by him as a serious one. In support of the idea
that women and girls should undergo the same gymnastic
and military exercises as men and boys Plato states:[3]
'While they are yet girls they should have practised
dancing in arms and the whole art of fighting — when
grown-up women, they should apply themselves to evolu-
tions and tactics, and the mode of grounding and taking
up arms; if for no other reason, yet in case the whole
military force should have to leave the city and carry on
operations of war outside, that those who will have to
guard the young and the rest of the city may be equal
to the task; and, on the other hand, when enemies,
whether barbarian or Hellenic, come from without with
mighty force and make a violent assault upon them, and
thus compel them to fight for the possession of the city,
which is far from being an impossibility, great would be
the disgrace to the state, if the women had been so
miserably trained that they could not fight for their
young, as birds will, against any creature however strong,
or die or undergo any danger, but must instantly rush to
the temples and crowd at the altars and shrines, and
bring upon human nature the reproach, that of all
animals man is the most cowardly!'

The main subjects in the curriculum proposed in the
Laws are the same as those given in the *Republic* — for the
early education music and gymnastic, and for the higher

---

[1] § 804.   Cf. Aristotle, *Politics*, viii. 1.
[2] *Laws*, §§ 804–6   [3] Ibid., § 814.

education mathematics; dialectic, the study to which the mathematical subjects were merely preparatory in the *Republic*, is alluded to only indirectly in the more practical *Laws*.

Gymnastic occupies a more prominent place than it does in the *Republic*, where it was treated merely in outline. It is now divided into two branches, dancing and wrestling, and these are, in turn, further subdivided. 'One sort of dancing imitates musical recitation, and aims at preserving dignity and freedom; the other aims at producing health, agility and beauty in the limbs and parts of the body, giving the proper flexion and extension to each of them, a harmonious motion being diffused everywhere, and forming a suitable accompaniment to the dance.'[1] In regard to wrestling, that form 'of wrestling erect and keeping free the neck and hands and sides, working with energy and constancy, with a composed strength, and for the sake of health' is useful and is to be enjoined alike on masters and scholars.[2] The general intent is that of all movements wrestling is most akin to the military art, and is to be pursued for the sake of this, and not for the sake of wrestling.[3]

Plato's treatment of music in the *Laws* follows the lines of that in the *Republic*, the old quarrel between poetry and philosophy being frequently renewed.[4] The same conclusion is reached, namely, that the compositions must impress on the minds of the young the principle 'that the life which is by the gods deemed to be the happiest is also the best'.[5]

The omission in the *Republic* of any reference to the education of the industrial or artisan class is partially rectified in the *Laws*. 'According to my view', Plato now says,[6] 'anyone who would be good at anything must practise that thing from his youth upwards, both in sport

---

[1] *Laws*, § 795.   Cf. ibid., §§ 814–16.   [2] § 796.   [3] § 814.
[4] Cf. §§ 659–70, 800–4, 811.   [5] § 664.   [6] § 643.

and earnest, in its several branches : for example, he who
is to be a good builder, should play at building children's
houses; he who is to be a good husbandman, at tilling
the ground; and those who have the care of their education should provide them when young with mimic tools.
They should learn beforehand the knowledge which they
will afterwards require for their art. For example, the
future carpenter should learn to measure or apply the line
in play; and the future warrior should learn riding, or
some other exercise, for amusement, and the teacher
should endeavour to direct the children's inclinations and
pleasures, by the help of amusements, to their final aim
in life. The most important part of education is right
training in the nursery. The soul of the child in his play
should be guided by the love of that sort of excellence in
which when he grows up to manhood he will have to be
perfected.'

As in the *Republic* so in the *Laws*, education cannot
begin too early;[1] 'Am I not right in maintaining that a
good education is that which tends most to the improvement of mind and body? And nothing can be plainer
than that the fairest bodies are those which grow up from
infancy in the best and straightest manner?' The care
of the child even before birth is dealt with by Plato.[2] The
early discipline is to be, as with Aristotle, habituation to
the good and the beautiful. 'Now I mean by education
that training which is given by suitable habits to the first
instincts of virtue in children; — when pleasure, and
friendship, and pain, and hatred are rightly implanted in
souls not yet capable of understanding the nature of them,
and who find them, after they have attained reason, to
be in harmony with her. This harmony of the soul,
taken as a whole, is virtue; but the particular training in
respect to pleasure and pain, which leads you always to
hate what you ought to hate, and love what you ought to

[1] § 788.   [2] §§ 788–92.

love from the beginning of life to the end, may be separated off; and, in my view, will be rightly called education.'[1]

The early training in the *Republic* comprising music and gymnastic was designed to occupy the first seventeen years of life. The ages at which the various parts of these subjects were to be taken up were not further particularised. In the *Laws*, however, Plato is most precise as to the occupations of the early years and the time to be allotted to each. 'Up to the age of three years, whether of boy or girl, if a person strictly carries out our previous regulations and makes them a principal aim, he will do much for the advantage of the young creatures. But at three, four, five or even six years the childish nature will require sports. . . . Children at that age have certain natural modes of amusement which they find out for themselves when they meet.'[2]

The sports which the children at these early ages engage in, it may be interpolated, are, in Plato's opinion, of supreme significance in maintaining the stability of the state. In the *Republic*[3] Plato repeatedly expresses his fear of innovations in music and gymnastic lest these should imperil the whole order of society. This was natural, for any change in an ideal state could only be regarded as a change for the worse. It was also in accordance with the Greek attitude of mind, to which the modern ideal of an infinite progress brought about by constant innovations was abhorrent, and which conceived of perfection after the manner of the plastic arts as limited and permanent. In the *Laws*, even when the constitution is but 'second-best', the dread of innovations still haunts Plato, and leads him to observe[4] 'that the plays of children have a great deal to do with the permanence or want of permanence in legislation. For when plays are ordered with a view to children having the same plays, and amusing themselves after the same manner, and finding delight in the same playthings, the more solemn institutions of the state are

[1] *Laws*, § 653.   [2] Ibid., § 794.   [3] Cf. § 424.   [4] § 794.

allowed to remain undisturbed. Whereas if sports are disturbed, and innovations are made in them, and they constantly change, and the young never speak of their having the same likings, or the same established notions of good and bad taste, either in the bearing of their bodies or in their dress, but he who devises something new and out of the way in figures and colours and the like is held in special honour, we may say that no greater evil can happen in the state; for he who changes these sports is secretly changing the manners of the young, and making the old to be dishonoured among them and the new to be honoured. And I affirm that there is nothing which is a greater injury to all states than saying this.'

Up to the age of six the children of both sexes may play together. After the age of six, however, they were to be separated — 'let boys live with boys, and girls in like manner with girls. Now they must begin to learn — the boys going to the teachers of horsemanship and the use of the bow, the javelin and sling, and the girls too, if they do not object, at any rate until they know how to manage these weapons, and especially how to handle heavy arms.'[1]

The musical is to alternate with the gymnastic training. 'A fair time for a boy of ten years old to spend in letters is three years; the age of thirteen is the proper time for him to begin to handle the lyre, and he may continue at this for another three years, neither more nor less, and whether his father or himself like or dislike the study, he is not to be allowed to spend more or less time in learning music than the law allows.'[2]

'There still remain three studies suitable for freemen. Arithmetic is one of them; the measurement of length, surface and depth is the second; and the third has to do with the revolutions of the stars in relation to one another. Not everyone has need to toil through all these things in a

[1] § 794.   [2] § 810.

strictly scientific manner, but only a few.'[1] All that is required for the many is such a knowledge as 'every child in Egypt is taught when he learns the alphabet', and which frees them 'from that natural ignorance of all these things which is so ludicrous and disgraceful'.[2] He who is to be a good ruler of the state, must, however, make a complete study of these subjects and of their interconnections; he must know these two principles — 'that the soul is the eldest of all things which are born, and is immortal and rules over all bodies; moreover, he who has not contemplated the mind of nature which is said to exist in the stars, and gone through the previous training, and seen the connection of music with these things, and harmonized them all with laws and institutions, is not able to give a reason of such things as have a reason. And he who is unable to acquire this in addition to the ordinary virtues of a citizen, can hardly be a good ruler of a whole state.'[3]

While in the *Republic* education was to be in the immediate charge of the guardians of the state, in the *Laws* it is to be delegated to a Director of Education.[4] The end of education nevertheless remains the same. Education is for the good of the individual and for the safety of the state. Thus Plato reaffirms in the *Laws*:[5] 'If you ask what is the good of education in general, the answer is easy — that education makes good men, and that good men act nobly, and conquer their enemies in battle, because they are good. Education certainly gives victory, although victory sometimes produces forgetfulness of education; for many have grown insolent from victory in war, and this insolence has engendered in them innumerable evils; and many a victory has been and will be suicidal to the victors; but education is never suicidal.'

Plato established the humanistic tradition in Western

---

[1] *Laws*, §§ 817–18.   [2] Ibid., § 819.   [3] § 967.
[4] §§ 765–6; § 809.   [5] § 641.

education. His influence on later educational thought can be traced in Quintilian, in the mediaeval curriculum, the studies constituting the *trivium* (grammar, rhetoric, logic or dialectic) and the *quadrivium* (music, arithmetic, geometry, astronomy), if different in order, being practically identical with those prescribed by Plato for the philosopher, in More's *Utopia*, Elyot's *Governour* and other renaissance writers, in the educational scheme of *The Book of Discipline* ascribed to John Knox, in Rousseau's *Article on Political Economy* and in Fichte's *Addresses to the German Nation*. Whether this influence has been for good or evil has been vigorously debated. That different interpretations can be derived from the writings of a thinker so original and fertile as Plato is only to be expected. Thus his static view of the state, with divisions into clearly demarcated classes, each of which is required to keep as much as possible to itself, has been condemned as undemocratic. Another evil side of Platonic culture, according to Whitehead,[1] was its total neglect of technical education as an ingredient in the complete development of ideal human beings. On the other hand, Whitehead recognises[2] that the Platonic ideal has rendered imperishable service to European civilisation by encouraging art, by fostering that spirit of disinterested curiosity which is the origin of science and by maintaining the dignity of mind in the face of material force. Dewey[3] likewise acclaims Plato's procedure of untrammelled inquiry, remarking: 'Nothing could be more helpful to present philosophising than a "Back to Plato" movement; but it would have to be back to the dramatic, restless, co-operatively inquiring Plato of the *Dialogues*, trying one mode of attack after another to see what it might yield;

[1] *The Aims of Education* (London: Williams & Norgate, 1929), p. 77.
[2] Ibid., p. 71.
[3] *Contemporary American Philosophy* (London: George Allen & Unwin, Ltd, 1930), ii. 21.

back to the Plato whose highest flight of metaphysics always terminated with a social and practical turn, and not to the artificial Plato constructed by unimaginative commentators who treat him as the original university professor.'

CHAPTER II

QUINTILIAN[1]

PLATO details for us the education of the philosopher, Quintilian that of the orator;[2] the former the education for speculative, the latter for practical life. The difference is typical of the national genius of the two peoples, Greek and Roman.[3]

This antithesis would nevertheless be rejected by Quintilian; the philosopher, he would admit, had become unpractical — and by philosopher he evidently intends the sophist[4] — but the ideal orator,[5] for whose education he prescribes, cannot be regarded as unspeculative or

[1] Born *c.* A.D. 35 — date of death unknown, but it was before A.D. 100. For life see F. H. Colson, *M. Fabii Quintiliani Institutionis Oratoriae, Liber I* (Cambridge University Press, 1924), pp. ix–xx; or C. E. Little, *The Institutio Oratoria of Marcus Fabius Quintilianus with an English Summary and Concordance* (Bureau of Publications, George Peabody College for Teachers, U.S.A., 1951), vol. ii, ch. i — 'His twenty years of teaching extended from about 70 or 71 to 90 or 91' (ibid., p. 16); W. M. Smail, *Quintilian on Education* (Oxford University Press, 1938).

[2] The Loeb Classical Library supplies text and translation: The *Institutio Oratoria of Quintilian* with an English translation by H. E. Butler, 4 vols. (London: William Heinemann. New York: G. P. Putnam's Sons, 1921).

The date of publication of the *Institutio Oratoria* should probably be fixed between A.D. 93 and 95. A. Gwynn, *Roman Education from Cicero to Quintilian* (Oxford: Clarendon Press, 1926), p. 185.

All references in this chapter not otherwise indicated are to the *Institutio Oratoria*.

For Roman education see A. S. Wilkins, *Roman Education* (Cambridge University Press, 1905); A. Gwynn, *Roman Education from Cicero to Quintilian*.

[3] 'In the *De Oratore* Cicero claims that jurisprudence is the Roman counterpart of Greek philosophy., Gwynn, p. 70.

[4] Cf. Quintilian's reference to 'the only professors of wisdom', a characterisation of the sophists employed by Plato in the *Laches*, § 186.

[5] Bk I. x. 4: 'I am not describing any orator who actually exists or has existed, but have in my mind's eye an ideal orator, perfect down to the smallest detail.'

unphilosophical. Plato's philosopher was also ruler or king; Quintilian's orator is sage as well as statesman. Both described the perfect man and the training which was to produce such.

Quintilian characterises his ideal as follows:[1] 'The perfect orator must be a man of integrity, the good man, otherwise he cannot pretend to that character; and we therefore not only require in him a consummate talent for speaking, but all the virtuous endowments of the mind. For an upright and an honest life cannot be restricted to philosophers alone; because the man who acts in a real civic capacity, who has talents for the administration of public and private concerns, who can govern cities by his counsels, maintain them by his laws, and meliorate them by his judgments, cannot, indeed, be anything but the orator. . . . Let therefore the orator be as the real sage, not only perfect in morals, but also in science, and in all the requisites and powers of elocution.' For brevity Quintilian would adopt the definition of the orator given by Cato, 'a good man skilled in the art of speaking';[2] with emphasis on the goodness, however, for he adds, 'not only that the orator ought to be a good man; but that he cannot be an orator unless such'.

Others had written of the training of an orator, but they had usually dealt with the teaching of eloquence to those whose education was otherwise completed. Quintilian, however, says,[3] 'for my part, being of opinion that nothing is foreign to the art of oratory . . . should the training up of an orator be committed to me, I would begin to form his studies from his infancy.' By reason of this, Quintilian's *Institutes of the Orator* is something more than a treatise on rhetoric; it has become an educational classic.

[1] Bk I, Int., §§ 9–18.
[2] Bk XII, ch. i, § 1. Cf. Bk II, ch. xv, § 1. Quintilian restricts the name of orators and the art itself to those who are good. Also Bk II, ch. xv, § 33. Gwynn (p. 40) claims that this definition was designedly opposed to Greek ideals. [3] Bk I, Int., § 1.

No training can produce the perfect orator unless a certain standard of natural endowment is presupposed; nature and nurture must co-operate. Thus Quintilian remarks:[1] 'It must be acknowledged that precepts and arts are of no efficacy unless assisted by nature. The person therefore that lacks a faculty will reap as little benefit from these writings as barren soils from precepts of agriculture. There are other natural qualifications, such as a clear, articulate and audible voice; strong lungs, good health, sound constitution and a graceful aspect; which, though indifferent, may be improved by observation and industry, but are somewhat wanting in so great a degree as to vitiate all the accomplishments of wit and study.'

The training of the orator falls into three stages: the early home education up to seven years of age; the general 'grammar' school education; and the specific training in rhetoric.[2]

With the early home education Quintilian would take as much care and exercise as much supervision as Plato devoted to the early education of the citizens and rulers of his ideal state. Recognising, like Plato, the great part which suggestion and imitation play in the early education of the child, Quintilian demands for his future orator that his parents — not his father only — should be cultured,[3] that his nurse should have a proper accent, that the boys in whose company he is to be educated should also serve as good patterns and that his tutors should be skilful or know their own limitations; the person who imagines himself learned when he is not really so is not to be tolerated. When such conditions do not prevail, Quintilian suggests that an experienced master of language

[1] Bk I, Int.
[2] 'It is plain from the outset that he is writing for the children of the rich. Not a word is said about the elementary schoolmaster (*ludi magister*) and his classes.' — Gwynn, p. 189.
[3] Typically Roman and in striking contrast to Greek sentiment.

should be secured to give constant attention and instantly correct any word which is improperly pronounced in the pupil's hearing in order that the boy may not contract a habit of it. And he adds:[1] 'If I seem to require too much, let it be considered how hard a matter it is to form an orator.'

Quintilian discusses[2] whether children under seven years of age should be put to learn, and, although he admits that little will be effected before that age, he nevertheless concludes that we should not neglect these early years, the chief reason — now regarded as invalid — being that the elements of learning depend upon memory, which most commonly is not only very ripe, but also very retentive in children.[3] He warns us, however, that great care must be taken lest the child who cannot yet love study, should come to hate it, and, after the manner of Plato, he declares that study ought to be made a diversion. The instruction at this early age is to include reading, and exercises in speech training which consist of repetition of rhymes containing difficult combinations of sounds; writing is also to be taught, the letters being graven on a plate so that the stylus may follow along the grooves therein, a procedure depending on practice in motor-adjustment and later revived in principle by Montessori.

Before proceeding to consider the second stage of education, Quintilian discusses the question whether public or private tuition is the better for children. Aristotle had maintained[4] that education should be public and not private; but the early Roman education had been domestic, and it was only under Greek influences that schools came to be founded in Rome. Aristotle's stand-

---

[1] Bk I, ch. i, § 2.   [2] § 4.
[3] In his chapter on memory, Bk XI, ch. ii, some of Quintilian's statements are surprisingly in accordance with experimental results.
[4] *Politics*, viii. 2. Cf. J. Burnet, *Aristotle on Education* (Cambridge University Press, 1903), p. 97.

point was political, that of Quintilian is practical and educational.[1]

Two objections were currently urged against public education, the first being the risk to a child's morals from his intercourse with other pupils of the same age, and the second the difficulty experienced by a tutor in giving the same attention to many as to one. Were the first objection valid, that schools are serviceable to learning but prejudicial to morals, Quintilian would rather recommend the training of a child in uprightness than in eloquent speaking. But he maintains that, though schools are sometimes a nursery of vice, a parent's house may likewise be so ; — there are many instances of innocence lost and preserved in both places — and children may bring the infection into schools rather than acquire it from them. In answer to the second objection Quintilian relies on the inspiration of numbers stimulating a master to give of his best : 'A master who has but one pupil to instruct, can never give to his words that energy, spirit and fire which he would if animated by a number of pupils.' 'I would not, however,' he adds, 'advise the sending of a child to a school where he is likely to be neglected ; neither ought a good master to burden himself with more pupils than he is well able to teach. . . . But if crowded schools are to be avoided, it does not follow that all schools are to be equally avoided, as there is a wide difference between avoiding entirely and making a proper choice.'

Having disposed of the objections to public education, Quintilian enumerates the advantages. At home the pupil can learn only what he is himself taught, but in school he can learn what is taught to others. At school he has others to emulate and to serve as patterns for imitation ; he also has the opportunities of contracting friendships. How, Quintilian asks, shall the pupil learn

[1] Bk I, ch. ii.

what we call 'common sense' when he sequesters himself from society? And for the orator who must appear in the most solemn assemblies and have the eyes of a whole state fixed upon him, public education has the special advantage of enabling the pupil early to accustom himself to face an audience.

The grammar-school training is considered by Quintilian in its two aspects, the moral and the intellectual.

He recognises that children differ in respect of moral disposition, and that training must be adapted to such differences. But he desires for his future ideal orator the lad who is stimulated by praise, who is sensible of glory and who weeps when worsted. 'Let these noble sentiments work in him; a reproach will sting him to the quick; a sense of honour will rouse his spirit; in him sloth need never be apprehended.'

Children must be allowed relaxation, but, as in other particulars, a mean has to be preserved; deny them play, they hate study; allow them too much recreation, they acquire a habit of idleness. Play also reveals their bent and moral character, and Quintilian observes that the boy who is gloomy, downcast and languid, and dead to the ardour of play affords no great expectations of a sprightly disposition for study.

The remarkable modernity of Quintilian's opinions is evident in his remarks on corporal punishment. 'There is a thing', he says, 'I quite dislike, though authorised by custom — the whipping of children. This mode of chastisement seems to me mean, servile and a gross affront to more advanced years. If a child is of so abject a disposition as not to correct himself when reprimanded, he will be as hardened against stripes as the vilest slave. In short, if a master constantly exacts from his pupil an account of his study, there will be no occasion to have recourse to this extremity. It is his neglect that most commonly causes the scholar's punishment.' Concluding, he asks, 'If there be no other way of correcting a child but whipping, what shall be done, when as a grown-up youth he is under no apprehension of such punishment and must learn greater and more difficult things?'

Having stated the disciplinary measures to be observed in moral training, Quintilian proceeds to consider the intellectual training which should be provided by the 'grammar school'.[1] To our surprise the first question which Quintilian raises is whether the Roman youth should begin his grammar-school training with Greek or with Latin. Heine's remark that had it been necessary for the Romans to learn Latin, they would not have conquered the world, derives its force from our ignorance of Roman education, for even though the Roman youths had not to learn Latin they had to learn Greek. It must nevertheless be remarked that Greek was then still a living language, that a knowledge of Greek was almost universal among the upper classes in Rome and that it was indeed the mother tongue of many of the slaves in the Roman households.[2] Quintilian consequently remarks[3] that it is a matter of no great moment whether the pupil begins with Latin or Greek, but in the early education he recommended the learning of Greek first, because Latin being in common use would be acquired unwittingly.

He would not have the boy even at the earliest stages speak only Greek, as in mediaeval schools boys were required to speak only Latin, for this he feared would affect his enunciation; consequently 'the Latin must soon follow and both in a short time go together; so it will come to pass that, when we equally improve both languages, the one will not be hurtful to the other.'

As music with Plato, so grammar with Quintilian

[1] Bk I, ch. iv.   [2] See Wilkins's *Roman Education*, pp. 19 et seq.
[3] Bk I, ch. iv.   Cf. Bk I, ch. i.

comprises literature, especially poetry.[1]   Grammar he divides into two parts : the knowledge of correct speaking and writing, and the interpretation of poetry. For good speaking, which must be correct, clear and elegant, reason, antiquity, authority and use are to be the guiding principles. As a practical preparation for the later training in rhetoric Quintilian proposes that the pupils should learn to relate Aesop's fables in plain form, then to paraphrase them into more elegant style.[2] With regard to correct writing or orthography 'unless custom otherwise directs', says Quintilian, 'I would have every word written as pronounced ; for the use and business of letters is to preserve sounds, and to present them faithfully to the eye of the reader, as a pledge committed to their charge. They ought therefore to express what we have to say.' This is a plea for 'simplified spelling'.

Like Plato, Quintilian recognises that children should be taught not only what is beautiful and eloquent, but in a greater degree what is good and honest. Homer and Virgil should consequently be read first, even although 'to be sensible of their beauties is the business of riper judgment'. Tragedy and lyric poetry may likewise be employed, but Greek lyrics being written with somewhat too great freedom and elegies that treat of love should not be put into children's hands. When morals run no risk, comedy may be a principal study. The general aim of reading at this stage is to get youths to read such books as enlarge their minds and strengthen their genius ; for erudition will come of itself in more advanced years. The study of grammar and love of reading should not, however, be confined to school-days, but rather extended to the last period of life.

Quintilian, after discussing grammar, proceeds to con-

---

[1] Quintilian, Bk II, ch. i, § 4, defines grammar as 'the science of letters'. Colson, p. xxxiv : 'Grammar was then a living study. . . . It held in fact in the mental outlook of the student of the time much the same position as science does today.'   [2] Bk I, ch. vi.

sider the other arts and sciences, a knowledge of which
the future orator ought to acquire at the grammar school;
and in justification of his selection he reiterates that he
has in mind 'the image of that perfect orator to whom
nothing is wanting'.[1]

Music must be included in the training of the orator,[2]
and Quintilian maintains that he might content himself
with citing the authority of the ancients, and in this connection instances Plato, by whom even grammar was
considered to fall under music. According to Quintilian,
music has two rhythms: the one in the voice, the other in
the body. The former treats of the proper selection and
pronunciation of words, the tone of voice, those being
suited to the nature of the cause pleaded:[3] the latter
deals with the gestures of action which should accompany
and harmonise with the voice. But this falls to be dealt
with in the school of rhetoric, and is considered at some
length by Quintilian towards the conclusion of his work.[4]

Geometry, which includes all mathematics, as in
Plato's scheme, is included by Quintilian,[5] but, unlike
Plato in the *Republic*, Quintilian does not despise its
practical advantages to the orator, who in a court might
make an error in calculation or 'make a motion with his
fingers which disagrees with the number he calculates,'
and thus induce people to harbour an ill opinion of his
ability; plane geometry is not less necessary as many
lawsuits concern estates and boundaries. Plato made
geometry a preparation for philosophy, and Quintilian
recommends it as a training for rhetoric. As order is
necessary to geometry, so also, says Quintilian, is it
essential to eloquence. Geometry lays down principles,
draws conclusions from them and proves uncertainties by
certainties; does not oratory do the same? he asks. It is

[1] Bk I, ch. vii.   [2] Bk I, ch. viii.
[3] Bk I, ch. x, and Bk XI, ch. iii.   [4] Cf. Bk XI, ch. iii.
[5] Bk I, ch. ix.

thus on the disciplinary value of geometry that Quintilian, following Plato, insists.

Quintilian would also have the pupil resort to a school of physical culture, there to acquire a graceful carriage. Dancing, too, might be allowed while the pupil is still young, but should not be long continued; for it is an orator, not a dancer, that is to be formed. 'This benefit, however, will accrue from it that without thinking, and imperceptibly, a secret grace will mingle with all our behaviour and continue with us through life.'

Having determined the selection of subjects, Quintilian inquires whether they can be taught and learned concurrently, even supposing that they are necessary.[1] The argument against this procedure is that many subjects of different tendency, if taught together, would bring confusion into the mind and distract the attention. It is also contended that neither the intellect, the physique nor the length of day would suffice; and though more robust years might undergo the toil, it should not be presumed that the delicate constitutions of children are equal to the same burden. But Quintilian replies that they who reason thus are not sufficiently acquainted with the nature of the human mind, which is so active, quick and keeps such a multiplicity of points of view before it that it cannot restrict itself to one particular thing, but extends its powers to a great many, not only during the same day, but likewise at the same moment. What, then, he asks, should hinder us applying our minds to many subjects, having several hours for reflection, especially when variety refreshes and renovates the mind? It is the opposite course, namely, to persevere in one and the same study that is painful. To be restricted for a whole day to one master fatigues greatly, but changes may be recuperative. In support of his argument Quintilian adduces the analogy of farming, asking, 'Why do we not advise our

[1] Bk I, ch. xii.

farmers not to cultivate at the same time their fields, vineyards, olive-grounds and shrubs?' Any of these occupations continued without interruption would prove very tiresome; in Quintilian's view, it is much easier to do many things than confine ourselves long to one.

The principle of the co-ordination of studies is also supported by Quintilian on the ground that no age is less liable to fatigue than childhood; but it would have been more scientific had he maintained that no age is more readily fatigued, hence the need of change. After concluding the survey of grammar-school education, Quintilian turns to consider that of the school of rhetoric, and at the outset complains of a certain overlapping in the work of the two types of schools, maintaining that it would be better if each confined itself to its own proper task.[1]

In selecting a school of rhetoric for the youth, the parents' first concern must be the character of the master. Quintilian describes his ideal teacher thus: 'Let him have towards his pupils the benevolent disposition of a parent, and assume the place of those by whom he has been entrusted with this charge. Let him be free from moral faults and not countenance such faults. Let him be severe but not harsh, affable but not lax, lest the former generate hatred and the second contempt. Let him speak frequently of what is honourable and good, for the oftener he admonishes the seldomer will he be obliged to punish. Not readily given to anger but not ignoring faults requiring correction. Unaffected in his manner of teaching, persevering and firm rather than excessive in his demands. Let him reply readily to his pupils' questions and stimulate those not inclined to put questions. In praising the recitations of his pupils he must neither be niggardly nor fulsome; the former will cause the work to be irksome, the latter will make the pupils negligent.

[1] Bk II, ch. i.

In correcting faults he must not be sarcastic, still less abusive, for the reproof which creates dislike will result in avoidance of work.'[1] The same high standard as in moral attainment is deemed requisite for the intellectual qualifications of the master of the school of rhetoric.

He characterises as silly the opinion of those who, when their boys are fit for the school of rhetoric, do not consider it necessary to place them immediately under the care of the most eminent, but allow them to remain at schools of less repute ; for the succeeding master will have the double burden of unteaching what is wrong as well as teaching what is right. Distinguished masters, it might be maintained, may think it beneath them or may not be able to descend to such small matters as the elements, but he who cannot, Quintilian retorts, should not be ranked in the catalogue of teachers, for it is not possible that he who excels in great should be ignorant of little things. The plainest method, he adds, is always the best, and this the most learned possess in a greater degree than others.

Having discussed the type of school to which the pupil of rhetoric should be sent, Quintilian considers the subjects to be taught and the methods to be employed. The treatment of rhetoric extending from Book III to Book XII of the *Institutes* is of a highly technical nature and of little value or interest to the student of education, although it may be a profitable study for the writer who seeks to improve his style[2] or for the teacher of classics, as it includes, in addition to choice and arrangement of material and the principles of style, a review of Latin literature from the point of view of the orator.[3]

[1] Bk II, ch. ii. Probably the first rating scale for teachers. Cf. the modern version : 'All that a teacher requires is a knowledge of his subject and a sense of humour.' Quoted by J. Adams, *The Herbartian Psychology Applied to Education* (London : D. C. Heath & Co.), n.d.

[2] Cf. A. T. Quiller-Couch, *On the Art of Writing* (Cambridge University Press, 1916), pp. 138-9.   [3] Bk X.

As the education which Quintilian prescribes is that of an orator, he does not deal with the education of women. From his remark that both parents of the orator should be cultured, it might be inferred, however, that he expected women to receive some form of education. There is no direct evidence of the existence of coeducational establishments in Rome, but it appears that girls were taught the same subjects as boys, although the early age of marriage would doubtless exclude them from the higher education in rhetoric in which, for Quintilian, the early and the grammar-school education culminate.

Quintilian's *Institutes* is the most comprehensive, if not the most systematic, treatise on rhetoric in existence;[1] it doubtless appeared too late to influence Roman education greatly, but it was regarded by the renaissance educators as the standard and authoritative work on education, and through them it assisted in fashioning educational training throughout Europe up to quite modern times.[2]

[1] Cf. Colson, p. xxv: 'While Quintilian's book is the great representative of the rhetorical school of educational thought and indeed of ancient pedagogy in general, it must be remembered that it is not as a whole a treatise on education, not even indeed a treatise on how to *teach* rhetoric. The great part of it, Book II. 14–XI, is a treatise *on* rhetoric.'

[2] See Colson, ch. iv, 'Knowledge and Use of Quintilian after 1416'; also John F. Downes, 'Quintilian Today', *School and Society*, vol. lxxiii, March 1951, pp. 165–7.

Milton mentions the first few books of the *Institutes* for moral edification. See below, p. 121.

CHAPTER III

ELYOT[1]

FROM the composition of Quintilian's *Institutes* in
A.D. 92–95 to the rediscovery of the complete text in 1416
during the later phase of the renaissance it was the
Church that kept learning alive. There was a minor
renaissance in the twelfth century, and thereafter the
universities — the offspring of the Church — assumed the
main burden of preserving and advancing culture. The
renaissance itself was a gradual movement, not a sudden
rebirth, as the traditional view assumed.[2] Originating in
Northern Italy it was assimilated, as it advanced north-
wards, to the climate — physical, cultural, social and
political — of the countries affected by it. While in Italy
it took a literary and aesthetic turn; in Northern Europe
it was ethical and religious; in England it was partly
political, but mainly educational, as we find in More's
Utopia, Elyot's *Governour* and Ascham's *The Scholemaster*.

The source from which the renaissance representatives
drew inspiration determined the direction of the movement. Socrates had turned from physical speculation as
an unprofitable study,[3] and thereafter fixed his thought

[1] 1490(?)–1546. For life see *Dictionary of National Biography* (London:
Smith, Elder & Co., 1889), vol. xvii, pp. 347–50; or, *The Boke named The
Governour*, devised by Sir Thomas Elyot, Knight, edited from the first
edition of 1531 by H. H. Stephen Croft (London: Kegan Paul, Trench
and Trübner & Co. Ltd., 1880), vol. i, pp. xix–clxxxix.

[2] Cf. L. E. Elliot-Binns, *England and the New Learning* (London: The
Lutterworth Press, 1937), p. 10. E. M. W. Tillyard, *The English Renaissance:
Fact or Fiction* (London: The Hogarth Press, 1952).

[3] Cf. Plato's *Apology*, § 19: 'The simple truth is that I have nothing to
do with physical speculation.'

upon man and his estate. His conversion had determined the course of Greek culture, which became rich in the products of the mind, in literature, philosophy and art, and thus the renaissance movement in education, in its attempt to reinstate in its entirety the golden age of Greece's greatest triumphs, was predestined to be humanistic rather than realistic.

The reinstatement of a past culture, even if completely attainable, must ultimately be unsatisfactory. The passage of time brings with it altered conditions, and in its new setting the old ideal appears obsolete. No age by reverting to the past can hope thus easily to escape the task of offering its own contribution to civilisation and history, and as the ideal of education reflects the general view of life current at the time, no past system of education can fully satisfy present demands. Thus humanism as an educational idea was doomed to failure; it must sooner or later exhaust itself and leave unsatisfied the new needs; and this was what actually did happen, for the aim of education was thought of in terms of language and literature instead of in terms of life. It was also an individualistic and aristocratic movement; and, although for a time it might satisfy the requirements of a specially favoured class in the community, it had nothing to offer to the rising commercial democracy and, like Plato's scheme of education in the *Republic*, it failed to make provision for the education of the producing and artisan class.

In 1416 Quintilian's *Institutes* was rediscovered, and became at once the authoritative work on education. So true is this that Erasmus (in 1512) apologises for touching upon methods or aims in teaching, 'seeing', he says, 'that Quintilian has said in effect the last word on the matter'. Quintilian's ideal personality had been the orator, that of the renaissance was the 'courtier', the English equivalent of which was the governor — governors including all officers paid or unpaid, involved in executive or legislative activity, royal secretaries, ambassadors, judges, etc.[1] The training in both cases, Roman and renaissance, was practically identical, namely, a training for public life; and Elyot in his *Governour* merely recapitulates the doctrines of Quintilian. It was only later in the Italian revival, after 1470, that the influence of Plato and of Aristotle came to be felt, and the influence of the former is most evident in More's *Utopia*.

Elyot's *Governour*[2] is a characteristic product of the renaissance in its final phase, the fact that the mother tongue, and not Latin, was the medium of his discourse indicates that the force of the renaissance was well-nigh spent. For its political standpoint it owed much to Italian writers and to Plato; Quintilian's *De Oratore* served as its educational pattern. Thus in the Proem to *The Governour* Elyot explains: 'I have now enterprised to describe in our vulgar tongue the form of a just public weal; which matter I have gathered as well of the sayings of most noble authors (Greeks and Latins) as by mine own experience.'

While earlier writers[3] had advocated the use of the mother tongue in education, Elyot was the first to use his native language in all his books, *The Governour* thus becoming the first work on education in English. Elyot recognised the deficiencies, and laboured 'for the augmentation of our language'. Like other reformers, as

[1] W. H. Woodward, *Studies in Education during the Age of the Renaissance* (Cambridge University Press, 1906), p. 272.

[2] *The Boke named The Governour*, devised by Sir Thomas Elyot, Knight. Edited from the first edition of 1531 by Henry Herbert Stephen Croft. Also Everyman's Library (London, J. M. Dent & Co., 1907), with an Introduction by Foster Watson, and new edition, 1963 — the only edition with modernised spelling and punctuation.

All references in this chapter not otherwise indicated are to the earlier Everyman edition.

[3] For example Vives (1492–1540): 'It is the duty of the parent and of the master to take pains that children speak their mother tongue correctly.' See W. H. Woodward, *Studies in Education during the Age of the Renaissance*, p. 197.

Croft observes,[1] he had to encounter the contemptuous opposition of those who hate all innovation : 'Divers men rather scorning my benefit than receiving it thankfully do show themselves offended with my strange terms.' But the King — Henry VIII — to whom it was dedicated, 'benignly receiving my book which I named *The Governour*, in the reading thereof soon perceived that I intended to augment our English tongue whereby men should as well express more abundantly the thing that they conceived in their hearts (wherefor language was ordained) having words apt for the purpose, as also interpreted out of Greek, Latin, or any other tongue into English, as sufficiently as any one of the said tongues into another. His Grace also perceived that throughout the book there was no term new made by me of a Latin or French word, but it is there declared so plainly by one mean or other to a diligent reader that no sentence is thereby made dark or hard to be understanded.'

An explanation of the title of the work is offered in the Proem : 'And forasmuch as the present book treateth of the education of them that hereafter may be deemed worthy to be governors of the public weal . . . I therefore have named it *The Governour*.' The plan is outlined after this manner :[2] 'But forasmuch as I do well perceive that to write of the office or duty of a sovereign governor or prince far exceedeth the compass of my learning, Holy Scripture affirming that the hearts of princes be in God's own hands and disposition, I will therefore keep my pen within the space that is described to me by the three noble masters, reason, learning, and experience, and by their enseignment or teaching I will ordinarily treat of the two parts of a public weal whereof one shall be named Due Administration, the other Necessary Occupation, which shall be divided into two volumes. In the first shall be comprehended the best form of education or

[1] Vol. i, p. lxvi. [2] Pp. 14–15.

bringing up of noble children from their nativity in such manner as they may be found worthy, and also able, to be governors of a public weal. The second volume which, God granting me quietness and liberty of mind, I will shortly after send forth, it shall contain all the remnant which I can either by learning or experience find apt to the perfection of a just public weal; in the which I shall so endeavour myself that all men, of what estate or condition soever they be, shall find therein occasion to be always virtuously occupied.' The first volume accordingly deals with the education of the sons of noblemen, the second, comprising Books II and III, with the principles of morality which should regulate their conduct when they have attained to manhood, and can be 'to their public weal profitable, for the which purpose only they be called to be governors'.[1]

On account of the diversity of gifts amongst men, it was natural, in Elyot's opinion, that there should be differences of position in the state, that some should be governors and that to such the others should minister, receiving in return from them direction as to the way of virtue and commodious living. The work being dedicated to Henry VIII, it was incumbent on Elyot to maintain that there should be in the state one sovereign governor, and that the subordinate governors, called magistrates, should be chosen or appointed by the sovereign governor. In a democracy, on the other hand, 'where all thing is common, there lacketh order; and where order lacketh, there all thing is odious and uncomely. And that have we in daily experience. . . . Similarly, the potter and tinker, only perfect in their craft, shall little do in the ministration of justice. A ploughman or carter shall make but a feeble answer to an ambassador. Also a weaver or fuller should be an unmeet captain of an army, or in any other office of a governor.'

[1] P. 297.

Like Quintilian, Elyot requires that care should be exercised in the choice of a nurse for the child so that the future governor should not in early infancy assimilate evil in any form. He would also, with Quintilian, have the child's instruction begin early, even before seven years of age, giving as his reason that, although certain of the Greek and Roman writers were of a contrary opinion, knowledge for them was to be found in works written in the mother tongue of the pupils, whereas in Elyot's time it was in Greek and Latin. For the learning of these languages much time was required; it was therefore necessary, he maintains, to encroach somewhat upon the years of childhood. The pupils are not, however, to be forced to learn, but, in accordance with the advice of Quintilian, to whom he refers, they are 'to be sweetly allured thereto with praises and such pretty gifts as children delight in'.

They are to be early trained to speak Latin, learning the names of objects about them and asking in Latin for things they desire. If it is possible, the nurses and those in attendance upon them are to speak Latin, or, at least, only pure English. This 'direct method' of learning Latin, as it would now be called, will prepare the way for writing Latin later on. Ascham in *The Scholemaster*,[1] '*or plain and perfect way of teaching children to understand, write, and speak in Latin tongue*', deprecates this method of learning, maintaining, 'If children were brought up in such a house or such a school, where the Latin tongue were properly and perfectly spoken, then the daily use of speaking were the best and readiest way to learn the Latin tongue. But now, commonly, in the best schools in England for words right choice is smally regarded, true propriety wholly neglected, confusion is brought in, barbarousness is bred up so in

---

[1] Roger Ascham, *The Scholemaster*, edited by Edward Arber (Westminster: A. Constable & Co., 1903). (Written 1563–8 and posthumously published in 1570.)

C

young wits, as afterward they be, not only marred for speaking, but also corrupted in judgment as with much ado or never at all they be brought to right frame again.' Ascham's aim is the same as that of Elyot, 'to have the children speak Latin', but he would not allow them to speak Latin till they had read and translated the first book of Sturm's *Epistles* [1565], 'with a good piece of a comedy of Terence also'. Speaking would come after writing in Ascham's proposals, which amounted to little more than a method of double translation.

Elyot advises that at seven years of age the pupil should be removed from the care of women and assigned to a tutor, who should be 'an ancient and worshipful man in whom is proved to be much gentleness mixed with gravity and as near as can be, such an one as the child by imitating may grow to be excellent. And if he be also learned, he is the more commendable.'

The first duty of the tutor is to know the nature of the pupil, approving and extolling any virtuous dispositions which the latter should happen to possess and condemning in no hesitating manner any which might later lead the pupil into evil. He should also take care that the pupil is not fatigued with continual learning, but that study is diversified with exercise. To this end Elyot recommends playing on musical instruments; this should lead to the proper understanding of music which, in its turn the tutor should declare, is necessary for the better attaining the knowledge of a commonwealth.[1] Other recreative subjects which may be taken up if the pupil has a natural taste for them include painting and carving. The former has practical advantages; it is not, however, for these but on account of its recreative value that it is to be studied. These subjects are not to be compulsory. 'My intention and meaning is', says Elyot, 'only that a noble child by its own natural disposition

[1] P. 28. Cf. Plato's idea that justice is a harmony.

and not by coercion, may be induced to receive perfect instruction in these sciences.'[1]

The tutor is likewise to seek out a master who is learned in both Greek and Latin and who is also of good character, and the pupil, when he knows the parts of speech and can separate one of them from another in his own language, is to be put under such an one. Elyot is of the same opinion as Quintilian concerning the order in which languages should be acquired; he would have the pupil study Greek and Latin authors both at one time or else to begin with Greek, 'for as much as that is hardest to come by'. If the child begins Greek at seven, he may read Greek authors for three years, using Latin meanwhile as 'a familiar language'. He is not to be detained long over grammar, either Latin or Greek, for grammar is but an introduction to the understanding of authors, and if too much time is spent on it, or it is dealt with too minutely, the desire for learning fails. The works to be read are mainly those enumerated in Quintilian : first Aesop's *Fables*, and later Homer and Virgil. These with the others which he names — most of the other classical authors being mentioned — will, he considers, suffice till the pupil is thirteen years of age when reason develops and he may proceed to the study of more advanced subjects.

From fourteen to seventeen years of age the pupil is to study logic, rhetoric, cosmography or geography which serves as a preparation for history. At the age of seventeen the pupil is considered ripe enough to pass to the study of philosophy, which Elyot contends should continue till twenty-one years of age. He protests against the early specialisation in law, which at that time seemed common, maintaining that the general training in philosophy would ultimately be more profitable.[2] In philosophy Aristotle's

[1] P. 31.
[2] Cf. pp. 68–69. Cf. K. Charlton, 'Liberal Education and the Inns of Court in the Sixteenth Century', *British Journal of Educational Studies*, vol. ix, No. 1, November 1960, p. 37 : 'Though writers like Elyot and his successors

Ethics, Cicero's *De Officiis,* and later, when the judgment of man is come to perfection, the works of Plato, the Proverbs of Solomon with the books of Ecclesiastes and Ecclesiasticus would provide excellent lessons, and the historical parts of the Old Testament should be studied by a nobleman after he is mature in years. The residue with the New Testament 'is to be reverently touched, as a celestial jewel or relic'.[1]

As continuous study without some manner of exercise, according to Elyot, exhausteth the vital spirits, he comments on the physical exercises which are regarded as befitting a gentleman. The attention which Elyot devotes to physical culture recalls Greek rather than Roman practice, and is characteristically English. Wrestling, running, swimming, handling the sword and battle-axe, riding and vaulting are advised on the ground of their utility as well as for the training they afford; and the inclusion of these exercises is further justified by copious references to the use made of them by classical heroes.

Other exercises recommended, the utility of which is not always evident, include hunting, mainly of deer, as lions and wild beasts were not to be found; not, however, hunting with dogs but rather with javelins after the manner of war. Hunting of the fox would only be followed in the deep winter when the other game is unseasonable, and hunting of the hare with greyhounds was regarded as a solace for men that be studious, and for gentlewomen 'which fear neither sun nor wind for impairing their beauty'. Tennis seldom used and for a little space is a good exercise for young men, bowling he hardly approves of, ninepins and quoiting are utterly abject, likewise football, 'wherein is nothing but beastly fury and extreme violence; whereof proceedeth hurt,

insisted on some legal training so that a gentleman might better serve the state, this remained very much an ideal to which the Inns of Court made little practical contribution.'   [1] P. 48.

and consequently rancour and malice do remain with them that be wounded, wherefore it is to be put in perpetual silence'.[1] No exercise can, in Elyot's opinion, compare with archery or shooting with the long-bow; on national grounds he considers that it ought to be practised because it is the characteristically English mode of warfare, and for killing game is as effective as any other means of shooting.

Above all, in regard to dancing[2] do we find Elyot adopting the Greek rather than the Roman standpoint. Not only would he permit it, but he would use dancing even as a means of training the pupil to prudence. In the various steps or movements he sees analogies with the different aspects of morality and concludes that 'dancing diligently beholden shall appear to be as well a necessary study as a noble and virtuous pastime'. In justification of his view Elyot cites classical and biblical instances of dancing as a religious rite or as the expression of religious thanksgiving.

In *The Governour* there is an interesting digression[3] on the decay of learning in England. More, in his *Utopia*,[4] had previously complained that in the England of his day more than two-fifths of the people could not read English, much less Latin or Greek. Elyot attributes this condition of affairs to two main causes: the pride, avarice and negligence of parents, and the lack of qualified teachers. To be well learned was likewise regarded as a reproach amongst gentlemen at that time, an opinion against which Ascham also inveighs,[5] and which Elyot rejects, citing from history instances of great rulers who were also great scholars. In regard to the avarice of parents he states that they take exceeding care in

[1] In the reign of James I of Scotland, 1406–37, the king ordered every man who played football to be fined fourpence. The time that was wasted on it, he thought, could more profitably be given to archery.
[2] Pp. 85–107. [3] Pp. 49–72. [4] 1515–16.
[5] *The Scholemaster*, p. 60.

engaging servants to inquire into their abilities, but when engaging a schoolmaster their only concern is for how little he can be secured.

Of the dearth of good teachers Elyot remarks : 'Lord God, how many good and clean wits of children be nowadays perished by ignorant schoolmasters,' and for his standard of perfection he resorts to Quintilian : 'I call not them grammarians which only can teach or make rules whereby a child shall only learn to speak suitable Latin, or to make six verses standing on one foot, wherein perchance shall be neither sentence nor eloquence. But I name him a grammarian by the authority of Quintilian, that speaking Latin elegantly, can expound good authors, expressing the invention and disposition of the matter, their style or form of eloquence, explicating the figures as well of sentences as words, leaving nothing, person or place named by the author, undeclared or hid from his scholars. Wherefore Quintilian saith, it is not enough for him to have read poets, but all kinds of writing must also be sought for ; not for the histories only, but also for the propriety of words, which commonly do receive their authority of noble authors.' Few answering this description, Elyot concedes, are to be found in the realm. Contributing causes of this are the early withdrawal of children from school, which takes from the master 'the worship that he above any reward coveteth to have by the praise of his pupil', also the opinion which Quintilian had previously characterised as silly, that any kind of master was good enough to teach the elements.

To remedy these defects Elyot wrote *The Governour*, and in his concluding paragraph he states : 'Now all ye readers that desire to have your children to be governors, or in any other authority in the public weale of your country, if ye bring them up and instruct them in such form as in this book is declared, they shall then seem to all men worthy to be in authority, honour and noblesse,

and all that is under their governance shall prosper and
come to perfection. And as a precious stone set in a rich
jewel they shall be beholden and wondered at, and after
the death of their body their souls for their endeavour
shall be incomprehensibly rewarded of the giver of
wisdom.'

In 1540 Elyot published *The Defence of Good Women*[1]
thus fulfilling the intention announced in *The Governour*[2]
of making 'a book for ladies wherein her praise shall be
more amply expressed'. Earlier in *The Governour*[3] he had
summarised his views of the natures of man and woman :
'A man in his natural perfection is fierce, hardy, strong
in opinion, covetous of glory, desirous of knowledge. . . .
The good nature of a woman is to be mild, timorous,
tractable, benign, of sure remembrance, and shame-
fast.'

The Defence of Good Women is in the form of a dialogue,
somewhat after the Socratic manner, in which one
imaginary character upholds Plato's view of the nature
and function of woman in a commonwealth and another
supports the view of Aristotle. According to the Preface,
Elyot 'devised a contention between two gentlemen, the
one named Caninius, the other Candidus. Caninius, like
a cur, at women's conditions is always barking, but
Candidus, which may be interpreted benign or gentle,
judgeth ever well and reproveth but seldom : between the
two the estimation of womankind cometh in question.
And after long disputation wherein Candidus (as reason
is) hath the pre-eminence at the last for a perfect conclusion, Queen Zenobia by the example of her life con-
firmeth his arguments and also vanquisheth the obstinate
mind of forward Caninius ; and so endeth the matter.'
Not quite. Woman-like, Zenobia has the last word,

[1] Sir Thomas Elyot's *The Defence of Good Women*. Edited by Edwin
Johnston Howard (Oxford, Ohio: The Anchor Press, 1940).
[2] P. 145.   [3] P. 95.

contending that the postponement of her marriage from
sixteen years of age to twenty enabled her to study moral
philosophy,[1] and that after her marriage the knowledge
of letters was profitable to her. In this we have an early
plea for the higher learning for women.

[1] P. 55.

CHAPTER IV

LOYOLA[1]

IN the Jesuit system founded by Ignatius of Loyola[2] the
aristocratic tendency which characterises the educational
systems with which we have already dealt, to some extent
survives. Ignatius, a knight of noble birth, recognised
that, for the crusade which the Company of Jesus was
enrolled to wage, all available gifts of intellect and birth
would be required; consequently it gave him peculiar
satisfaction when the tests imposed on candidates for
admission to the Society were passed by youths of noble
birth.[3] The Society devotes itself mainly, although not
exclusively, to higher education, but for this restriction
there is historical justification. Its aim was to arrest the
disintegrating forces in the religious life of Europe,[4] and

[1] 1491–1556. For the life of Ignatius Loyola see Francis Thompson,
Saint Ignatius Loyola (London: Burns & Oates, 1909); Paul Van Dyke,
Ignatius Loyola: The Founder of the Jesuits (New York and London: Charles
Scribner's Sons, 1927); Leonard von Matt and Hugo Rahner, St Ignatius
of Loyola: A Pictorial Biography. Translated from the German by John
Murray (London: Longmans, Green & Co., 1956); James Brodrick,
Saint Ignatius Loyola: The Pilgrim Years (London: Burns & Oates, 1956).

[2] For origin and history of the Society of Jesus see James Brodrick, The
Origin of the Jesuits (Longmans, Green & Co., 1940), and The Progress of
the Jesuits (1947). Also T. Corcoran, 'Jesuit Education', The Encyclopaedia
and Dictionary of Education, edited by F. Watson (London: Sir Isaac Pitman,
1921), vol. ii, pp. 913–16.

On 27th September 1540 formal approval was given by the Bull of
Pope Paul III to the members of the Company of Jesus to incorporate
themselves into a religious order. Seven months afterwards Ignatius was
elected the first General.

[3] Francis Thompson, Saint Ignatius Loyola, pp. 171–2.

[4] It is unhistorical to assume that the Society was founded to combat Protestantism. It represents rather an original development within
the Church itself. The Jesuit educational system is likewise a phase of
the Renaissance movement, and the general practice of the Jesuit schools
corresponded with the practice of all Western and Central Europe of

to effect this it was necessary to attack the evils at their source, namely, in the universities, hence the Society's concern for higher education.[1]

While the Jesuits are expressly adjured to address themselves to higher education, they do not hesitate, when necessity compels, to devote themselves to primary instruction.[2] As the Jesuit system is sometimes charged

whatever religion. See R. Schwickerath, *Jesuit Education: Its History and Principles* (St Louis: B. Herder, 1903), p. 77; also F. Charmot, *La Pédagogie des Jésuites* (Paris: Spes, 1943), pp. 32-47.

[1] The official publications of the Society of Jesus are *The Spiritual Exercises*, *The Constitutions of the Society* and the *Ratio Studiorum*.

Various translations of *The Spiritual Exercises* are available. *Spiritual Exercises of St Ignatius of Loyola*. Edited by O. Shipley (London, 1870). W. H. Longridge, *The Spiritual Exercises of St Ignatius of Loyola* (London: A. R. Mowbray & Co., 1930). *The Text of the Spiritual Exercises of St Ignatius* (London: Burns & Oates, 1880). *Manresa or the Spiritual Exercises of St Ignatius*, new edition (London: Burns & Oates, 1881).

The *Constitutiones Societatis Jesu. Romae, in aedibus Societatis Jesu* 1558. *Reprinted from the Original Edition: with an Appendix containing A Translation, and Several Important Documents* (London: J. G. & F. Rivington, 1838) does not include the Declarations or Clarifications. The Appendix contains The First Approbation of the Society of Jesus by Paul III, 1540. A Translation of the Bull for the Effectual Suppression of the Order of Jesuits by Clement XIV, 1773. A Translation of the Bull for the Restoration of the Order of Jesuits by Pius VII, 1814. *Saint Ignatius' Idea of a Jesuit University* by George E. Ganss (Milwaukee: Marquette University Press, 1956), includes Pt IV of the *Constitutions* of the Society of Jesus Translated from the Spanish of Saint Ignatius of Loyola, together with an account of the origin of the *Constitutions* and titles of the ten Parts. E. A. Fitzpatrick also included Pt IV of the *Constitutions* in *St Ignatius and the Ratio Studiorum* (New York and London: McGraw-Hill, 1933).

The *Ratio Studiorum et Institutiones Scholasticae Societatis Jesu* in G. M. Pachtler, *Monumenta Germaniae Paedagogica* (Berlin, 1887-94), vol. v, contains the Latin text of the 1586 *Ratio*, and Latin texts and German translations of the 1599 and 1832 versions. The 1591 version was evidently not known to Pachtler (see Farrell, p. 308). T. Corcoran issued for academic use in University College, Dublin, the *Renatae Litterae saeculo a Chr. XVI in Scholis Societatis Jesu Stabilitae* containing portions of the three versions of the *Ratio* in Latin which he designated *Ratio Studiorum Prima* (1586), *Ratio Studiorum Intermedia* (1591), *Ratio Studiorum Definitiva* (1599). In 1938 the Bruce Publishing Company, Milwaukee, issued *The Jesuit Code of Liberal Education: Development and Scope of the Ratio Studiorum* by Allan P. Farrell. This traces the development of the *Ratio* and includes the 1832 version prepared after the Restoration of the Society.

[2] In the 1832 revision of the *Ratio Studiorum*, Reg. Praef. Stud. Inf. 8, § 12, reference is made to elementary schools.

with intentionally and unnecessarily restricting education
to its higher forms, it is advisable to state the Society's
attitude in its own terms. According to the *Constitutions*[1]
of the Society instructing others in reading and writing
would be a work of charity if the Society had enough
members to be able to attend to everything; but because
of the lack of members, these elementary branches are not
ordinarily taught. Aquaviva, the fifth General of the
Society, writing[2] on 22nd February 1592, regarding the
admission of young pupils to the schools of the Society,
states that only those are to be admitted who are sufficiently versed in the rudiments of grammar and know how
to read and write; nor is any dispensation to be granted
to anyone, whatever be his condition of life; but those
who press the petitions upon us are to be answered, 'that
we are not permitted'. In the *Ratio Studiorum* the twenty-
first rule for the Provincial or Superior of a Province
provides that for the lower studies there are to be not
more than five classes: one for rhetoric, one for humanities
and three for grammar. Where there are fewer classes,
the Provincial is to see that the higher classes are to be
retained, the lower ones being dispensed with.[3] The
charge that the Society selected, as a special field for its
endeavours, the sphere of education in which it believed
its efforts were most required and likely to be most
effective, has only to be formulated to be rendered
meaningless.

It is evident that there was no intention to further a
social exclusiveness, as originally the instruction which the
Jesuits did afford was free,[4] even including the university

[1] Ganss, ch. 12, Clarification C, p. 332.
[2] Cf. Pachtler, *Monumenta Germaniae Paedagogica*, vol. ii, p. 311.
[3] *Ratio Studiorum*, Reg. Provincialis, 21, § 4. Cf. Pachtler, vol. ii, p. 258.
[4] *Constitutions*, Pt IV, ch. xv, § 4: 'Just as the Society teaches free.'
In the *Constitutions*, Pt IV, ch. vii, § 3, Ignatius decrees that gifts to which
special conditions are attached are not to be accepted by the Society. On
the principle of gratuity in Jesuit education see Farrell, pp. 436–40.

stage, and when tempted to impose fees by the advantages accruing to their competitors who did not scruple to charge for education, no text was more frequently quoted[1] than 'Freely ye have received, freely give'. In this respect the Jesuit system realised a principle which many modern democracies have not yet fully attained, the Jesuit practice in this regard recalling the disinterested Greek attitude to knowledge.

If aristocrats, the Jesuits are not individualists, and for much the same reasons as Quintilian, they extol public education. 'For this moral strengthening of character, no less than for the invigorating of mental energies, the system of Ignatius Loyola prescribes an education which is public — public, as being that of many students to-gether, public as opposed to private tutorism, public, in fine, as requiring a sufficiency of the open, fearless exercise both of practical morality and of religion.'[2]

The aim of the Society of Jesus is avowedly religious. Its characteristic features were its missionary enterprise and its educational activities. Thus Francis Thompson, distinguishing the duties of its members, writes :[3] 'Nor was any order bound to foreign missions. But, above all, their educational obligations were a new thing. The teaching of children and the poor had no body of men vowed to its performance, and its neglect was among the abuses which drew down the censure of the Council of Trent ; while, in gratuitously undertaking the higher education of youth, the Jesuits were absolutely original.

[1] T. Hughes, *Loyola and the Educational System of the Jesuits* (London : William Heinemann, 1892), pp. 67, 117. Cf. also *Constitutions*, Pt IV, ch. vii, § 3 ; ch. xv, § 4.

The *Ratio Studiorum*, Reg. Praef. Stud. Infer. 9, enacts that no one shall be excluded because he is poor or of lowly station.

The Reg. Com. Prof. Class. Infer. 50, declares that the professor is to slight no one, to care as much for the progress of the poor pupil as of the rich. Cf. Fitzpatrick, p. 155.

[2] T. Hughes, *Loyola*, p. 99.

[3] *Saint Ignatius Loyola*, p. 179.

In his missionary assault, by preaching and ultimately by writing, upon the people of power and intellect, who were the brain and marrow of the anti-Catholic movement, he confronted the present; in his masterly seizure of the school, he confronted the future. He not only confronted, but anticipated it: he tore from the revolt the coming generation, and levied immediate posterity under the Catholic banner. If the coming years prospered a counter-reformation, a sudden return-tide of Catholicism which swept back and swamped the Renascence, that counter-movement was prepared in the Jesuit schools.'

After his surrender to the Christian life, it was early borne in upon Loyola, while reading in the Gospel, 'they understood none of these things', that without proper education his labours would be of no avail. He forthwith resolved, when over thirty years of age, to acquire from the beginning the rudiments of Latin and patiently to learn his lessons among the ordinary pupils. Bringing to his studies an adult mind of a surprisingly practical type and an unerring judgment, he could reflect upon the methods employed, and from his own initial failures deduce a procedure from which others might profit. 'One knows not whether more to admire his astonishing determination or his astonishing mental power, when it is reflected that he carried through his philosophical studies at the age of forty-four, having begun his whole education from the very elements others acquire in boyhood.'[1]

In the original draft of what might be termed the articles of association of the new Society, mention is made of teaching. On the 3rd May 1539, a series of resolutions was adopted by the few companions to whom Ignatius had communicated his ideas of founding a society, agreeing (1) to take an explicit vow of obedience to the Pope; (2) to teach the Commandments to children or anyone else; (3) to take a fixed time — an hour more or less —

[1] Ibid., p. 73.

to teach the Commandments and Catechism in an orderly way; (4) to give forty days in the year for this work.[1]   In the First Papal Approbation it is affirmed that the members of the Society 'shall have expressly recommended to them the instruction of boys and ignorant people in the Christian doctrine of the ten commandments, and other the like rudiments, as shall seem expedient to them according to the circumstances of persons, places and times'.   In the last vows which the Jesuit takes[2] he promises 'peculiar care in the education of boys'.

In the *Constitutions* of the Society, a work begun at the request of the Pope in 1541, Ignatius set forth the fundamental principles of the Society.   This work consists of ten Parts,[3] the fourth and largest of which presents in outline the plan of studies which was later more fully elaborated in the *Ratio Studiorum*.   Part I of the *Constitutions* prescribes the conditions of Admission of Applicants, and Part II the causes justifying the Dismissal of Those Found Unsuitable.   The qualifications which, according to Ignatius, the Society should demand of its entrants recall in several particulars the qualities which Plato in the *Republic* required of his philosophers.   'It is needful', Ignatius states,[4] 'that those who are admitted to aid the Society in spiritual concerns be furnished with these following gifts of God.   As regards their intellect: of sound doctrine, or apt to learn it; of discretion in the management of business, or, at least, of capacity and judgment to attain to it.   As to memory: of aptitude to perceive, and also to retain their perceptions.   As to intentions: that they be studious of all virtue and spiritual perfection;

---

[1] Francis Thompson, *Saint Ignatius Loyola*, p. 136.

[2] *Constitutions*, Pt V, ch. iii, § 3.

[3] A table of contents is provided by Ganss, p. 287.

All the quotations from Pt IV of the *Constitutions* are taken, by permission, from the translation from the Spanish by G. Ganss, *St Ignatius' Idea of a Jesuit University*, pp. 281–345.

[4] Ibid., Pt I, ch. ii, §§ 6–13.   Cf. qualifications in First Papal Approbation: 'prudent in Christ and conspicuous in learning'.

calm, steadfast, strenuous in what they undertake for God's
service; burning with zeal for the salvation of souls, and
therefore attached to our Institute; which directly tends
to aid and dispose the souls of men to the attainment of
that ultimate end, from the hand of God, our Creator
and Lord. In externals: facility of language, so needful
in our intercourse with our neighbour, is most desirable.
A comely presence, for the edification of those with whom
we have to deal. Good health, and strength to undergo
the labours of our Institute. Age to correspond with
what has been said; which in those admitted to probation should exceed the fourteenth year and in those
admitted to profession the twenty-fifth. As the external
gifts of nobility, wealth, reputation and the like are not
sufficient, if others are wanting; so, if there be a sufficiency
of others, these are not essential; so far, however, as they
tend to edification, they make those more fit for admission,
who, even without them, would be eligible on account of
the qualities before mentioned; in which, the more he
excels who desires to be admitted, so much the more fit
will he be for this Society, to the glory of God our Lord,
and the less he excels, so much the less serviceable will he
be. But the sacred unction of the divine Wisdom will
instruct those who undertake this duty to His service and
more abundant praise, what standard should be maintained in all these things.'

Part III of the *Constitutions* is devoted to the Preservation and Improvement of Those who Remain for Probation in the Novitiate, and what more especially concerns
the educationist, a chapter is included 'Of the Super-
intendence of the Body'. Loyola, speaking from his own
experience, frequently warned his companions against the
subversive influence of an enfeebled bodily condition.
Thus we find him writing to Borgia :[1] 'As to fasting and

[1] Cf. Francis Thompson, *Loyola*, p. 282. Borgia became the third
General of the Order.

abstinence, I think it more to the glory of God to preserve and strengthen the digestion and natural powers than to weaken them. . . . I desire then that you will consider that, as soul and body are given you by God, your Creator and Maker, you will have to give an account of both, and for His sake you should not weaken your bodily nature, because the spiritual could not act with the same energy.' The same sentiment inspires the treatment in the *Constitutions* :[1] 'As over-much solicitude in those things which pertain to the body is reprehensible ; so a moderate regard for the preservation of health and strength of body to the service of God is commendable, and to be observed by all. . . . Let a time for eating, sleeping and rising be appointed for general observation. In all those things which relate to food, clothing, habitation and other things needful for the body, let care be taken with the divine aid, that in every probation of virtue and act of self-denial, nature be nevertheless sustained and preserved for the honour of God and his service, due regard being paid to persons in the Lord. As it is not expedient that anyone be burdened with so much bodily labour that the intellect be overwhelmed, and the body suffer detriment ; so any bodily exercise, which aids either, is generally necessary for all, those not excepted who ought to be occupied in mental pursuits which should be interrupted by external employments, and not continued nor taken up without some measure of discretion. The castigation of the body should neither be immoderate nor indiscreet in vigils, fastings, and other external penances and labours, which usually do harm and hinder better things. . . . Let there be some one in every house to preside over everything that relates to the good health of the body.' The charge frequently made against the Jesuit system of education, that it does not regard the physical care of the pupil, is

[1] Pt III, ch. ii. Also Pt IV, ch. iv, § 1. Cf. Ganss, p. 303.

accordingly not warranted by the *Constitutions* of the Society.

While the vows to be taken, the conduct of missions and the administration of the Society are the subjects treated in the later sections of the *Constitutions*, the Fourth Part is devoted to the regulations governing the instruction in literature and other studies of those who remain in the Society after their two years' period of probation. The first ten chapters of this Part are concerned with the organisation and management of the colleges, the remaining seven with the universities of the Society.

The aim and scope of the work of colleges is thus defined :[1] 'the end of the learning acquired in this Society is, with the help of God, to aid the souls of its own members and those of their neighbours. This, therefore, is the criterion to be used in deciding, both in general and in the case of individual persons, what subjects members of the society ought to learn, and how far they ought to progress in them. To speak in general, the humane letters of the various languages, and logic, natural philosophy, moral philosophy, metaphysics, scholastic theology, positive theology, and Sacred Scripture are helpful. These are the branches to which those who are sent to the colleges should apply themselves. They will devote themselves with greater diligence to the parts which are more helpful for the end mentioned above. Furthermore, account is to be taken of circumstances of time, place, persons, and other such factors, according to what seems best in our Lord to him who holds the chief responsibility.'

The order of studies to be followed is first the Latin language, then the liberal arts, thereafter scholastic, then positive theology. Scripture can be studied either concomitantly or later on.[2]

[1] *Constitutions*, Pt IV, ch. v, § 1. Ganss, pp. 306–7.
[2] *Constitutions*, Pt IV, ch. vi, § 4. Ganss, p. 310.

The students should be faithful in attendance at the lectures, diligent in preparing for them beforehand, and afterwards in reviewing them. They must ask about points they do not understand, and note down what may be useful later on to assist the memory.[1] Latin was commonly to be spoken by all, but especially by the students of the humanities;[2] and since the practice of debating is useful, especially to the students in arts and scholastic theology, instructions are given[3] as to when and how these debates or disputations are to be arranged and conducted. There should be in each college a general library, of which the key is to be given to those who in the rector's judgment ought to have it. Furthermore, each one should have the books which are necessary for him.[4]

Those scholars who intend to devote their lives to the work of the Society are further instructed in the performance of the ordinances of the Church;[5] and to discharge this duty they should endeavour to learn the vernacular language well.[6]

The universities which the Society establishes or maintains will be divided into the three faculties: languages, arts and theology;[7] 'the study of medicine and laws, being rather remote from our Institute, will not be taught in the universities of the Society, or at least the Society will not undertake this activity through its own members'.[8] The curriculum in arts shall extend over three and a half years, and that in theology over four years. In the arts curriculum reference is made to the natural sciences which prepare the intellectual powers for theology, and are highly serviceable for the perfect understanding and

---

[1] *Constitutions*, Pt IV, ch. vi, § 8. Ganss, p. 312.
[2] Ibid., § 13. Repeated in *Ratio Studiorum*, Reg. Com. Prof. Class. Infer. 18, and modified slightly in 1832 *Ratio*.
[3] *Constitutions*, Pt IV, ch. vi, §§ 10–12.
[4] Ibid., § 7.   [5] Ch. viii.   [6] § 3.
[7] Ch. xvii, § 5.   [8] Ch. xii, § 4.

use of it, and also of themselves help to attain the same ends,[1] and it is further enjoined, and is an interesting comment on the criticism that the Society neglects the natural sciences, that they 'should be treated with fitting diligence and by learned teachers. In all this, the honour and glory of our Lord should be sincerely sought.'

Provision was made by Ignatius in the *Constitutions*[2] for modification of his outline plan of studies. 'According to circumstances of place and persons there must be great variety in particular details.' That this concession should not be abused and the uniformity of the system destroyed, it was considered expedient that an authoritative yet more detailed plan of studies than that outlined in the *Constitutions* should be issued for the guidance of the schools and colleges of the Society.

The *Ratio atque Institutio Studiorum Societatis Jesu*, usually referred to as the *Ratio Studiorum*, was accordingly prepared, becoming the main source of the educational doctrines of the Society; and Jouvancy's *Ratio Discendi et Docendi*[3] is regarded as the official complement to, and commentary on, the *Ratio Studiorum*.

The first draft of the *Ratio Studiorum* was the result of the labours of six Jesuits summoned to Rome in 1584 by Aquaviva, the fifth General of the Order. Availing themselves of all the material regarding methods and administration of education which they could assemble and of the experience which the practice of the Society itself afforded, they were able after a year's collaboration to

[1] Ch. xii, § 3.
[2] Cf. Pt IV, ch. vii, § 2; also ch. xiii, § 2. In the *Ratio Studiorum* the same freedom is retained. Cf. Regulae Praepositi Provincialis, 39.
[3] Jouvancy's *Ratio Discendi et Docendi*, first published in 1692, was reissued in 1703 — revised and adapted to meet the requirements of a decree passed by the General Assembly of the Order in 1696–7. French and German editions of Jouvancy's *Ratio* exist, but no English translation. Hughes's *Loyola*, pp. 163–6, gives an outline. For account of Joseph de Jouvancy, 1643–1719, see F. Charmot, *La Pédagogie des Jésuites* (Paris: Spes, 1943), pp. 559–63.

present in August 1585 to the General of the Society the results of their efforts. In 1586 the report was sent by the General to the Provinces for examination and comment. A new report was issued in 1591 as *Ratio atque Institutio Studiorum*, and after further revision the final plan of studies was published at Naples in 1599 under the title *Ratio atque Institutio Studiorum Societatis Jesu.*[1]

The *Ratio Studiorum*, unlike the *Constitutions*, deals exclusively with education. It sets forth the regulations which are to direct the Superior of a Province in dealing with education in his Province, then the regulations which the rector of a college is to apply in governing a college, thereafter rules for the guidance of the prefect of studies. General regulations for the professors of the higher faculties — theology and philosophy — are followed by special rules for the professors of each subject in these faculties, namely, sacred writings, Hebrew, scholastic theology, ecclesiastical history, canonical law and moral or practical theology, moral philosophy, physics and mathematics. Regulations for the prefects of the lower studies, together with regulations for the conduct of written examinations and for the awarding of prizes, are also prescribed, and these are succeeded by the general regulations for the professors of the lower classes and by detailed regulations for the professors of rhetoric, humanity and higher, intermediate and lower grammar. Rules for the pupils for the management of academies,[2] etc., are added. So comprehensive, systematic and exhaustive are the regulations that the modern reader is inclined to forget that the *Ratio Studiorum* is one of the first attempts on record at educational organisation, management and method, at a time when it was unusual even to grade

[1] No great originality was claimed for the *Ratio*, but it did claim to embody the best practice of the day and to have systematised this.

[2] In these on specified days the pupils hold lectures, debates, etc., among themselves.

pupils in classes; and one is tempted to compare it, not always to the disadvantage of the *Ratio*, with the regulations of a modern school system which have only after some generations been evolved and perfected. The *Ratio Studiorum* comprehends all subjects from the principles governing the educational administration of a Province to the fixing of school holidays, the textbooks to be used in teaching Latin grammar and the method of correcting exercises.

The general organisation of the educational work of the Society may be gathered from the regulations issued for the direction of the Provincial.[1] The theological course of four years is the highest, and this is preceded by a course of philosophy extending over three years. Although the course for the study of humanity and rhetoric cannot be exactly defined, it is enacted that the Provincial shall not send pupils to philosophy before they have studied rhetoric for two years. All students in the philosophical course must, according to the *Ratio* of 1599, attend lectures in mathematics; and provision is made that students who show special proficiency in any subject should have the opportunity of extending their study of that subject. The classes for the lower studies are not to exceed five : one for rhetoric, another for humanity and three for grammar. These classes are not to be confused with one another, a warning which recalls the complaint of Quintilian. Where the number of pupils warrants it, parallel classes for the various grades are to be instituted.

In the regulations for the rector of a college[2] the need of trained teachers even for the lowest classes is recognised. That the teachers of the lower classes should not take up the work of teaching without training, it is there enacted[3]

---

[1] Regulae Praepositi Provincialis. Cf. Fitzpatrick, pp. 121–37.
[2] Regulae Rectoris. Cf. Fitzpatrick, pp. 137–43.
[3] Reg. 9. The same view was expressed in a criticism of the 1586 *Ratio*. See Hughes, *Loyola*, pp. 160–1.

that the rector of the college from which the teachers of humanity and grammar are wont to be taken should select someone specially skilled in teaching, and that towards the end of their studies the future teachers should come to him three times a week for an hour to be trained for their calling in methods of exposition, dictation, writing, correcting and all the duties of a good teacher.

In colleges the rector appoints a prefect of studies as his assistant,[1] the position of the latter being somewhat analogous to that of the dean of a faculty. He is responsible to the rector for the proper organisation of studies and the regulating of classes so that those who attend may make as much advancement as possible in uprightness of life, the arts and doctrine.[2] The prefect of lower studies, analogous to a head master, aids the rector in ruling and governing schools in such a way that those who attend may progress no less in uprightness of life than in the liberal arts. In day schools the prefect of studies is ordinarily responsible for both studies and discipline and in boarding schools he exercises both functions within class hours.[3] But the rules for the rector[4] provide, where necessary, for a prefect of studies having as assistant a prefect of discipline whose duties in a boarding school would be somewhat analogous to those of a bursar in an English public school or in a university college.

In the general regulations for all the professors of the higher faculties[5] the educational aim of the Society is recalled, namely, to lead the pupil to the service and love of God and to the practice of virtue. To keep this before him each professor is required to offer up a suitable prayer before beginning his lecture. Directions are given as to

---

[1] Rules for Rector, 2. Fitzpatrick, p. 138.

[2] Rules for Prefect of Studies. Fitzpatrick, pp. 143–50.

[3] Rules for Prefect of Lower Studies. Fitzpatrick, pp. 176–90.

[4] Rule 22. Fitzpatrick, p. 142.

[5] Regulae Communes Omnibus Professoribus Superiorum Facultatum. Cf. Fitzpatrick, pp. 150–5.

the extent to which authorities are to be followed and used by the professors in lecturing, and how they are to lecture that the students may be able to take proper notes.[1] After each lecture the professor is to remain a quarter of an hour that the students may interrogate him about the substance of the lecture.[2] A month is to be devoted at the end of each session to the repetition of the course.[3] And the last of the general rules for all the professors declares that the professor is not to show himself more familiar with one student than with another; he is to disregard no one, and to further the studies of the poor equally with the rich; he is to promote the advancement of each individual student.[4]

Detailed directions for the professors of each of the subjects in the faculties of theology and philosophy follow; and of these it need only be mentioned here that in the 1832 revision of the *Ratio* special provision was made for the teaching of physics, which had previously been treated under the general title philosophy, and the regulations for the teaching of mathematics were modernised. That the Society did not neglect the natural sciences is confirmed by these statements, and the charge that the Society ignores changing conditions is refuted by a glance at the parallel columns on these subjects in Pachtler's edition of the *Ratio Studiorum*.[5]

Amongst the rules for the prefect of the lower studies[6] the following may be noted. He is to help the masters and direct them, and be especially cautious that the esteem and authority due to them be not in the least impaired.[7] Once a fortnight he is to hear each one teach.[8] He is to see that the teacher covers the class-book

---

[1] Cf. Reg. 9.   [2] Reg. 11.
[3] Reg. 13, 1599 *Ratio*. No definite time is specified in the 1832 *Ratio*.
[4] Reg. 20.
[5] *Monumenta Germaniae Paedagogica*, vol. v, pp. 346–51.
[6] Regulae Praefecti Studiorum Inferiorum. Cf. Fitzpatrick, pp. 176–90.
[7] Reg. 4.   [8] Reg. 6.

in the first half-year, and repeats it from the beginning in the second term.[1] The reasons for the repetition are two :[2] what is often repeated is more deeply impressed on the mind ; it enables the boys of exceptional talents to pass through their course more rapidly than the others, as they can be promoted after a single term. Promotion is generally to take place after the long vacation ; but where it would appear that a pupil would make better progress in a higher class he is not to be detained in the lower, but after examination to be promoted at any time of the year.[3] When there is a doubt whether a pupil should ordinarily be promoted, his class record is to be examined, and his age, diligence and the time spent in the class are to be taken into consideration.[4] In intimating promotions the names of pupils gaining special distinction are to be announced first ; the others are to be arranged in alphabetic order.[5] A censor is to be appointed, one who is held in esteem by his fellow-pupils and who shall have the power to impose small penalties.[6] For the sake of those who are wanting in diligence and in good manners and on whom advice and exhortation have no effect, a corrector, who is not to be a member of the Society, is to be appointed. When this is not possible some other suitable plan is to be devised.[7] When reformation is despaired of, and the pupil is likely to become a danger to his fellows, he is to be expelled.[8]

Among the general regulations for the professors of the lower studies[9] are those dealing with the *praelectio*, or method of exposition of a subject or lesson, and those concerning emulation. In the exposition of a lesson or passage four stages are to be distinguished :[10] (i) The

---

[1] Reg. 8, § 3.   [2] Reg. 8, § 4.   [3] Reg. 13.
[4] Reg. 23.   [5] Reg. 26.   [6] Reg. 37.
[7] Reg. 38.   Cf. Ganss, p. 319.   [8] Reg. 40.
[9] Regulae Communes Professoribus Classium Inferiorum.   Cf. Fitz-patrick, pp. 195–208.   [10] Reg. 27.

whole passage, when not too long, is to be read through. (*ii*) The argument is to be explained, also, when necessary, the connection with what went before. (*iii*) Each sentence is to be read, the obscure points elucidated; the sentences are to be connected together, and the thought made evident. (*iv*) The whole is to be repeated from the beginning.

In this section the subject of emulation is also introduced.[1] Throughout the *Constitutions* and the *Ratio* anything likely to excite contention or produce invidious distinctions is deprecated. Graduates are not to occupy special seats in the university classes, and except in cases in which pupils have specially distinguished themselves, the class lists are to be in alphabetic order. That emulation is not a dominant or integral part of the Jesuit system may be judged from the fact that only four regulations are here devoted to it.[2] It was merely one among other devices to enliven instruction and develop in the pupils a ready command of the knowledge which they had acquired. The directions governing its use state that the *concertatio*, or contest, is usually so conducted that either the teacher puts the question, and the *aemulus* or adversary corrects the answer, or the adversaries question one another. The contest is to be held in the highest regard, and to take place as frequently as time permits, so that an honourable rivalry (*honesta aemulatio*), which is a great incitement to study, may be fostered. The contest may be engaged in by one or more on either side, especially by the better pupils of the class against one another, and a contest of one against many may even be allowed. An average pupil may sometimes challenge a distinguished pupil, and if he overcomes, he succeeds to the superior office. Public contests may be allowed on occasion, but only the better pupils should take part. One class may contend with the

---

[1] Cf. A. P. Farrell, *The Jesuit Code of Liberal Education*, pp. 292–6.
[2] Reg. 31, 32, 34, 35.

class next to it on a common subject of study, both teachers presiding.

The spirit in which this and the other measures indicated above were conducted, can be gathered from the quaint account of the actual practice of an early Jesuit school given by John Dury in his *Description of a Transmarine School*.[1]

As a precedent for the introduction of emulation the Jesuits could cite Quintilian, who, likewise advocating public in preference to private education, says of the boy educated at school that he will hear indolence rebuked and industry commended. This will excite him to emulation. Though ambition may be a fault in itself, it is often the mother of virtues.[2] The classical apology of emulation is that given by Petavius (1583–1652), a Jesuit Father who, in an Inaugural Address entitled 'The Duty of Using Emulation in Schools',[3] instances emulation in play and games, refers to Virgil's desire to emulate Homer, and Cicero's effort to emulate Demosthenes. Between the living, too, there may be emulation without the necessity to imitate. It is exceptionally effective in youth, he claims; equals in age and ability should be regular rivals in knowledge, industry, acquisition of skill. Pupils will find in their teachers' lives and example a great stimulus to emulation. Teachers themselves may even engage in friendly rivalry to promote the knowledge, love of learning and character of their pupils. Herbart[4] virtually summarises the argument of Petavius: 'Emula-

[1] T. Corcoran, *Studies in the History of Classical Teaching* (London: Longmans, Green & Co., 1911), pp. 229–47. For Dury (1596–1680) see also G. H. Turnbull, *Hartlib, Dury and Comenius* (University Press of Liverpool, 1947). Dury was also the author of *The Reformed School* (1650); see J. Dury, *The Reformed School*, edited by H. M. Knox (University Press of Liverpool, 1958).

[2] *Institutes*, Bk I. ii. 21–22.

[3] *Petavius on Emulation in Schools*. Printed for academic use in the Department of Education, University College, Dublin, 1928.

[4] *Outlines of Educational Doctrine*, § 183.

tion, which is not contention, is a welcome feature of sport and play', he says. 'Mental activity likewise affords suitable opportunities for excelling; it also provides occasions for making comparisons; but relative excellence, children must understand distinctly, is not to be advanced by them as a basis for claims.'

Into the specific directions for the various professors of rhetoric, humanity and grammar, the conduct of academies and the training of scholastics, we cannot here enter. To trace the history of the system is also beyond the scope of this work; in truth, to the treatment of the *Ratio Studiorum* given in this chapter objection might be taken, since the *Ratio* is not the work of Ignatius; it nevertheless represents more fully, and doubtless more justly, his views on, and practices in, education than his *Constitutions*, in which the subject could be treated only as part of the general work of the Society. As more criticism than study has been devoted to this system by writers on the history of education, it is advisable incidentally to enumerate some of the topics in regard to which the Jesuits have anticipated modern practice, and by implication to reply to the unfounded criticisms of these writers.

To the Jesuits must be given the credit of providing education with a uniform and universal method. 'So far as the evidence of history extends,' it has been said,[1] 'an organised caste of priests, combining the necessary leisure with the equally necessary continuity of tradition, was at all times indispensable to the beginnings of scientific research'; it appears also to have been necessary, as it was undoubtedly advantageous, for the beginnings of teaching method. The need of a uniform and universal method in teaching was thus declared in the Proem to the 1586 *Ratio* :[2] 'Unless a ready and true method be adopted much labour is spent in gathering but little fruit. . . .

[1] T. Gomperz, *Greek Thinkers*, English translation (London, John Murray, 1901), vol. i, p. 43.   [2] Pachtler, vol. v, p. 27.

We cannot imagine that we do justice to our functions, or come up to the expectations formed of us, if we do not feed the multitude of youths, in the same way as nurses do, with food dressed up in the best way, for fear they grow up in our schools, without growing up much in learning.'

The Jesuit system does not, however, exalt the method at the expense of the teacher, as Comenius did later. In the selection of teachers something of the same discrimination as Ignatius exercised in his choice of the first members of the Society is still demanded; and the selected candidates are subjected to a training which in length and thoroughness no other educational system, with the possible exception of that sketched by Plato in the *Republic*, has attempted to approach.[1] Even yet the educational authorities in many modern countries have failed to realise the importance of thorough professional training for all engaged in higher education, including university teaching. The value of training was recognised in the draft *Ratio* of 1586 in the statement:[2] 'It would be most profitable for the schools, if those who are about to be preceptors were privately taken in hand by some one of great experience, and for two months or more were practised by him in the method of reading, teaching, correcting, writing, and managing a class. If teachers have not learned these things beforehand, they are forced to learn them afterwards at the expense of their scholars; and then they will acquire proficiency only when they have already lost in reputation; and perchance they will never unlearn a bad habit. Sometimes such a habit is neither very serious nor incorrigible, if taken at the beginning; but if the habit is not corrected at the outset, it comes to pass that a man, who otherwise would have been most useful, becomes well-nigh useless. There is no

---

[1] Cf. Hughes, *Loyola*, chs x, xii. Schwickerath, *Jesuit Education*, ch. xv.
[2] Pachtler, vol. v, p. 154; Schwickerath, pp. 432-3.

describing how much amiss preceptors take it, if they are corrected, when they have already adopted a fixed method of teaching, and what continual disagreement ensues on that score with the prefect of studies. To obviate this evil, in the case of our professors, let the prefect in the chief college, whence our professors of humanities and grammar are usually taken, remind the rector and Provincial, about three months before the next scholastic year begins, that, if the Province needs new professors for the following term, they should select someone eminently versed in the art of managing classes, whether he be at the time actually a professor or a student of theology or philosophy, and to him the future masters are to go daily for an hour, to be prepared by him for their new ministry, giving prelections in turn, writing, dictating, correcting, and discharging the other duties of a good teacher.'

The predominant place assigned to classics in the Jesuit curriculum has historical justification. The Society has not, however, as is frequently laid to its charge, bound itself slavishly to a seventeenth-century curriculum. From the outset provision was made for extension and modification of the curriculum, and of this liberty the Society has availed itself. While it has not rashly incorporated in its educational system every innovation, it has adopted such changes as seem to it permanent and valuable. The widening of the conception of culture to connote not only the classical languages but also a precise use of the mother tongue, an appreciation of modern literature, the principles of mathematics and the methods of natural science, has been recognised by the Jesuits; and the new subjects, when admitted to the curriculum, have been taught with the same thoroughness as the old. Indeed the changes which time has brought have been more fully recognised and more effectively met by the Jesuits than by some of the schools whose pupils have condemned in quite unmeasured terms the conservatism of the Jesuits.

In order of time the mathematical subjects follow the classical subjects; the subjects are taught successively, not simultaneously. While the Jesuits defend on pedagogical grounds the successive teaching of different branches of instruction in preference to the simultaneous treatment of a number of subjects, they modify this procedure when the educational requirements of any government system require this. Their arrangement, while it does not find favour with other schools of educational thought, is partly recognised in the demand of present-day educators who advocate successive periods of 'intensive study' of the various school subjects.[1]

In retaining the drama as an educational instrument[2] the Jesuits anticipated the modern movement represented by what is termed the dramatic method of teaching history.[3] In insisting on the speaking of Latin they likewise anticipated the direct method of teaching the classics. In repeating the work of the class twice in the year, and thus enabling the abler pupils to spend only half a session in a grade and be promoted more rapidly, they introduced a procedure now adopted by some modern school systems.

The Jesuits' contribution to school discipline was as notable as the advance made by the *Ratio* in the teaching practice it displaced. To the early Jesuits we owe the substitution of supervision for compulsion, and while later

[1] T. Corcoran, 'Jesuit Education', *The Encyclopaedia and Dictionary of Education*, edited by Foster Watson (London: Sir Isaac Pitman, 1921), vol. ii, pp. 913-16. 'The changes from the old Order are very considerable. Uniformity is now limited to principles, for national distinctiveness in education has become dominant. The loss of foundations and endowments makes "free education" rarely possible. Boarding-schools have become more common, in all lands, for secondary education; modern subjects are fully provided for, and taught concurrently with classics.'

[2] Cf. Reg. Rectoris, 73: 'The subject of tragedies and comedies, which would be in Latin and but rarely performed, must be pious and edifying.'

[3] Bacon would have the art of acting (*actio theatralis*) made a part of the education of youth. The Jesuits, he says, do not despise it; and he thinks they are right; for though it be of ill repute as a profession, yet as a part of discipline it is of excellent use.

writers have generally condemned the Jesuit policy,[1] it has only to be contrasted with the barbarities of the disciplinary measures current in their day to realise the revolution they effected. The principle implied is that prevention is better than cure. They did not, however, dispense with punishment altogether, for the *Ratio* of 1599[2] recommended the introduction of a corrector. The office of corrector was later dispensed with, but the principle of dissociating punishment from teaching has been retained. It must not be inferred that there is undue severity in their methods. Gentleness is especially enjoined towards the pupils, Ignatius prescribing as the maxim of the Society that it 'must always govern by love'.[3] That obedience is one of the vows taken by the members of the Society must lighten the work of teaching, and in the confession and the communion the Society possesses powerful instruments for the moral and religious education of the pupil. Whatever others may think of the confessional, the Jesuit Society recognises that it is of inestimable value in the moral training of the pupil,[4] and through the communion the Society secures practice in worship, an exercise which distinguishes the religious from the moral attitude to life, and a training in which is essential to a complete and generous education.[5]

[1] In one of his *Aphorisms* Herbart declared: 'The old pedagogy betrayed its weakness in nothing as much as its dependence on compulsion; the modern in nothing so much as in the emphatic value it places on supervision. Great perplexity can alone be the motive for exclusively recommending a measure at once so prejudicial, insufficient and costly. The hindrance of offences is only good when a new activity continually takes the place of that which is restrained.' In his *Outlines of Educational Doctrine*, § 178, he says, however, 'Gambling must be forbidden, and in case compliance with this prohibition is doubtful, obedience must be secured by watchful supervision.'

[2] Rules for Prefects of Lower Studies, 38. Cf. Fitzpatrick, p. 187, and Rules Common to Professors of Lower Studies, 40. Cf. Fitzpatrick, p. 206.

[3] Cf. Francis Thompson, *Loyola*, p. 295.

[4] Cf. Schwickerath, pp. 553–5.

[5] See Chap X of this work for incompleteness of Herbart's conception of the end of education as morality.

The Jesuit system has survived since its approval by the Pope in 1540, and has adapted itself with a certain measure of success to changing conditions.[1] Its limitations are mainly self-imposed, and its defects are doubtless best known to, and can be best stated by, those who are applying it, the criticisms of others tending to be beside the mark. As its exponents are not merely educators, but missionaries of a religious faith, it has been applied in almost every country in the world. For these reasons its founder is as worthy of a place amongst the great educators as amongst the saints.

Although with a chivalrous self-effacement the modern exponents of this system attribute its success to the original methods of the *Ratio Studiorum*, it is doubtless to be attributed in part also to the thoroughness of the training and the devotion to their vocation of the exponents themselves. Francis Thompson, writing of Loyola — and the statement may be taken to apply to his present-day representatives — says : 'When he spoke, it was not what he said, it was the suppressed heat of personal feeling, personal conviction which enkindled men. This has ever been the secret of great teachers, were they only schoolmasters ; it is the communication of themselves that avails.'[2] Their reward, it may be added, is the respect and affection of their pupils, the only reward of the true teacher ; and probably no class of teachers has constrained such affection in their pupils as the Jesuits have done and still do. The Jesuit educational system, then, has taught the world the value of a uniform and universal method in education, and the economy of a cultured and highly-trained teaching profession.

[1] See *The Times*, 2nd January 1958, 'Jesuit Fathers : Training and Functions in the Modern World'.
[2] *Saint Ignatius Loyola*, p. 181.

CHAPTER V

COMENIUS[1]

THE early educators had confined their attention to the training of the governing classes of the community, and until the time of Comenius it was only idealists like More who could hazard the suggestion that 'all in their childhood be instruct in learning . . . in their own native tongue'.[2] Comenius not only proposed to teach 'all things to all men', but also set about in a practical fashion planning a universal system of education, devising methods of teaching which would hasten the attainment of his ideal, and even preparing school books to illustrate how his principles should be applied in practice. It was not that foreseeing the triumph of democracy he would take time by the forelock and 'educate our masters', nor was it on the grounds of an abstract political principle like the equality of man that he based his belief, but rather by reason of the infinite possibilities in human nature and of the uncertainty as to the position to which providence might call this or that man that he advocated that education should be accessible to all. It was only on religious grounds that such a faith in the universal education of the people could at that time be based, for the

[1] 1592–1670. For life see Matthew Spinka, *John Amos Comenius: That Incomparable Moravian* (University of Chicago Press, 1943). Also *The Teacher of Nations* (Cambridge University Press, 1942).
  For visit to England see *The Times Educational Supplement*, 10th March 1928, and R. F. Young, *Comenius in England* (Oxford University Press, 1932). Also G. H. Turnbull, 'Plans of Comenius for his Stay in England', *Acta Comeniana*, II, i, pp. 7–23, and *Hartlib, Dury and Comenius* (University Press of Liverpool, 1947), pp. 349–70.
[2] *Utopia*, §§ 182, 183.

D   89

idea of universalising education has proved more difficult of realisation than could possibly have been foreseen by Comenius.[1]

Apart from his exertions to succour his persecuted and exiled people and his endeavours to assuage the bitter dissensions between the factions of the Reformed Church, his most influential gift to the religious life of his nation was *The Labyrinth of the World and the Paradise of the Heart*, the supplementary title of which reads — 'a book that clearly shows that this world and all matters concerning it are nothing but confusion and giddiness, pain and toil, deceit and falsehood, misery and anxiety, and lastly, disgust of all things and despair; but he who remains in his own dwelling within his heart, opening it to the Lord God alone, will obtain true and full peace of mind and joy'.[2]

The Labyrinth is in many respects analogous to Bunyan's *Pilgrim's Progress* and in Czech literature has become a classic and one of the great books of mystical devotion.[3] The sections in *The Labyrinth* having educational significance are those in which he describes the current pedagogical practice and what Comenius considers ought to be the practice. 'I speak not of their pouches,' he says,[4] 'but of their skins which had to suffer, for fists, canes, sticks, birch rods struck them on their cheeks, heads, backs and posteriors till blood streamed forth, and they were almost entirely covered with stripes, scars, spots and

---

[1] Cf. M. Spinka, *John Amos Comenius*, p. 32: 'He became an educational reformer more by accident than by primary design; and it would be doing him less than justice if we were to fail to recognise his primary and dominant life-motive.'

[2] John Amos Komensky, *The Labyrinth of the World and the Paradise of the Heart* (1623), edited and translated by Count Lutzow (London: Swan Sonnenschein, 1901). Or J. A. Comenius, *The Labyrinth of the World and the Paradise of the Heart* (London: Dent's Temple Classics, 1905).

There is also a translation by Matthew Spinka (Chicago, 1942).

[3] M. Spinka, *John Amos Comenius*.

[4] Count Lutzow's translation, pp. 116–17.

weals.' In the ideal state, the paradise of the heart, however, Comenius describes[1] how he found 'no few learned
men, who, contrary to the customs of the world, sur-
passed the others in humility as greatly as they did in
learning, and they were sheer gentleness and kindness. It
befell that I spoke to one of them, from whom it was
thought no earthly learning was concealed, yet he bore
himself as a most simple man, sighing deeply over his
stupidity and ignorance. The knowledge of languages
they held in slight value, if the knowledge of wisdom was
not added to it. For languages, they said, give not wisdom, but have that purpose only that by means of them
we can converse with many and diverse inhabitants of
the terrestrial globe, be they alive or dead. Therefore,
not he, they said, who can speak many languages, but he
who can speak of useful things, is learned. Now they call
useful things all God's works, and they said that arts are
of some use for the purpose of understanding Him; but
they also say that the true fountain of knowledge is Holy
Writ, and the Holy Ghost our teacher, and that the purpose of all true knowledge is Christ, He who was crucified.'

Although Comenius's efforts for educational reform
were undoubtedly inspired by religious motives, the great
interest of his life, apart from religion, lay in a scheme of
universal knowledge or pansophism, and this influenced,
and on occasion diverted him from, his educational
activities. Pansophism is not to be identified with mere
encyclopaedism, as Kenneth Richmond in *The Permanent
Values in Education*[2] was at pains to point out: 'Encyclo-
paedic teaching is neither practicable nor desirable;
pansophic teaching is both. The one aims at making the
learner an inexhaustible mine of information upon every
subject, the other would make him capable of wisdom in
his regard for any subject and able to see any subject in

---

[1] *The Labyrinth*, pp. 335-6.
[2] London: Constable & Co., 1917, p. 36.

relation to others and to general principles.' Nor is it merely 'the correlation of sciences in a unity' as Laurie in his *Comenius*[1] proposes, for correlation is, after all, a somewhat artificial and external process. Pansophism is best understood when expressed in modern terms as a recognition of the organic conception of knowledge — the 'flower in the crannied wall'. In a sketch of his pansophic work Comenius himself explains that it was to be 'an accurate anatomy of the universe, dissecting the veins and limbs of all things in such a way that there shall be nothing that is not seen, and that each part shall appear in its place and without confusion'. The purpose, as he explains at length in *The Way of Light*,[2] is not so much to make men learned as to make them wise, to give them understanding of their own ends and of the end of all things. This pansophic conception reflects the influence of Bacon and recalls the *New Atlantis* rather than the scientific method of the *Advancement of Learning* or the *Novum Organum*. In the *New Atlantis* the central feature is Salomon's House, 'which house or college is the very eye of the kingdom'. This foundation is the embodiment of the scientific spirit which Bacon hoped might bring happiness to humanity. Salomon's House is a great laboratory equipped with all manner of scientific instruments, and associated with it is an organised army of scientific investigators. All the processes of nature are there artificially reproduced, and the results made to serve mankind.[3] While Comenius failed to appreciate the value

[1] S. S. Laurie, *John Amos Comenius* (Cambridge University Press, 1899), p. 20.

[2] John Amos Comenius, *The Way of Light* (1668), translated into English with Introduction by E. T. Campagnac (University Press of Liverpool, 1938), pp. 148–51.

[3] R. F. Young (*Times Educational Supplement*, 10th March 1928) traced the development of a great college for scientific research from the Accademia Platonica at Florence in the fifteenth century, the Accademia Secretorum Naturae founded at Naples in 1560, the Accademia dei Lincei established at Rome in 1603, and similar Italian scientific societies of the sixteenth and early seventeenth centuries.

of experiment in science on which Bacon insisted, he believed that the progress of humanity could be materially advanced by the collection of all available knowledge of God, nature and art, and by its reduction, on what he considered scientific principles, to a system which he denoted by the term Pansophia or Universal Wisdom.

Although *The Great Didactic*[1] belongs to the earlier period of Comenius's life — to the religious rather than to the pansophic — the title 'The Great Didactic setting forth the whole Art of Teaching all Things to all Men' nevertheless reveals 'the desire for omniscience' which, according to Adamson,[2] is very rarely absent from the seventeenth-century writers. The sub-title likewise formulates Comenius's democratic attitude; it runs: 'a certain Inducement to found such schools in all the Parishes, Towns and Villages of every Christian Kingdom that the entire youth of both sexes, none being excepted, shall quickly, pleasantly and thoroughly become learned in the Sciences, pure in Morals, trained to Piety, and in this manner instructed in all things necessary for the present and for the future life.'

That a reorganisation of educational institutions and a revolution in educational methods were urgent is evident from the complaint as to the condition of the schools of their day common to all the pedagogical writers of the period; of these schools Comenius wrote:[3] 'they are the terror of boys and the slaughter houses of minds — places where a hatred of literature and books is contracted, where ten or more years are spent in learning what might

[1] Written in Czech between 1628 and 1632, published in Latin 1657-8. The Czech version was not published till 1849. English translation by M. W. Keatinge, *The Great Didactic of John Amos Comenius* (London: A. & C. Black, 1910). Cf. V. Jelinek, *The Analytical Didactic of Comenius* (University of Chicago Press, 1954).

[2] J. W. Adamson, *Pioneers of Modern Education* (Cambridge University Press, 1905), p. 149. Bacon, for example, took all knowledge for his province.

[3] Quoted S. S. Laurie, *John Amos Comenius*, p. 55.

be acquired in one, where what ought to be poured in gently is violently forced in and beaten in, where what ought to be put clearly and perspicaciously is presented in a confused and intricate way, as if it were a collection of puzzles — places where minds are fed on words'. In *The Great Didactic* he dismisses existing schools more succinctly as 'terrors for boys and shambles for their intellects'.

In accordance with the ideal of the universal school expressed in the sub-title of *The Great Didactic* Comenius would establish such a system of education that all the young, 'not the children of the rich or of the powerful only but all alike, boys and girls, both noble and ignoble, rich and poor, in all cities and towns, villages and hamlets, should be sent to school. Let none therefore be excluded unless God has denied him sense and intelligence.'[1] His plea for the inclusion of girls runs : 'They are endowed with equal sharpness of mind and capacity for knowledge, and they are able to attain the highest positions since they have often been called by God Himself to rule over nations. Why, therefore, should we admit them to the alphabet, and afterwards drive them away from books?'

Like Quintilian, Comenius contends that school education is preferable to home education, schools being necessary since it is seldom that parents have adequate ability or the necessary leisure to instruct their children. 'And although there might be parents with leisure to educate their own children, it is nevertheless better that the young should be taught together and in large classes, since better results and more pleasure are to be obtained when one pupil serves as an example and a stimulus for another. For to do what we see others do, to go where others go, to follow those who are ahead of us, and to keep in front of those who are behind us is the course of action to which we are all most naturally inclined. Young children especially are always more easily led and

[1] *The Great Didactic*, ch. ix.

ruled by example than by precept. If you give them a precept, it makes little impression; if you point out that others are doing something, they imitate without being told to do so.'[1] Comenius is likewise an advocate of the common school. 'We wish all men to be trained in all the virtues, especially in modesty, sociability and politeness, and it is therefore undesirable to create class distinctions at such an early age, or to give some children the opportunity of considering their own lot with satisfaction and that of others with scorn.'[2]

Comenius would organise schools on the following plan: a mother or nursery school[3] for children up to the age of six, a vernacular or primary school in every village for pupils of six to twelve, a Latin or secondary school in every city for pupils of twelve to eighteen, and a university in every kingdom or province for youths from eighteen to twenty-four preparing for the professions. Promotion was throughout to be by ability: 'When boys are only six years old, it is too early to determine their vocation in life, or whether they are more suited for learning or for manual labour. At this age neither the mind nor the inclinations are sufficiently developed. Nor should admission to the Latin school be reserved for the sons of rich men, nobles and magistrates, as if these were the only boys who would ever be able to fill similar positions. The wind blows where it will, and does not always begin to blow at a fixed time.'[4] University entrance is to be more stringently restricted:[5] 'The studies will progress with ease and success if only select intellects, the flower of mankind, attempt them. The rest had better turn their attention to more suitable occupations, such as agriculture, mechanics or trade', a recommendation that

[1] Ibid., ch. viii, § 7. [2] Ch. xxix, § 2.
[3] Ch. xxviii. Also *The School of Infancy*, translated by D. Benham (London: W. Mallalieu & Co., 1858). Or *The School of Infancy*, edited by E. M. Eller (University of North Carolina Press, 1957).
[4] *The Great Didactic*, ch. xxix, § 2. [5] Ibid., ch. xxi, § 4.

recalls the advice of Montaigne, who, for a pupil having no aptitude for learning, suggests as the best remedy 'to put him prentice to some base occupation, in some good town or other, yea, were he the son of a Duke'.[1]

The lack of internal organisation of the existing schools sorely distressed Comenius. Among the defects which he diagnosed were that each school, even each teacher, used a different method, that one procedure was followed in one language and another in a second, and even in the same subject the method was so varied that the pupil scarcely understood in what way he was expected to learn. No method was known by which instruction was given to all the pupils in a class at the same time; the individual only was taught.[2] To remedy these defects he proposed[3] that there should only be one teacher in each school or at any rate in each class; only one author should be used for each subject studied; the same exercises should be given to the whole class; all subjects and languages should be taught by the same method; everything should be taught thoroughly, briefly and pithily; all things that are naturally connected ought to be taught in combination; every subject should be taught in definitely graded steps, that the work of one day may thus expand that of the previous day, and lead up to that of the morrow; and finally, everything that is useless should be invariably discarded.

Not only would Comenius make instruction more methodical but he would also make it more agreeable to the pupil. He suggests[4] that the school should be situated in a quiet spot, far from noise and distraction,

---

[1] *Essays*: 'Of the Institution and Education of Children' (1580). From a manuscript emendation (cf. S. S. Laurie, *Studies in the History of Educational Opinion from the Renaissance* (Cambridge University Press, 1903), p. 105, it appears that Montaigne would give such pupils even shorter shrift, as he there advises the masters to 'strangle such youths if they can do it without witnesses'.

[2] *The Great Didactic*, ch. xix, §§ 7, 8.   [3] Ibid., ch. xix, § 14.

[4] Ch. xvi, § 56 (ii).

and explains further :[1] 'The school itself should be a pleasant place, and attractive to the eye both within and without. Within, the room should be bright and clean, and its walls should be ornamented by pictures. These should be either portraits of celebrated men, geographical maps, historical plans, or other ornaments.[2] Without, there should be an open place to walk and to play in (for this is absolutely necessary for children), and there should also be a garden attached, into which scholars may be allowed to go from time to time and where they may feast their eyes on trees, flowers and plants. If this be done, boys will in all probability go to school with as much pleasure as to fairs, where they always hope to see and hear something new.'

With greater insistence than any of his predecessors Comenius reiterates the principle that the child should be first instructed in things before being taught to express them in language,[3] that everything should be first learned-through the medium of the senses.[4] 'Men must,' he explains,[5] 'as far as possible, be taught to become wise by studying the heavens, the earth, oaks, and beeches, but not by studying books ; that is to say, they must learn to know and investigate the things themselves, and not the observations that other people have made about the things. We shall thus tread in the footsteps of the wise men of old, if each of us obtain his knowledge from the originals, from things themselves, and from no other sources.' And echoing Bacon, he adds : 'That no information should be imparted on the grounds of bookish authority, but should be authorised by actual demonstration for the senses and to the intellect.'

The common school for all pupils from six to twelve years of age necessitates not only that the teaching of other languages should be carried on through the mother

[1] Ch. xvii, § 17.   [2] Cf. ibid., § 42.   [3] Ch. xvi, § 19.
Ch. xvii, § 2 (viii). Cf. § 38 (iii).   [5] Ch. xviii, § 28. Cf. ch. xx.

tongue,[1] but also that direct instruction in the mother tongue itself should be given. 'To attempt to teach a foreign language before the mother tongue has been learned is', says Comenius,[2] 'as irrational as to teach a boy to ride before he can walk. Cicero declared that he could not teach elocution to those who were unable to speak, and, in the same way, my method confesses its inability to teach Latin to those who are ignorant of their mother tongue, since the one paves the way for the other. Finally, what I have in view is an education in the objects that surround us, and a brief survey of this education can be obtained from books written in the mother tongue which embody a list of the things that exist in the external world. This preliminary survey will render the acquisition of Latin far easier, for it will only be necessary to adapt a new nomenclature to objects.' Montaigne had earlier recommended[3] learning first the mother tongue, but, unlike Comenius, he was proposing an education suitable for 'a complete gentleman born of noble parentage'.

Comenius's curriculum would include 'all those subjects which are able to make a man wise, virtuous and pious'.[4] He requires, in fact, that every pupil should, in Milton's phrase, have a universal insight into things, and the qualification which he adds is apparent rather than real :[5] 'But do not, therefore, imagine that we demand for all men a knowledge (that is to say, an exact or deep knowledge) of all the arts and sciences. It is the principles, the causes, and the uses of all the most important things in existence that we wish all men to learn ; all, that is to say, who are sent into the world to be actors as well

---

[1] *The Great Didactic*, Cf. ch. xvii, §§ 27, 28.

[2] Ibid., ch. xxix, §§ 3–4. For the teaching of the vernacular see whole chapter.

[3] *Essays* (1580): 'Of the Institution and Education of Children': 'I would first know my own tongue perfectly, then my neighbours with whom I have most commerce.'

[4] *The Great Didactic*, ch. xii, § 2.   [5] Ibid., ch. x, § 1.

as spectators. For we must take strong and vigorous measures that no man in his journey through life may encounter anything unknown to him that he cannot pass sound judgment upon it and turn it to its proper use without error.'

All the errors of the past could be avoided and all his aims achieved, Comenius assumed, by the adoption of the principles of order. Order, he believed, was education's, as well as heaven's, first law; he accordingly contended that the art of teaching demands nothing more than the skilful arrangement of time, of the subjects taught and of the method. Just as Bacon, however, with his new inductive methods failed to appreciate the part which the mind must play in originating hypotheses, so Comenius belittled the importance in education of the teacher;[1] as Bacon believed that by his method truth could straightway be attained, so Comenius assumed that it could be easily conveyed to all. Thus we find him adding:[2] 'As soon as we succeed in finding the proper method it will be no harder to teach schoolboys in any number desired than with the help of the printing press to cover a thousand sheets daily with the neatest writing.'

The right order, or proper method, Comenius conceives, can be secured if, after the manner of the writers of his time, we 'follow nature'; thus he declares:[2] 'That order which is the dominating principle in the art of teaching all things to all men, should be, and can be, borrowed from no other source but the operations of nature. As soon as this principle is thoroughly secured, the processes of art will proceed as easily and as spontaneously as those of nature.' For Comenius, 'following nature' nevertheless consists merely in adducing analogies from natural processes in support of preconceived and

[1] See nevertheless the significance assigned to the teacher in the *Pampaedia* below, p. 105.
[2] *The Great Didactic*, ch. xxx, § 15. Cf. ch. xix, §§ 16–29.

independently acquired principles; the analogies are in many instances quite fanciful and lend no authority to the maxims of method which are supposed to be based on them.

Among the precepts of Comenius are to be found certain of the traditional maxims of teaching method, for example, 'Proceed from what is easy to what is more difficult',[1] and instead of the maxim 'Proceed from the particular to the general' we find 'Proceed from the general to the particular'.[2] The principle of correlation or integration of studies is implied in the admonitions: 'Great stress [should] be laid on the points of resemblance between cognate subjects';[3] and 'all things that are naturally connected ought to be taught in combination'.[4] The inductive method of teaching, or what Adams terms 'anticipatory illustration',[5] is expressed thus:[6] 'It is necessary that examples come before rules.' Herbart's doctrine of interest is anticipated in such remarks as: 'The desire to know and to learn should be excited in the boy in every possible manner.'[7] 'Every study should be commenced in such a manner as to awaken a real liking for it on the part of the scholars';[8] and although Comenius's own psychology was of the most primitive type, he anticipated the psychological principle of Pestalozzi when he affirmed[9] that nothing should be taught the young unless it is not only permitted but actually demanded by their age and mental strength.

Some of the principles and methods recommended by Comenius are common to him and to the Jesuits, the success of whose practices he cites[10] in support of the procedures he advocated. Thus Comenius advises that

---

[1] *The Great Didactic*, ch. xvi, § 25; xvii, § 2.
[2] Ibid., ch. xvii, § 2.   [3] Ch. xviii, § 4.
[4] Ch. xix, § 14.   [5] *Exposition and Illustration*, p. 31.
[6] *The Great Didactic*, ch. xvi, § 19.   [7] Ibid., ch. xvii, § 13.
[8] Ch. xviii, § 16. Cf. ch. xix, § 20 (ii).   [9] Ch. xvii, § 38. Cf. § 35.
[10] Cf. Spinka, *John Amos Comenius*, pp. 129–30.

care should be exercised in the selection of texts put into pupils' hands; he maintains[1] that the books which the scholars use should be such as can rightly be termed sources of wisdom, virtue and piety; and he deplores the fact that more caution has not been exercised in the matter.[2] The *Ratio Studiorum* instructs the Provincial[3] to secure that school books which might do harm to virtue or good morals should be withheld from pupils till the offensive passages are expurgated, and the professors of the lower studies are advised[4] to refrain from introducing words prejudicial to good morals, and not only to abstain from expounding these but also to deter pupils as far as possible from reading them out of school. Comenius also recommends[5] the use of epitomes, the use of which by the Jesuits has been criticised.[6] The following extracts from *The Great Didactic* read almost like a translation of the Jesuit regulations:[7] 'If the scholars are to be interested, care must be taken to make the method palatable, so that everything, no matter how serious, may be placed before them in a familiar and attractive manner; in the form of a dialogue, for instance, by pitting the boys against one another to answer and explain riddling questions, comparisons and fables. . . .' 'The civil authorities and the managers of schools can kindle the zeal of the scholars by being present at public performances (such as declarations, disputations, examinations and promotions), and by praising the industrious ones and giving them small presents (without respect of person).' Even emulation is commended by Comenius as 'by far the best stimulus'[8] with school pupils.

---

[1] *The Great Didactic*, ch. xvii, § 62 (ii).
[2] Ibid., ch. ix, § 6. Cf. ch. xix, § 52.   [3] Reg. Provincialis, 34.
[4] Reg. Com. Prof. Class. Inf. 8.   [5] *The Great Didactic*, ch. xxi.
[6] Cf. A. P. Farrell, *The Jesuit Code of Liberal Education*, pp. 248–51.
[7] *The Great Didactic*, ch. xvii, §§ 19–20. For further references to contests see ch. xix, § 25; xxvi, § 5; to public debates or dissertations, ch. xxxi, § 5.
[8] Ibid., ch. xix, § 16.

On school discipline Comenius held enlightened views, and his recommendations follow the principles enunciated by Quintilian[1] on this subject. Thus he affirms :[2] 'That no blows be given for lack of readiness to learn (for, if the pupil do not learn readily, this is the fault of no one but the teacher, who either does not know how to make his pupil receptive of knowledge or does not take the trouble to do so)'; and in his chapter 'Of School Discipline'[3] the analogy he there employs lends force to his argument. Thus he says : 'A musician does not strike his lyre a blow with his fist or with a stick, nor does he throw it against the wall, because it produces a discordant sound; but, setting to work on scientific principles, he tunes it and gets it into order. Just such a skilful and sympathetic treatment is necessary to instil a love of learning into the minds of our pupils, and any other procedure will only convert their idleness into antipathy and their lack of industry into downright stupidity.'

The need of suitable textbooks was early felt by Comenius. Like the other educators of his time and in spite of the prominence he assigned to the teaching of the vernacular, Comenius was compelled to devote attention to the teaching of languages, especially of Latin. Here, nevertheless, he met with his greatest practical success, for the manuals he prepared to facilitate the learning of Latin won ready acceptance, his *Janua Linguarum Reserata* being doubtless the most celebrated school book ever published and his *Orbis Pictus* one of the earliest to introduce visual aids.[4]

[1] See above, Ch. II.
[2] *The Great Didactic*, ch. xvii, § 41 (i). [3] Ibid., ch. xxvi.
[4] For comparison of the *Janua* of Comenius with that published earlier by Bathe, a Jesuit priest of the Irish College at Salamanca, see T. Corcoran, *Studies in the History of Classical Teaching*, pp. 1–130.

If Comenius's *Janua* was not original, he must be given credit for preparing a series of textbooks in a graded manner — Janua, Vestibulum, Atrium and Palladium. It was not until more than a century later that it became common to write textbooks in series — John A. Nietz, 'Some

A manuscript work in Latin by Comenius — the *Pampaedia*, doubtless his last word on education, was discovered by Professor Dmitrij Tschizewskij at Halle in Germany in 1935.[1] The Latin text with a German translation was published at Heidelberg in 1960.[2] The *Pampaedia* was one of a series of seven volumes, each of the titles having the prefix *pan* — the Greek for 'all', and the whole collection the general title : General Considerations concerning Human Improvement. By Pampaedia is to be understood instruction in the true knowledge of the whole, that is, in pansophia.[3]

In an appendix[4] to the German edition of *Pampaedia* H. Geissler claims that pansophia, formerly regarded as irrelevant to Comenius's educational doctrine, is now seen to be the framework of this, and he quotes W. Dilthey to the effect that the connection of pansophia with the *Didactic* is the vantage point from which Comenius's system should be viewed and understood.

In another appendix[5] K. Schaller explains that Comenius's metaphysics is not a subjectivism derived

Findings from Analyses of Old Textbooks', *History of Education* (Spring 1952), vol. iii, No. 3, p. 81.

On picture books see *The Great Didactic*, ch. xxviii, §§ 25–26. The *Orbis Pictus* was not the first illustrated textbook. See letter on 'Early Textbooks' by W. Brickman, *Journal of Education* (London, June 1947). Comenius evidently derived the suggestion of a school book with pictures from Eilhard Lubinus (1565–1621), Professor of Theology at Rostock. For origin of *Orbis Pictus* and photograph of an early incomplete version see G. H. Turnbull, 'An Incomplete Orbis Pictus of Comenius. Printed in 1653', *Acta Comeniana*, i, i, pp. 35–54 (Prague, 1957).

The boys of G. W. Leibniz's time (1646–1716) appear to have been brought up on 'the picture book of Comenius and the little catechism [Luther's]' — R. Latta, *Leibniz: The Monadology* (1898), p. 1. Kant in his Lectures on education also mentions the *Orbis Pictus*.

[1] An account of the discovery of the manuscript is given in the German edition of the *Pampaedia*, pp. 490–5, also in an article 'Schools in the *Pampaedia* of J. A. Comenius' by A. Turek, *Research Review*, The Research Publications of the Institute of Education, University of Durham, No. 2, September 1951, pp. 29–39 (University of London Press).

[2] Quelle Meyer.   [3] *Pampaedia*, ch. 3, § 19.   [4] Pp. 507–11.

[5] *Pampaedia*, pp. 498–507, 'Über die Stellung der Pampaedia im pansophischen Gesamtwerk des Comenius.'

from such a formula as Descartes's *Cogito ergo sum*, for man cannot realise his self by withdrawing into himself; he can only attain his full stature as he sets the world in opposition to himself — as the derivation of the German term for 'object', *Gegenstand*, suggests — and overcomes and incorporates it. On the other hand, it is not a pure objectivism, assuming the existence of a world completely estranged from the mind that knows it, or like the view of modern science — indifferent to man or subordinating him to events, or like Bacon's, where nature can only be commanded by obeying. The objects of the world, too, can only become what they were designed to be, by being known and used. To designate Comenius, by reason of his emphasis on things, a realist, as has been usual in the past,[1] evinces consequently a complete misunderstanding.[2]

Pampaedia itself argues at considerable length, supported freely by texts from the Scriptures, that all should be educated, irrespective of class, creed, sex or age, in all things, and according to their true nature. All life is to be a school from the cradle, or even prior, to the grave. Seven stages or schools are distinguished:[3] (*i*) the antenatal, (*ii*) infancy, (*iii*) boyhood, (*iv*) adolescence, (*v*) youth, (*vi*) adulthood, (*vii*) senescence; death completes the series. The first school has its location in the womb, the second in every home, the third in every village, the

[1] See, however, earlier editions of this work. Spinka has designated Comenius 'the incurable idealist'.

[2] Comenius's metaphysical doctrine has also been summarised as follows by G. H. Turnbull in an article, 'The Pansophiae Diatyposis of Comenius and its Continuation', *Acta Comeniana*, I, ii, pp. 113–51 (Prague 1957): 'For Comenius wisdom is the true knowledge of all things knowable. The general basis of this wisdom is knowledge of the highest general classes of all things, the structure of all things, the laws of all things. Such knowledge is obtainable by the guidance of the common ideas, innate in every human mind, which need no proof but, illustrated only by examples, are thereupon admitted by every sane mind, and which are the principles of knowledge, on which are based all the other sciences. . . . The principles of knowledge are the principles of things, and these proceed from God, whose image the mind of man is.'

[3] *Pampaedia*, ch. 5, § 6.

fourth in every town, the fifth in every kingdom or province, the sixth in the whole world, and the seventh wherever old men congregate. The first two may be designated 'private schools'; the middle three 'public schools' since they are under the supervision of the Church or the community; and the last two 'personal', since every man thus far advanced in years is, or should be, the architect of his own fortune, and his education is in the hands of himself and of God.[1] Provision for each stage of life in the way of schools, books and teachers must be made, and in the *Pampaedia* a chapter is devoted to each of these.[2] The fact that Comenius devotes a chapter to the characteristics to be possessed by the teacher may help to correct the general impression that he insists unduly on the significance of method in education. The requisites of the true teacher are: he himself should be all that he expects his pupils to become; he should possess the technique of making them so; he should be zealous in his task, that is, he should be able, knowing and willing to make 'pansophes'. Accordingly the makers of men should be picked people, pious, honourable, serious, keen, industrious and tactful. Teachers must know the aim or purpose of their calling, all the means to attain this, and the whole range of methods.[3] Under twenty-four headings, termed Problems, the issues in teaching are set forth: for example, under Problem VI it is affirmed that examples, principles and practice must be combined, for without examples nothing can be taught easily, without rules or principles nothing orderly, and without practice nothing permanent. Also for correct insight into the natural world analysis, synthesis and syncresis are necessary, the last being the comparison of part with part or whole with whole.[4]

In the succeeding chapters Comenius applies his general

---

[1] Ibid., ch. 5, § 7.   [2] Ch. 5, schools; ch. 6, books; ch. 7, teachers.
[3] Ch. 7, §§ 3–5.   [4] Ch. 7, § 16.

maxims to the different age-groups, indicating how the
various schools, from the ante-natal to senescence, are to
be conducted.[1] In the chapter[2] on the first so-called
school, that is, before birth, Comenius offers us what
reads like an early attempt to formulate the regulations of
a marriage-guidance council and an ante-natal clinic
conducted by the mother — and father. The infant
school,[3] from birth to six years of age, is comparable with
the mother school of *The Great Didactic*[4] to which
Comenius refers us. To the objection that this age is too
early to instruct the child, Comenius retorts that it is the
age at which the child learns to speak, and he speaks only
what he learns. He stresses the importance of right
beginnings, averring that a mistake made in infant education cannot be rectified in later life. A novel feature, not
occurring in any of Comenius's other writings, is the
proposal of a nursery school from the age of four to the
age of six, an idea attributed to one Sophonias Hasen-
müller. This anticipates Froebel's kindergarten, but some
of the exercises — building up words from sounds, display
a formalism analogous to what we shall later encounter in
Pestalozzi. The school, Comenius nevertheless keeps re-
minding us, is to be a place of happiness for the child.
The aim of the boyhood stage[5] is to make the body, the
senses and the innate mental powers more responsive.
Not only do pupils more quickly imbibe what is taught
them as boys, but they do so more precisely. The teachers
of the younger classes, however, need to be more highly
skilled than other teachers, and, according to Comenius,
ought to receive higher salaries. The principles in accordance with which the appropriate textbooks should be
prepared are elaborated, for example, for the third class

[1] Cf. Shakespeare's seven ages of man in *As You Like It*, III. vii — (*i*)
infant, (*ii*) schoolboy, (*iii*) lover, (*iv*) soldier, (*v*) justice, (*vi*) pantaloon, (*vii*)
second childishness.
[2] *Pampaedia*, ch. 8.   [3] Ibid., ch. 9.   [4] Ch. 28.
[5] *Pampaedia*, ch. 10.

of this school moral maxims are deduced from natural phenomena, thus, the rose smells sweetly but has thorns, so erudition and virtue are worthy but work and discipline are necessary for their attainment, and these represent the thorns. Religious exercises are planned for this and later years. In addition, handwriting is prescribed throughout, calligraphy for the first two years, rapid writing for the next two, and orthography for the final two. Comenius advises beginning handwriting with large roman capitals, then proceeding to small letters. He advocates a form of simplified spelling in which sound and symbol should correspond. In arithmetic, exercises in number, mass and weight are necessary for all. Music is included, and for pupils of ten and eleven the beginnings of a modern language.[1]

At the adolescent state we must survey the world, the mind and Holy Writ to get an insight into the grounds of all things ; as means thereto we must enlist philosophy, politics and theology respectively ; the corresponding methods are dialogue, disputation, dramatic presentation and letters. The three divisions of the curriculum are : (*i*) languages, (*ii*) sciences and arts, (*iii*) morals. Languages comprise one or two modern languages of neighbouring peoples, together with Latin, Greek and Hebrew. All can be mastered in six years — Latin in three, Greek in two and Hebrew in one. The sciences and arts include a study of nature, of the technical achievements of man, and of the Scriptures for faith, hope and action. On the analogy of the care of the body Comenius prescribes for the training of character. The three factors which must be considered are (*i*) environmental influences, (*ii*) bodily humours, (*iii*) natural tendencies of the mind or otherwise acquired imaginings ; these properly directed lean to virtue's side, neglected they precipitate us into evil.

[1] A fuller account of the activities at the elementary-school stage appears in Turek's article, 'Schools in the *Pampaedia* of J. A. Comenius'.

The aim of the school of youth[1] is fuller wisdom. Through the senses, intellectual deliberation and the witnesses of Holy Writ together, will an integrated knowledge of the whole be attained, since the perfecting of understanding depends on pure insight into the natural world, the perfecting of the will on the choice of the right things, and the perfecting of skill on the deft handling of all things. This school or stage of young manhood has three divisions : (i) academy, (ii) travel, (iii) vocational preparation. An academy is a permanent body of students and scholars, a library and a laboratory, where theoretical exercises and mechanical demonstrations can be undertaken. This is also the appropriate stage for travel, the benefits of which are enumerated, and warnings issued against the temptations incidental to it.

The aim of the stage of manhood is expressed in the text : Seek ye first the kingdom of heaven. This is the one thing needful. We must, however, take care that nothing acquired in the earlier stages in the way of erudition, morals or piety is forfeited ; it is foolish to forgo the advantages of previous training. Thus books are not to be abandoned as most people do at this time of life, but are to be used wisely. The books that should be read are the books of the mind, of the world, of Holy Writ ; in addition, history, philosophy and theology ; further, to improve one's style, oratory and poetry ; lastly, moral and technical authors to enable one to perform his work properly and wisely. As the school demands examples, precepts and practice, so at the school of manhood men must concern themselves with history for examples, seek abstract wisdom in books, and engage in regular practice. This is the stage of self-education. A man's calling is a school in which he himself is master, and sets examples, precepts and exercises to himself. A definite vocation is to be chosen which will serve both

[1] *Pampaedia*, ch. 12.

God and humanity; the choice lies between agriculture, trade and commerce, and Comenius shows an undoubted preference for the first. The career should be one suitable to a man's natural inclinations and powers, and he ought to be able to say, — it is the job for him — the ideal of vocational guidance. Since emulation is a characteristic of school life, man should engage in righteous rivalry to attain the good — a justification of emulation borrowed from the Jesuits. Finally, man must so live at this stage that he will be able to enjoy what remains of life.

Comenius's reflections on the school of old age or the stage of senescence read like a lecture on geriatrics. This stage of life is not to be regarded as a grave with the cessation of all labour, as Ecclesiastes bemoans: 'there is no work, nor desire, nor knowledge, nor wisdom in the grave where thou goest.' It is part of life, in which Job counsels: 'O that they were wise, that they understood this, that they consider the latter end.' Its aim should be to bring to a successful conclusion what has already been begun; nothing in the foregoing stages must be made to appear useless or in vain. Comenius modifies a saying of Seneca to the effect that the young shall prepare, the adult use, and the old bring everything to fruition. The aged are not to seek satisfaction in idleness, but are to continue in well doing, and even to undertake, when the opportunity presents itself, work they had not previously thought of, but they should avoid what is beyond their strength, and must not attempt through rashness or presumption — faults at any stage — any new project which can only lead to disaster if they lack the necessary foresight. Old age has its peculiar faults, and its habits reveal special defects; these should be guarded against. Throughout this still active period of life the aged should reflect on the past, rejoicing in what was good, and considering how what was done could have been improved and what was defective could be amended; they should

review the present, look upon it as the Sunday of their
week; should consider what remains to be done and
plan how it can be carried out; take care to avoid such
mishaps as the aged are prone to; and guard against
infirmities and illnesses by taking more care than hitherto.

As an afterthought Comenius added a brief chapter on
Death — the final school; it balances the first school —
birth, and correlates with the eight planes or worlds: (*i*)
possible, (*ii*) ideal, (*iii*) angelic, (*iv*) material, (*v*) technical, (*vi*) moral, (*vii*) spiritual, (*viii*) eternal.

Such an education as set forth in the *Pampaedia*, he
claims, is salutary for the world; it can be attained
through the means described which make it easy and
pleasant, and as a consequence, such a culture will afford
for the human race an open paradise of joy. A prayer
for eternal wisdom concludes this work.

There is much repetition and some contradiction among
the principles of Comenius; but throughout his writing
is evinced a sincere sympathy with childhood, issuing in
an earnest aspiration to make education available to all,
to lighten the drudgery of learning for the child, and to
introduce into schools a humane treatment of the pupil.
It has been claimed[1] that the establishment of the United
Nations Educational, Scientific and Cultural Organisation marks the culmination of a movement for the creation
of an international agency for education which began with
Comenius, and in support Comenius is quoted: 'Universal harmony and peace must be secured for the whole
human race. By peace and harmony, however, I mean
not that external peace between rulers and peoples among
themselves, but an internal peace of mind inspired by a
system of ideas and feelings.' To guarantee the stability
of the world there must be 'some universal rededication
of minds', and on this Kandel comments: 'The "uni-

[1] I. L. Kandel in 'National Education in an International World',
N.E.A. Journal (April 1946), p. 175.

versal rededication of minds", the guidance of "will and purpose and the desires of the peoples and nations of the world" must begin in the schools of each nation.' And Ulich sums up : 'For Comenius education was the instrument to lead a suffering and divided world out of war and divisions toward peace and international understanding.'[1]

[1] R. Ulich, *Professional Education as a Humane Study* (New York : The Macmillan Co., 1956), p. 115.

CHAPTER VI

MILTON[1]

THE account of his own life which Milton interpolates in *The Second Defence of the People of England*[2] affords the occasion of explaining how he came to pen the tractate *Of Education*: 'When, therefore, I perceived that there were three species of liberty which are essential to the happiness of social life — religious, domestic and civil; and as I had already written concerning the first, and the magistrates were strenuously active in obtaining the third, I determined to turn my attention to the second, or the domestic species. As this seemed to involve three material questions, the conditions of the conjugal tie, the education of the children, and the free publication of the thoughts, I made them objects of distinct consideration. I explained my sentiments, not only concerning the solemnization of the marriage but the dissolution, if circumstances rendered it necessary. . . . I then discussed the principles of education in a summary manner, but sufficiently copious for those who attend seriously to the subject; than which nothing can be more necessary to principle the minds of men in virtue, the only genuine source of political and individual liberty, the only true safeguard of states, the bulwark of their prosperity and renown.'

The keynote of Milton's political writings is liberty,

[1] 1608–74. For life and work see E. M. W. Tillyard, *Milton* (London: Chatto & Windus, 1930).

[2] *The Prose Works of John Milton* (London: Henry G. Bohn, 1848–53), vol. i, pp. 254–61. It begins: 'I will now mention who and whence I am. I was born in London, of an honest family. . . .' For personal appearance see pp. 235–6.

liberty in the State, in the Church, and in personal life, for, as he writes in one of his letters[1] 'what can be more noble or more useful than to vindicate the liberty of man'. And in *The Second Defence of the People of England*[2] he asks : 'What can conduce more to the beauty or glory of one's country than the recovery not only of its civil but its religious liberty?' And he even there speaks of 'the sweetness of liberty'. 'Real and substantial liberty is rather to be sought from within than from without, and whose existence depends, not so much on the terror of the sword, as on sobriety of conduct and integrity of life.'[3] He further explains :[4] 'Know that to be free is the same thing as to be pious, to be wise, to be temperate and just, to be frugal and abstinent, and lastly, to be magnanimous and brave ; so to be the opposite of all these is the same as to be a slave.' The highest liberty is liberty of conscience : 'Give me liberty to know, to utter, and to argue freely according to conscience, above all liberties.'[5] In *The History of Britain* he observes that 'liberty hath a double edge, fit only to be handled by just and virtuous men ; to bad and dissolute, it becomes a mischief unwieldy in their own hands'.[6]

That there can be no liberty without discipline Milton unequivocally declares.[7] To those who 'for the ease of their inconsequent opinions' would offer the excuse that it can be left to the discretion of men, he retorts :[8] 'To this conceit of theirs I answer, that it is both unsound and untrue ; for there is not that thing in the world of more grave and urgent importance throughout the whole life of man than is discipline. What need I

---

[1] *Prose Works*, iii, p. 506. *Familiar Letters*, Letter xiv (1564).
[2] *Prose Works*, i, p. 217.   [3] Ibid., p. 258.
[4] Ibid., p. 298.   [5] *Areopagitica, Prose Works*, ii, p. 95.
[6] *Prose Works*, v, p. 239.
[7] E. M. W. Tillyard, *Milton*, p. 134 : 'Discipline is for him primarily self-discipline, not external discipline ; it is consonant with, and necessary to, liberty.'
[8] *The Reason of Church Government* (1641). *Prose Works*, ii, pp. 441–2.

instance! He that hath read with judgment of nations and commonwealths, of cities and camps, of peace and war, sea and land, will readily agree that the flourishing and decaying of all civil societies, all the moments and turnings of human occasions are moved to and fro as upon an axle of discipline. So that whatever power or sway in mortal things weaker men have attributed to fortune, I durst with more confidence (the honour of Divine Providence ever saved) ascribe either to the vigour or slackness of discipline. Nor is there any sociable perfection in this life, civil or sacred, that can be above discipline; but she is that which with her musical cords preserves and holds all their parts together . . . and certainly discipline is not only the remover of disorder; but if any visible shape can be given to divine things, the very visible shape and image of virtue, whereby she is not only seen in the regular gestures and motions of the heavenly paces as she walks, but also makes the harmony of her voice audible to mortal ears.' The application to the Church runs: 'how much less can we believe that God would leave his frail and feeble, though not less beloved Church here below to the perpetual stumble of conjecture and disturbance in this our dark voyage without the card and compass of discipline?'

For the task he was undertaking Milton had only a very limited practical experience. Of his own education he records:[1] 'My father had me daily instructed in the grammar schools, and by other masters at home.' He followed for a brief interval what Dr Johnson characterised as 'the mean employment' of a schoolmaster.[2] His nephew, who had been one of his pupils, in his account

---

[1] *Second Defence of the People of England. Prose Works*, i, p. 254.

[2] Johnson in *Lives of the Poets* says: 'Milton was not a man who could become mean by a mean employment.' Earlier in the same essay, referring to Milton's teaching interlude, Johnson wrote: 'His father was alive; his allowance was not ample; and he supplied its deficiencies by an honest and useful employment.'

of his schooldays insists that Milton 'never set up for a public school to teach all the young fry of a parish, but only was willing to impart his learning and knowledge to relations, and the sons of some gentlemen that were his intimate friends; besides, that neither his converse, nor his writings, nor his manner of teaching ever savoured in the least anything of pedantry'.[1] A. F. Leach, writing on 'Milton as Schoolboy and Schoolmaster',[2] remarks : 'Milton's life as a schoolmaster is as barren of facts as his life as a schoolboy. It lasted only about seven years. It was carried on first in the house in Aldersgate Street, then a suburb [of London], the houses having gardens, while the end of the street bordered on the open country. Later, in 1645, as there was a prospect of more pupils, Milton removed to a larger house in the Barbican. And after his father's death in 1647 . . . Milton abandoned schoolmastering for political pamphleteering. Professor Masson has drawn up a list of ascertained pupils, who with barely an exception are of an aristocratic kind, sons of people with handles to their names, when a handle was by no means so common as now.'

Of Education is dedicated to Samuel Hartlib[3] in response to whose 'earnest entreaties' Milton was induced to set down in writing his thoughts on education. Hartlib, a foreigner by birth, was a semi-official go-between in the endeavours of the Commonwealth parliament to maintain contact with such religious and educational reformers

[1] *Milton* (London : Macmillan's English Classics, 1963), p. 93.

[2] A. F. Leach, 'Milton as Schoolboy and Schoolmaster', *Proceedings of the British Academy* (1907–8) (London : Oxford University Press), p. 313.

[3] For Hartlib (born within the last few years of the sixteenth century – 1662) see G. H. Turnbull, *Samuel Hartlib : A Sketch of his life and his relation to J. A. Comenius* (London : Oxford University Press, 1920). Also G. H. Turnbull, *Hartlib, Dury and Comenius: Gleanings from Hartlib's Papers* (University Press of Liverpool, 1947).

If Turnbull's surmise is confirmed that Hartlib was at Emmanuel College, Cambridge, between 1621 and 1626, Milton being at Christ's from 1625 to 1632, they would be contemporaries at Cambridge in adjacent colleges. See, however, Turnbull, pp. 39–40, for supposed first meeting.

on the Continent as were favourably disposed to its régime. He was in regular correspondence with Comenius and John Dury,[1] and he furthered the publication of Comenius's works in England, in one case at least too precipitately. Milton's testimonial to him in the opening pages of the tractate reads : 'Nor should the laws of any private friendship have prevailed with me to divide thus, or transpose my former thoughts, but that I see those aims, those actions which have won you with me the esteem of a person sent hither by some good providence from a far country to be the occasion and the incitement of great good to this island. And, as I hear, you have obtained the same repute with men of most approved wisdom, and some of highest authority among us ; not to mention the learned correspondence which you hold in foreign parts, and the extraordinary pains and diligence which you have used in this matter both here and beyond the seas ; either by the definite will of God so ruling, or the peculiar sway of nature, which also is God's working.' Yielding to Hartlib's solicitations, Milton penned his 'few observations' on the subject, elaborating 'the incidental discourses' which they had previously enjoyed. The topic itself was one fully worthy of attention for its own sake ; the times conspired to increase the urgency of such an undertaking, and the claims of friendship added to the appeal which constrained Milton to produce a general view in writing. Other compelling interests prevented him from doing justice to the subject to the extent it warranted, and from beginning 'as some have done, from the cradle, which might be worth many considerations, if brevity had not been my scope'.

In the tractate *Of Education* Milton first disposes of the current practice in learning, both school and university. Education at both stages suffers from too many idle vacations. School education, in addition, is too ambitious ;

[1] See above, p. 82, note 1.

it is adapted not to the undeveloped capacities of the
pupils but rather to adult intelligence with ripe experience, and he instances the composition of essays, verses
and orations. Instead he advocates committing to memory elementary rules of grammar before practising
them in 'some short book lessoned thoroughly to them'.
An analogous error is that instead of being introduced to
concrete studies which they can understand, students
first coming up to the university find they must commence with subjects remote from experience — logic and
metaphysics, abstractions beyond their comprehension,
with the result that they grow into hatred and contempt
of learning, 'and these are the errors, and these are the
fruits of misspending our prime youth at the schools and
universities, as we do, either in learning mere words, or
such things chiefly as were better unlearnt'.

Although Milton expressed the most grateful appreciation of the treatment he received, and an affectionate
regard for all the Fellows of Christ's College,[1] he holds
in the utmost contempt the universities of his day; he
dismisses them as 'nurseries of superstition and empty
speculation',[2] elaborating that 'honest and ingenuous
natures coming to the universities to store themselves
with good and solid learning, and these unfortunately fed
with nothing else but the scragged and thorny lectures of
monkish and miserable sophistry; were sent home again
with such a scholastic bur in their throats, as hath stopped
and hindered all true and generous philosophy from
entering; cracked their voices for ever with metaphysical
jurgarisms'. And if he thought little of his own university, he naturally thought less of that other one, 'which
as in the time of her better health, and mine own younger
judgment, I never greatly admired, so now much less'.[3]

As an alternative to 'that asinine feast of sow thistles

[1] *Prose Works*, iii, p. 111.   [2] Ibid., p. 146.
[3] Ibid., p. 112. See also p. 511.

and brambles which is commonly set before them as all the food and entertainment of their tender and most docible age' Milton proposes 'a complete and generous education, that which fits a man to perform justly, skillfully, and magnanimously all the offices, both private and public of peace and war'. This he elaborates in *The Ready Way to Establish a Free Commonwealth*.[1] His purpose is: 'To make the people fittest to choose, and the chosen fittest to govern, will be to mend our corrupt and faulty education, to teach the people faith, not without virtue, temperance, modesty, sobriety, parsimony, justice; not to admire wealth or honour; to hate turbulence and ambition; to place everyone his private welfare and happiness in the public peace, liberty, and safety. They shall not then need to be much mistrustful of their chosen patriots in the grand council; who will be then rightly called the true keepers of our liberty.' To this end:[2] 'They should have here also schools and academies at their own choice, wherein their children may be bred up in their own sight to all learning and noble education. They would soon spread much more knowledge and civility, yea, religion, through all parts of the land, by communicating the natural heat of government and culture more distributively to all extreme parts, which now be numb and neglected; would soon make the whole nation more industrious, more ingenious at home, more potent, more honourable abroad.' And to improve the state of the clergy he even proposes that public libraries should be instituted: 'And yet we may be confident, if these things be thought needful, let the state but erect in public good store of libraries, and there will not want men in the church, who of their own inclinations will become able in this kind.'[3]

---

[1] *Prose Works*, ii, p. 126. [2] Ibid. ii, p. 136.
[3] *The Likeliest Means to Remove Hirelings Out of the Church. Prose Works*, iii, p. 38.

To provide for such an education as Milton proposes a spacious house and ground round about it fit for an academy, and big enough to lodge one hundred and fifty persons is to be procured. This place, for pupils between twelve and twenty-one, is to be both school and university, and except for those who would later proceed to the study of law or of medicine, is to afford a liberal education sufficient in itself. That an academy is selected for his ideal educational institution emphasises the practical nature of the education which Milton regards as better suited to a gentleman than that traditionally offered by grammar schools and universities.[1]

The tractate[2] represents a reversion to the Renaissance attitude to education,[3] and is quite at variance with the robust views of Milton's later polemical writings vindicating the Revolution and pleading for liberty.

[1] For academies see above, p. 92, footnote 3 and T. L. Jarman, *Landmarks in the History of Education* (London: The Cresset Press, 1951), ch. xi, 'The Beginnings of Educational Reform: The Academies'. Foster Watson in *Vives: on Education*. A translation of the *De Tradendis Disciplinis* of Juan Luis Vives (Cambridge University Press, 1913), Introduction, cli, says: 'We can hardly help thinking that Milton had Vives's Academy before his mind when he suggests "the spacious house and grounds" to be at once a school and university, not needing a remove "but to be 'absolute' for all studies"'. It is nevertheless just as likely that he had his own Cambridge college in mind; the number in residence — a hundred and fifty — would support this contention. Milton went up to Cambridge when he was sixteen years old.

[2] Oscar Browning, *Milton's Tractate on Education* (Cambridge University Press, 1897). The treatise was first published in 1644, and was reprinted in 1673. The text of Browning's edition is a facsimile of the reprint of 1673. M. Davis, Milton's *Areopagitica* and *Of Education* (London: Macmillan's English Classics, 1963), pp. 89–117. K. M. Burton, *Milton's Prose Writings* (Everyman's Library. London: J. M. Dent & Sons Ltd.), pp. 319–30. O. M. Ainsworth, *Milton on Education: The Tractate of Education with supplementary extracts from other writings of Milton* (New Haven: Yale University Press, 1928).

As the tractate is short, page references are omitted from quotations from it.

[3] E. M. W. Tillyard, *Milton*, pp. 152–3, referring to the tractate writes: 'It is, too, perhaps more than any other prose writing of Milton, a document of the Renaissance. . . . The charms of learning are described in the tones of Sidney, and the ideal of manhood is the many-sided one of the Renaissance.'

The curriculum that Milton plans for his proposed educational institution comprises : studies, exercises, diet.

The studies prescribed by Milton correspond to what the Greeks termed 'music', and, after the manner of Plato, who had condemned Spartan educational practice for its restriction to training in the arts of war and for its neglect of culture, 'the institution of breeding' delineated by Milton 'shall be', he repeats, 'equally good both for peace and war'. As any one nation cannot provide all that is useful in every branch of learning, it behoves us to learn the languages of such peoples as have been 'most industrious after wisdom', not for the training of the mind afforded in acquiring them but for their content, for 'language is but the instrument conveying to us things useful to be known. And though a linguist should pride himself to have all the tongues that Babel cleft the world into, yet if he have not studied the solid things in them as well as the words and lexicons, he were nothing so much to be esteemed a learned man as any yeoman or tradesman competently wise in his mother-dialect only.'[1]

Latin had undoubtedly the first claim to be the source book of the arts and sciences. The pupils accordingly begin 'with the chief and necessary rules of some good grammar'. Milton was evidently dissatisfied with the Latin grammar then in use, for he later prepared one,[2] 'For the use of such as, younger or elder, are desirous without more trouble than needs, to attain the Latin tongue, the elder sort especially, with little teaching and his own industry.' He also prefers that the pronunciation of the Latin words should be 'after the Italian manner'. At the same time as they are learning the grammar, they are to have read to them for moral training — 'to win

---

[1] Cf. *A Defence of the People of England. Prose Works*, i, p. 141 : 'And know for the future that words must be comformable to things and not things to words.'

[2] See *Prose Works*, v, pp. 432–79.

them easily to the love of virtue and true labour, some easy and delightful book of education, whereof the Greeks have store, as Cebes, Plutarch, and other Socratic discourses, but in Latin we have none of classic authority extant, except the two or three first books of Quintilian and some select pieces elsewhere. But here the main skill and groundwork will be to temper them such lectures and explanations upon every opportunity as may lead them in willing obedience, inflamed with the study of learning and the admonition of virtue.' Later in their college days they are to read for themselves certain moral treatises, thus perfecting themselves 'in the knowledge of personal duty'. 'And either now or before this they may have easily learned at any odd hour the Italian tongue.' At the same time as they are acquiring Latin grammar 'some other hour of the day might be taught them the rules of arithmetic, and, soon after, the elements of geometry, even playing, as the old manner was'.[1]

The next step is to study authors on agricultural subjects, then the use of globes and all maps, geography,[2]

[1] Milton is doubtless here referring to Plato's *Laws* (§ 819). Writing of Egypt, Plato remarks: 'In that country arithmetical games have been actually invented for the use of children, which they learn as a pleasure and amusement. They have to distribute apples and garlands, using the same number sometimes for a larger and sometimes for a lesser number of persons; and they arrange pugilists and wrestlers as they pair together by lot or remain over, and show the order in which they follow. Another mode of amusing them is by distributing vessels, some in which gold, brass, silver and the like are mixed, others in which they are unmixed; as I was saying, they adapt to their amusement the numbers in common use, and in this way make more intelligible to their pupils the arrangements and movements of armies and expeditions, and in their management of a household they render people more useful to themselves, and more wide awake.' And of the more advanced arithmetical processes Plato adds: 'These pastimes are not so very unlike a game of draughts'; and 'The learning of them will be an amusement, and they will benefit the state.'

[2] In *A Brief History of Moscovia* (*Prose Works*, v, pp. 394–431) Milton refers to the study of geography as 'both profitable and delightful', and describes the northern latitudes relating the experiences encountered by ambassadors journeying to Moscow.

In *The History of Britain* (*Prose Works*, v, pp. 164–93) his justification of history (p. 185) reads: 'For worthy deeds are not often destitute of worthy

E

astronomy and natural philosophy, and, to enable them to read with profit the historical physiology of Aristotle, Greek is to be acquired. Having mastered the general principles of the sciences they are to proceed to applied trigonometry, and pass from thence to fortification, architecture, engineering or navigation; thereafter from the history of meteors, minerals, plants to living creatures as far as anatomy. A course in medicine might prove useful in warfare. To give concrete content to such studies the experience of practitioners — hunters, fowlers, fishermen, shepherds, gardeners, apothecaries, and in other sciences — architects, engineers, mariners and anatomists should be enlisted 'and this would give them such a real tincture of natural knowledge as they shall never forget, but daily augment with delight'. Milton's aim is nevertheless not to qualify his pupils to practise the numerous arts detailed, but merely to enable them to acquire such a familiarity with the various topics as might be expected of a gentleman no matter in what company he chanced to be. To counteract the technical studies some Latin poetry is to be read.

After becoming acquainted with their personal duty the students are to proceed to acquire knowledge of their social duties, of 'economics' — the term used by Milton, but by which we now understand household and business management. The field of studies comprises the legal codes from the earliest Biblical times down to the common law of England. 'When all these employments are well conquered, then will the choice histories, heroic poems and Attic tragedies of stateliest and most regal argument, with all the famous political orations, offer themselves;

relaters, as by a certain fate great acts and great eloquence have most commonly gone hand in hand, equalling and honouring each other in the same ages' — a sentiment echoed by Herbart in the *Allgemeine Pädagogik* (*The Science of Education*), p. 74, but expressed negatively: 'Periods which no master has described, whose spirit no poet breathes, are of little value to education.'

which if they were not read, but some of them got by memory, and solemnly pronounced with right accent and grace, as might be taught, would endue them even with the spirit and vigour of Demosthenes or Cicero, Euripides or Sophocles.' And lastly, logic, rejected at the earlier stage, is introduced to improve their style in composition and facilitate the transition to rhetoric. 'From hence, and not till now, will be the right reason of forming them to be able writers and composers in every excellent matter, when they shall be fraught with an universal insight into things; or whether they be to speak in parliament or council, honour and attention would be waiting on their lips.'

As 'the end of learning', according to an alternative statement of Milton 'is to repair the ruins of our first parents by regaining to know God aright', provision is naturally made for instruction in religion; thus at an early stage 'after evening repast till bed-time their thoughts would be best taken up in the easy grounds of religion and the story of Scripture'; later, to complement their ethical studies, 'they close the day's work under the determinate sentence of David or Solomon, or the evangels and apostolic scriptures', and when mature enough to study law and politics 'Sundays also and every evening may now be understandingly spent in the highest matters of theology and church history, ancient and modern, and ere this time at a set hour the Hebrew tongue might have been gained, and the Scriptures may now be read in their own original; whereto it would be no impossibility to add the Chaldee and the Syrian dialect'.

During intervals of relaxation and recuperation from their physical exercises the students are to be entertained with incidental music discoursed to them on the organ, also after meals 'it would not be inexpedient, sending their minds back to study in good tune and satisfaction'.

'These are the studies wherein our noble and our gentle youth ought to bestow their time in a disciplinary way from twelve to one-and-twenty, unless they rely more upon their ancestors dead than upon themselves living.'

Had Milton professed to be presenting a complete treatise on education, then the criticism which Rousseau in the *New Héloïse* passed on Locke — 'he speaks much more of what should be required of children than of the means to be employed in getting it' might more aptly have been directed against him. He nevertheless formulates two general principles of educational method, one that knowledge should be based on sensory experience, the other that there should be a revision of work previously learned : 'But because our understanding cannot in this body found itself but on sensible things, nor arrive so clearly to the knowledge of God and things invisible, as by orderly conning over the visible and inferior creature, the same method is to be followed in all discreet teaching.' For studies in general he recommends : 'In which methodical course it is so supposed they must proceed by the steady pace of learning onward, as at convenient times for memory's sake to retire back into the middle ward, and sometimes into the rear of what they have been taught, until they have confirmed, and solidly united the whole body of their perfected knowledge, like the last embattling of a Roman Legion.'

The physical training which Milton recommends for his students must be consonant with their intellectual and moral training. 'Now will be worth the seeing what exercises and recreations may best agree and become those studies.' Rather surprisingly, the pursuits which he advocates as meeting this requirement are swordsmanship and wrestling. Milton was a consistent exponent of physical fitness. His own practice he discloses in *The Second Defence of the People of England* :[1] 'My stature

[1] *Prose Works*, i, p. 235.

certainly is not tall, but it rather approaches the middle than the diminutive. . . . Nor, though very thin, was I ever deficient in courage or in strength ; and I was wont constantly to exercise myself in the use of the broadsword, so long as it comported with my habit and my years.' And later, when resident in London :[1] 'Those morning haunts are where they should be, at home ; not sleeping or concocking the subjects of an irregular feast ; but up and stirring, in winter often ere the sound of any bell awaken men to labour or devotion ; in summer as oft with the bird that first rouses, or not much tardier, to read good authors, or cause them to be read, till the attention be weary, or memory has its full fraught ; then, with useful and generous labours preserving the body's health and hardiness.' In addition he indicates military exercises and manœuvres, on foot or on horseback according to age, and to extend their acquaintanceship beyond the exercises at home 'there is another opportunity of gaining experience to be won from pleasure itself abroad : in those vernal seasons of the year, when the air is calm and pleasant, it were an injury and sullenness against nature not to go out and see her riches and partake in her rejoicing with heaven and earth. I should not, therefore, be a persuader to them of studying much then, after two or three years that they have well laid their grounds, but to ride out in companies with prudent and staid guides to all the quarters of the land, learning and observing all places of strength, all commodities of building and of soil for towns and tillage, harbours, and ports for trade. Sometimes taking sea as far as to our navy, to learn there also what they can in the practical knowledge of sailing and sea-fight.'

To conclude : 'These ways would try all their peculiar gifts of nature, and if there were any secret excellence among them, would fetch it out and give it fair

[1] Ibid. iii, p. 112.

opportunity to advance itself by, which could not but mightily redound to the good of this nation, and bring into fashion again those old admired virtues and excellences, with far more advantage now in the purity of Christian knowledge.'

The tractate *Of Education* is inspirational; it was composed merely 'for light and direction', and is not to be judged by ordinary canons. The summing-up of Leach may suffice:[1] 'Milton's *Tractate* suffers under the same disadvantage as Elyot's *De regimine Principum*, Ascham's *Scholemaster*, Locke's *Theory* and most treatises on education. It proceeded not from experience of a public school but from that of a private tutor. Theories of education which may be all very well when applied by a single master of exceptional ability and enthusiasm to one or two pupils, to whom individual and exclusive attention is given, are incapable of application to the common crowd in a common school by a common man. Still, Milton the Schoolmaster anticipated in theory what has since been partly realised in practice, the danger of exclusive bookishness, and the necessity of combining practical work with theoretical instruction. As a schoolmaster, as in everything else, he was miraculous in industry, magnificent in ideas and splendid in style. In a word, he was Miltonic'.

In *An Apology for Smectymnuus* (1642)[2] Milton relents somewhat, and as a concession to human frailty confesses: 'For as in teaching doubtless the spirit of meekness is most powerful, so are the meek only fit persons to be taught.'

[1] *Proceedings of the British Academy* (1907–8), p. 318.
[2] *Prose Works*, iii, p. 101.

CHAPTER VII

LOCKE[1]

ALTHOUGH Locke's name is inevitably associated with *An Essay Concerning Human Understanding*[2] which may be said to have opened a new era in philosophical thought, his political ideas as set forth in the *Two Treatises of Government*[3] had a more far-reaching influence on world opinion. In comparison with these epoch-making works his *Some Thoughts Concerning Education*[4] may be regarded merely as a literary diversion, and, like the *Essay*, written 'in patches and at distant times'. But for the fact that the *Thoughts* were by the same person as the *Essay* it would hardly merit attention; as Laslett puts it:[5] 'Everything else which he wrote was important because he, Locke of the *Human Understanding*, had written it. It was so with his *Thoughts Concerning Education* (1694).'

In the early chapters of the *Second Treatise of Government* Locke declares that in a state of nature all men are born free and equal.[6] The law of nature is, for Locke,[7] also

---

[1] 1632–1704. Maurice Cranston, *John Locke: A Biography* (London: Longmans, Green & Co., 1957). Peter Laslett, *John Locke: Two Treatises of Government* (Cambridge University Press, 1960), ch. 2, 'Locke the Man and Locke the Writer'. D. J. O'Connor, *John Locke* (London: Penguin Books, 1952). [2] Published 1690.

[3] The *Second Treatise* was first in time, 1679; amended and extended 1689.

[4] 1693. R. H. Quick, *Some Thoughts Concerning Education by John Locke* (Cambridge University Press, 1895). [5] P. 38.

[6] Ch. 2, § 4; Laslett, p. 287; ch. 2, § 6, Laslett, p. 289; ch. 8, § 95, Laslett, p. 348. Cf. also J. Milton, *Prose Works*, ii, p. 8: 'No man, who knows aright can be so stupid to deny that all men naturally were born free, being the image and semblance of God Himself, and were, by privilege above all creatures, born to command and not to obey.'

[7] Treatise I, ch. 9, § 101; Laslett, p. 233. Cf. J. Milton, *A Defence of the People of England, Prose Works*, i, p. 108: 'I am of opinion that the law

the law of reason, and both have a divine origin. In the state of nature all men are naturally in 'a state of perfect freedom to order their actions and dispose of their possessions', 'a state also of equality . . . no one having more than another . . . and the use of the same faculties should also be equal one amongst another . . . without subordination or subjection'.[1] Although all men are equal politically, in actual life differences must be recognised :[2] 'Though I have said above that all men by nature are equal, I cannot be supposed to understand all sorts of equality; age or virtue may give men a just precedency; excellence of parts and merit may place others above the common level; both may subject some and alliance or benefits others, to pay an observance to those to whom nature, gratitude or other respects may have made it due; and yet all this consists with the equality which all men are in.' The inequality of parts, or talents, here mentioned is also recognised in Locke's *Conduct of the Understanding* :[3] 'There is, it is visible, great variety in men's understandings, and their natural constitutions put so wide a difference between some men in this respect that art and industry would never be able to master, and their very natures seem to want a foundation to raise on it that which other men easily attain unto. Amongst men of equal education there is great inequality of parts.' The concept of equality must also be qualified in the case of children.[4] 'Children, I confess, are not born

of God does exactly agree with the law of nature'; also iv, pp. 211–12. M. Cranston, pp. 64–65, says of the law of nature : 'It is a notion as old as Stoic philosophy. It had an important place in the theory, if not in the practice of Roman jurisprudence. In mediaeval Christendom it was identified with the law of God, and the Church assumed the duty of upholding it over the heads of temporal rulers.'

[1] *Second Treatise*, ch. 2, § 4; Laslett, p. 287.
[2] *Second Treatise*, ch. 6, § 54; Laslett, p. 322.
[3] T. Fowler, *Locke's Conduct of the Understanding* (Oxford : Clarendon Press, 1901), p. 5, section 2, 'Parts'. Also, *Essay*, The Epistle to the Reader : 'We have our understandings no less different than our palates.'
[4] *Second Treatise*, ch. 6, § 55; Laslett, p. 322.

in their full state of equality though they are born to it. Their parents have a sort of rule and jurisdiction over them when they come into the world and for some time after, but 'tis but a temporary one.'

As regards freedom Locke likewise recognises certain limitations in the case of children.[1] Only in a community with an established system of law can man be regarded as politically free, according to Locke. 'Where there is no law, there is no liberty.' Freedom is not a liberty for every man to do as he likes, but a liberty to dispose of his person and property within the allowance of the laws and not to be subject to the arbitrary will of another. To appreciate the law on which liberty is dependent a man must have reason. To turn a child loose before he has reason to guide him is not to grant him freedom 'but to thrust him out amongst brutes and abandon him to a state as wretched and as much beneath that of man as theirs'. Thus[2] 'we are born free as we are born rational, not that we have actually the exercise of either ; age that brings one brings with it the other too, and thus we see how freedom and subjection to parents may consist together and are both founded on the same principle'.

Having thus disposed of equality and freedom we can now consider the duties and rights of parents. In the chapter headed 'Paternal Power'[3] Locke prefaces his treatment by remarking that the title should rather be 'Parental Power', as such power is vested in both parents and not in the father only.[4] The rights of parents he defines thus :[5] 'Paternal or parental power is nothing

[1] *Second Treatise*, ch. 6, §§ 57–58 ; Laslett, pp. 323–5.

[2] § 61 ; Laslett, p. 326.

[3] Laslett, pp. 321–36.

[4] This distinction Locke had elaborated in the *First Treatise of Government* by citing numerous texts from the Scriptures where both father and mother are included, his aim being to controvert the arguments adduced by Sir R. Filmer in defence of absolute monarchy and the divine right of kings.

[5] *Second Treatise*, ch. 15, § 170 ; Laslett, p. 399.

E 2

but that which parents have over their children, to govern them for the children's good till they come to the use of reason or a state of knowledge wherein they may be supposed capable to understand that rule whether it be the law of nature or the municipal law of their country they are to govern themselves by, capable, I say, to know it as well as several others who live as free men under the law. The affection and tenderness which God hath planted in the breasts of parents towards their children makes it evident that this is not intended to be a severe arbitrary government but only for the help, instruction and preservation of their offspring.' The child's rights are summed up in the statement :[1] 'All that a child has right to claim from his father is nourishment and education, and the things nature furnishes for the support of life.' In return, the child is expected to honour his parents.

An approach to Locke's educational position from another angle — the psychological, is through the famous *An Essay Concerning Human Understanding*.[2] Although an educational system cannot be based on psychological considerations, it cannot afford to neglect such data ; these qualify any pronouncements made on philosophical or social grounds. It is for this reason that Locke's *Essay* has significance for the educationist.[3]

Locke's intention in the *Essay* is to make an analysis and reconstruction of mental content, or in his own words[4] 'to examine our own abilities and see what

[1] *First Discourse*, ch. 9, § 93 ; Laslett, p. 228.

[2] Epistle to the Reader — 'Having been begun by chance, was continued by entreaty, written by incoherent parcels, and, after long intervals of neglect, resumed again, as my humour or occasions permitted, and at last in a retirement where an attendance on my health gave me leisure, it was brought into that order thou now seest it.' Published 1689.

[3] Laslett, p. 86, says : 'Even between the *Essay* and the work on education, where the barrier of anonymity is absent on both sides and the connection is intimate, Locke makes no cross-references. It is pointless to look upon his work as an integrated body of speculation and generalisation, with a general philosophy at its centre and as its architectural framework.'   [4] Epistle to the Reader.

objects our understandings were or were not fitted to deal
with'. His method is the method of introspection : 'I
could look into nobody's understanding but my own to
see how it wrought'.[1] Before proceeding to his main task,
however, Locke finds it necessary, as he puts it,[2] 'to clear
my way to those foundations which I conceive are the
only true ones' by disposing of two general misconcep-
tions, namely, the presence in the mind of innate ideas,
and of mental faculties. The term 'idea' Locke uses in
a wide sense : 'It being that term which I think serves
best to stand for whatsoever is the object of the understanding when a man thinks, I have used it to express
whatever is meant by phantasm, notion, species, or whatever it is which the mind can be employed about in
thinking.'[3] It thus comprises all the contents of the mind
including what later psychologists designate by sensations, percepts, images and concepts.

There are two types of innate ideas — speculative, and
practical or moral, and Locke contends that both types
are acquired and are not innate. He refutes the arguments advanced on behalf of such ideas, maintaining that
nothing should be regarded as innate the presence of
which in the mind can be accounted for otherwise ; the
analogy he uses in support is :[4] 'It would be impertinent
to suppose the ideas of colour innate in a creature to
whom God had given sight.' The conviction that truths
which are generally or universally accepted must be
innate is challenged by citing the example of mathematical propositions. Moral principles he also maintains[5]
require reasoning and discourse and some exercise of the
mind to discover the certainty of their truth, and he adds :[6]
'Were there any such innate principles, there would be

---

[1] *Essay*, Bk I, ch. 1, note.   [2] Bk I, ch. 4, § 25.
[3] Bk I, ch. 1, § 8, Bk I, ch. 1, note.
[4] Bk I, ch. 2, § 1. Cf. Bk I, ch. 4, § 12.
[5] Bk I, ch. 3, § 1.   [6] Bk I, ch. 3, § 14. Cf. § 22.

no need to teach them.' He nevertheless recognises '
law knowable by the light of nature', such an one bein
'a desire of happiness and an aversion to misery'.[1] An
in the *Second Treatise of Government* he instances[2] 'that Cai
was so convinced that everyone had a right to destro
such a criminal that after the murder of his brother h
cries out: "Everyone that findeth me shall slay me."
So plain was it writ in the hearts of all mankind.' Laslett
comments that the final phrase is the most conspicuous
instance in the whole book of Locke's willingness to take
advantage of the belief in innate ideas and innate practical
principles.

In dealing with 'Power'[3] Locke refers to the powers of
the mind — perceiving and preferring, and remarks that
the ordinary way of speaking 'is that the understanding
and the will are two faculties of the mind, a word proper
enough if it be used . . . so as not to breed any confusion in man's thoughts by being supposed to stand for
some real beings in the soul that performed those actions
of understanding and volition'. He adds :[4] 'For if it be
reasonable to suppose and talk of faculties as distinct
beings that can act as we do when we say "The will
orders" and "The will is free" it is fit that we shall make
a speaking faculty, and a walking faculty, and a dancing
faculty, by which these actions are produced, which are
but several modes of motion.' He further explains :[5] 'But
the fault has been that faculties have been spoken of and
represented as so many distinct agents. For it being
asked, what it was that digested the meat in our stomachs,
it was a ready and very satisfactory answer to say that it
was the digestive faculty . . . and so on in the mind, the
intellectual faculty, or the understanding, understood ;
and the elective faculty, or the will, willed or commanded ;
which is, in short, to say that the ability to digest, digested ;

---

[1] *Essay*, Bk I, ch. 3, § 13 ; also § 3.   [2] Ch. 2, § 11 ; Laslett, p. 292.
[3] *Essay*, Bk II, ch. 21, § 6.   [4] Ibid., Bk II, ch. 22, § 17.   [5] Bk II, ch. 21, § 20.

and the ability to move, moved; and the ability to understand, understood. For "faculty, ability, and power", I
think, "are but different names for the same thing".'

Having thus disposed of innate ideas and of mental
faculties Locke first classifies the contents of mind under
two main heads — understanding[1] and volition. Modern
psychologists distinguish three aspects of the mental
process — cognition, conation and feeling. Locke does
nevertheless recognise the existence of feeling:[2] 'The
term operations I use in a large sense as comprehending
not barely the actions of the mind about its ideas, but
some sort of passions arising sometimes from them, such
as is the satisfaction or uneasiness arising from any
thought', but he is in doubt whether to regard pleasure
and pain as independent and analogous to sensations or as
merely 'annexed' to sensations.[3] His rejection of mental
faculties enables him to deal somewhat drastically with
the vexed problem of the freedom of the will. To the
question — What is it that determines the will? Locke
replies:[4] 'the true and proper answer is the mind'. Or[5]
more precisely: 'Every man is put under a necessity by
his constitution as an intelligent being to be determined in
willing by his own thought and judgment, what is best for
him to do.' Locke thus preserves man's freedom by
sacrificing the will. Man's actions are regulated by the
understanding through desire. One condition nevertheless must be observed; the idea or the desire that motivates
the will or leads man to act must be regarded as attainable: 'desire is stopped or abated by the opinion of the
impossibility or unattainableness of the good proposed'.[6]

Understanding, for Locke, comprises all the cognitive
processes — sensation, perception, imagination and thinking, the bases of all which are 'simple ideas' and, what

---

[1] Note the use of this term in the title of the *Essay*, where it is equated
to Mind.   [2] Bk II, ch. 1, § 4.
[3] Bk II, ch. 7, § 1; Bk II, ch. 20, § 1.   [4] Bk II, ch. 21, § 29.
[5] Bk II, ch. 21, § 48.   [6] Bk II, ch. 20, § 6. Cf. ch. 21, § 40.

he calls 'ideas of reflection', the latter merely being the mental processes themselves regarded as objects or ideas. Locke usually refers to simple ideas and to ideas of reflection as if they were of equivalent standing, but ideas of reflection must come later in the child's development, since, as Locke says,[1] they 'require attention', or, as we should now say, they involve introspection. When we ask how we acquire simple ideas or sensations, all that Locke can offer in reply is — by experience.[2] His doctrine thereby came to be designated empiricism. As Locke's classification of ideas is not restricted to sensory percepts, he is not strictly speaking an empiricist.[3] Empiricism assumes that the mind is constituted of independent impressions passively imprinted on it from without. Rationalism, to which it is opposed, assumes that knowledge is derived by deduction from certain first principles intuitively apprehended. Locke does not carry his analysis further, and inquire, as did Kant in effect later, how experience is possible. Kant's answer in *The Critique of Pure Reason*, given here in a line, is that the structure of the mind determines the type of experience we have; the experience of minds otherwise constituted than ours would be in another dimension. Experience is thus mentally conditioned, and idealism rather than empiricism would accordingly appear to be the ultimate answer.

Locke's assumption that simple ideas or simple sensations were unrelated and essentially disconnected necessitates an agency or agencies in the mind to arrange and combine these, whereas the mind that registers the impressions is conceived by Locke merely as a blank sheet or plain surface — a *tabula rasa*, the ideas being related only by the laws of association. To enable Locke's psychology

---

[1] *Essay*, Bk II, ch. 1, § 8.   [2] Ibid., Bk II, ch. 20, § 1.
[3] Cf. Gilbert Ryle, 'Locke on the Human Understanding', in *John Locke: Tercentenary Addresses* (Oxford University Press, 1933), pp. 26, 34.

to be profitable the notion of the simple idea would require to be abandoned; 'the pure sensation we may regard as a psychological myth', says James Ward;[1] it is a product of psychological abstraction and never encountered in actual experience. Some synthetic activity must also be attributed to mind, as Kant later affirmed, if science, or even experience itself, is to be possible. In metaphysics the view of mind as constituted of simple unrelated ideas led to Hume's scepticism, for such a hypothesis, as he confessed, rendered it impossible to account for the necessary connection implied in causality which science demanded. Some recent philosophers who have appropriated the title 'realists' base their system on sense-data which are merely hypothetical elements of psychological abstraction, and analogous to Locke's simple ideas. Had Locke adopted the genetic, instead of the introspective, standpoint he would have come to realise that the original state of mind is an undifferentiated continuum out of which single objects gradually emerge, and that the child's earliest mental experience is, in William James's words, 'a great big blooming buzzing confusion'.

Locke's contribution to education has been variously assessed. The publication in 1690 of the *An Essay Concerning Human Understanding* has been said to mark the opening of an epoch in the history of education.[2] While it undoubtedly initiated a new era in philosophic thought, its influence on education was mainly indirect. Adamson in his Introduction to the *Educational Writings of John Locke* later admitted[3] that these have proved much less influential than his philosophy. Adams, on the other hand, claims :[4] 'Locke's influence far exceeds his fame.

[1] *Psychological Principles* (Cambridge University Press, 1918), p. 143.

[2] J. W. Adamson, *A Short History of Education* (Cambridge University Press, 1919), p. 204.

[3] Cambridge University Press (1922), p. 11.

[4] J. Adams, *Herbartian Psychology Applied to Education*, p. 33.

Most of his followers do not know their master. His point of view coincides so completely with that of the ordinary intelligent man in the street that his following in all English-speaking countries is infinitely greater than any other philosophical writer can command.' His influence on education on the Continent, where theories of education are taken more seriously than in this country, has also been considerable.

An explanation that may be offered to account for such a discrepancy is that no systematic account of education was ever contemplated by Locke. He repeatedly protests : 'I would not have it thought that I looked on it as a just treatise on this subject'; 'But to enter into particulars would be beyond the design of this short treatise'; 'I am far from imagining that it contains all those particulars which his growing years or peculiar temper may require'.[1] Publication was justified on the grounds that 'it may give some light to those . . . that dare venture to consult their own reason in the education of their children rather than wholly rely upon old custom', also 'it is every man's indispensable duty to do all the service he can to his country' and 'the well educating of their children is so much the duty and concern of parents, and the welfare and prosperity of the nation so much depends on it that I would have every one lay it seriously to heart'.[2]

The occasion of committing his thoughts to paper is thus explained. When resident in Holland and engaged on the great *Essay*, Locke in the latter half of 1684 began to append to his letters to his friend Edward Clarke of Chipleigh House in Somerset, advice on the upbringing of his friend's children, especially of the eldest boy — Edward. The 'Directions'[3] served as the first draft of

[1] *Thoughts*, §§ 217, 139, 133.   [2] Ibid., § 217, The Epistle Dedicatory.
[3] B. Rand, *The Correspondence of John Locke and Edward Clarke*, also *John Locke : Directions concerning Education*. Being the First Draft of his *Thoughts Concerning Education* now printed from Add. MS. 38777 in the British Museum with an introduction by Frederick George Kenyon (Oxford, 1933).

Some Thoughts Concerning Education and constituted the opening sections of the work eventually printed in 1693 and addressed to Clarke.[1] The age of Clarke's eldest boy, namely, eight years, when Locke began his letters, explains the emphasis in the early sections on physical well-being and on conduct,[2] the later sections on intellectual education being added as the lad grew older. The contents of his library suggest that Locke was not quite so unprepared for the task he undertook as has generally been supposed.[3]

Locke's standpoint in producing the *Thoughts* he defines in another connection. In reply to a request for advice on the education of her son, Locke wrote in 1697 to Lady Peterborough :[4] 'I have always thought that to direct a young gentleman's studies right, it is absolutely necessary to know what course of life — either by the destination of his quality or fortune or the choice and determination of his parents — he is designed to.' Instead of a uniform classical training for all Locke insisted that education should be tailored to fit the prospective mode of life of the pupil ; this is more definitely formulated in the *Thoughts* : 'I think a prince, a nobleman and an ordinary gentleman's son, should have different ways of breeding.'[5] His

[1] See Epistle Dedicatory to the *Thoughts*.

[2] Letter of Locke in Ninehead Collection. See Rand, p. 25 note 2 : 'Thus you have my first chapter on this subject calculated to the age your son is now of.'

[3] J. R. Harrison and Peter Laslett, 'The Library of John Locke', *The Times Literary Supplement*, 27 Dec. 1957. H. C. Hughes, 'Locke's Library', *Book Collectors' Quarterly*, vol. iii, nos ix–xii, 1933. J. Lough, 'Locke's Reading during his Stay in France' (1675–9), *The Library* (5th series), vol. viii, Oxford University Press, 1953. P. Laslett, *John Locke: Two Treatises on Government*, Appendix B, pp. 130–45.

See Appendix to this chapter for list of works on Education in Locke's library, supplied by Mr John Harrison of the University Library of Cambridge.

[4] Maurice Cranston, *John Locke: A Biography*, p. 427.

[5] *Thoughts*, § 217. For Locke's project for the maintenance and upbringing of pauper children see R. H. Quick, *Some Thoughts Concerning Education by John Locke*, Appendix A.

main concern in the *Thoughts*, however, is with 'the breeding of a young gentleman', who would in the natural course of events fall heir to the family estates. Referring to *Some Thoughts Concerning Reading and Study* and for everything else he published Laslett says:[1] 'They were to be part of the assimilated atmosphere of the English gentleman, the member of Parliament, the administrator and politician, at home and overseas, but above all the landowner, the local notable'; and later, 'The ideal of the English gentleman is with us today, and in part it is Locke's invention.' Locke's conception of the ideal gentleman, interposed in his condemnation of affectation,[2] is : 'he that will examine wherein that gracefulness lies which always pleases, will find it arises from the natural coherence which appears between the things done and such a temper of mind as cannot but be approved of as suitable to the occasion. We cannot but be pleased with an humane, friendly, civil temper wherever we meet with it. A mind free and master of itself and all its actions, not low and narrow, not haughty and insolent, not blemished with any great defect is what everyone is taken with.'

Locke's virtually vocational outlook on education implies a pragmatic attitude in the sense that the outcomes must have practical worth : 'we shall not have reason to complain of the narrowness of our minds, if we but employ them about what may be of use to us.'[3] This is reflected in his emphasis on practical studies, and Newman in *The Idea of a University* accuses Locke, 'that celebrated philosopher',[4] of having anticipated the Edinburgh reviewers in advocating 'that no good could come of a system which was not based upon the principle of utility'.

---

[1] Pp. 4, 51.   [2] *Thoughts*, § 66.   [3] *Essay*, Introduction.
[4] *Discourses on University Education*, viii, 'Philosophical Knowledge viewed in relation to professional' (Dublin, 1852).

Unlike Milton and Comenius, Locke does not assume that man should be omniscient: 'How short soever their knowledge may come of an universal or perfect comprehension of whatever is, yet secures their great concernments that they have light enough to lead them to a knowledge of their Maker and the sight of their own duties',[1] and in the Introduction to the *Essay* he says: 'Our business here is not to know all things, but those which concern our conduct.' In the *Thoughts*[2] it is not the tutor's business 'to teach them all that is knowable'. In his essay 'Of Study' he elaborates:[3] 'The extent of knowledge of things knowable is so vast . . . that the whole time of our life is not enough to acquaint us with all those things, I will not say which we are capable of knowing, but which it would not be only convenient but very advantageous to know.' In accordance with this view Locke formulates the principle which has come to be known as 'frequency of use', a principle extensively exploited by modern curriculum makers: 'And since it cannot be hoped he [the pupil] should have time and strength to learn all things, most pains should be taken about that which is most necessary, and that principally looked after which will be of most frequent use to him in the world.'[4]

Whether the young gentleman should be educated at home under a tutor or sent to a public school is a problem that perplexes Locke. 'I confess both sides have their inconveniences.'[5] But whether as a result of his own experience or not under the famous Dr Busby at Westminster School he, in opposition to Quintilian and Comenius, decided: 'I cannot but prefer breeding of a young gentleman at home in his father's sight under a good governor as much the best and safest way to this

---

[1] *Essay*, Bk I, ch. 1 : cf. 'out of an affectation of an universal knowledge'.
[2] § 195.   [3] R. H. Quick, *Some Thoughts*, Appendix B.
[4] *Thoughts*, § 94.   [5] Ibid., § 70.

great and main end of education when it can be had
and is ordered as it should be.' Locke's prescription for
the upbringing of the lad as set forth in the *Thoughts* does
not seem to have worked so efficaciously as he had intended, for we find from one of his letters[1] that he recommended a change of tutor, and then, as he suspected want
of application, he even suggested[2] to his father that the
boy might be sent to 'Westminster, or some other severe
school, where if he were whipped soundly while you are
looking out another fit tutor for him, he would perhaps be
more pliant and willing to learn at home afterwards'.

'A sound mind in a sound body is a short but full
description of a happy state in this world. He that hath
these two, has little more to wish for; and he that wants
either of them, will be but little the better for anything
else.'[3] Such are the opening sentences of the *Thoughts*.
Locke, who had some pretensions to medical skill,[4] disposes first of health education, advocating a hardening
régime which is the natural lot of the children of the
poor but necessary to give Locke's pupil, who might
otherwise become pampered and spoiled, some of the
advantages of what has been termed 'the education of
the gutter'.[5] Thus Locke recommends[6] that the youth is
'to have his shoes made so as to leak water', and he sums
up his advice on the physical upbringing of the boy thus :[7]

[1] Maurice Cranston, *John Locke: A Biography*, pp. 25, 349–50.

[2] Ibid., p. 355.

[3] Laslett explains (p. 28): 'What had begun as a medical undertaking,
turned itself into an educational experiment, and the third earl [of Shaftes-
bury] tells us that he and his five brothers and sisters were all educated by
Locke "according to his own principles (since published by him)".'

[4] See K. Dewhurst, *John Locke, Physician and Philosopher: A Medical
Biography* (London: Wellcome Historical Medical Library, 1963); *British
Medical Journal*, 5 Oct. 1963, 'An Oxford Medical Quartet'. Also *British
Medical Journal*, 4 April 1964, 'John Locke's Medical Notes'.

[5] Cf. J. Adams, *Modern Developments in Educational Practice* (London:
University of London Press, 1922), p. 30. For the slogan 'from the gutter
to the university' see S. S. Laurie, *The Training of Teachers and Methods of
Instruction* (Cambridge University Press, 1902), pp. 194–5; cf. pp. 149–50.

[6] *Thoughts*, § 7.   [7] Ibid., § 30.

'Plenty of open air, exercise and sleep, plain diet, no wine or strong drink, and very little or no physic, not too warm and strict clothing, especially the head and feet kept cold, and the feet often used to cold water and exposed to wet.' In his chapter on 'Physical Education' in *Education: Intellectual, Moral and Physical*, Herbert Spencer comments on Locke's rigorous régime in the following terms :[1] 'The common notion about "hardening" is a grievous delusion. Not a few children are "hardened" out of the world; and those who survive, permanently suffer either in growth or constitution. . . . The reasoning on which this hardening theory rests is extremely superficial. Wealthy parents, seeing little peasant boys and girls playing about in the open-air only half-clothed, and joining with this fact the general healthiness of labouring people, draw the unwarrantable conclusion that the healthiness is the result of the exposure and resolve to keep their own offspring scantily covered! It is forgotten that these urchins who gambol upon village-greens are in many respects favourably circumstanced — that their lives are spent in almost perpetual play; that they are all day breathing fresh air; and that their systems are not disturbed by over-taxed brains. For aught that appears to the contrary, their good health may be maintained not in consequence of, but in spite of, their deficient clothing. This alternative conclusion we believe to be the true one; and that an inevitable detriment results from the loss of animal heat to which they are subject. For when, the constitution being sound enough to bear it, the exposure does produce hardness, it does so at the expense of growth.'

In fashioning his ideal type of personality four things, according to Locke, are necessary :[2] virtue, wisdom,

[1] Locke's *Thoughts* was among the books heading Spencer's article in *The British Quarterly Review* for January and April 1858.

[2] *Thoughts*, § 134.

breeding and learning. Wisdom is beyond the reach of children since it implies natural good temper, application of mind and experience.[1] Breeding is largely a matter of right company: 'such as his company, such will be his manners.'[2] Its aim is to secure 'a carriage suitable to his rank', and the rule to be observed is: 'Not to think meanly of ourselves, and not to think meanly of others.'[3]

Of virtue Locke says:[4] ''Tis virtue, then, direct virtue, which is the hard and valuable part to be aimed at in education. . . . All other considerations and accomplishments should give way and be postponed to this. This is the solid and substantial good [on] which tutors should not only read lectures, and talk of, but the labour and art of education should furnish the mind with, and fasten there, and never cease till the young man had a true relish of it, and placed his strength, his glory, and his pleasure in it.' The foundations of virtue are to be laid in religion: 'There ought to be imprinted on his mind a true notion of God as of an independent supreme being, author and maker of all things, from Whom we receive all our good, Who loves us, and gives us all things', a confession of faith similar to that which Rousseau in *Émile* later formulates for Sophy.

Learning Locke puts last, and regards it as the least part of education. 'This may seem strange in the mouth of a bookish man; and this making usually the chief, if not only hustle and stir about children, this being almost that alone which is thought on when people talk of education, makes it the greater paradox.'[5] The explanation that he offers in *Thoughts Concerning Reading and Study for a Gentleman* is that 'a gentleman's proper calling is the service of his country, and so is most properly concerned in moral and political knowledge; and thus the studies which more immediately belong to his calling are those

[1] *Thoughts*, § 140.   [2] Ibid., § 145.   [3] § 94.   [4] § 70.   [5] § 147.

which treat of virtue and vices, of civil society and the arts of government, and will take in also law and history'.[1]

Rousseau's criticism of Locke in the *New Héloïse*, that he speaks much more of what should be required of children than of the means that have to be employed in getting it, is hardly justified, for Locke does recognise the importance of method in education. 'Order and constancy are said to make the great difference between one man and another: This I am sure, nothing so much clears a learner's way, helps him so much on in it, and makes him go so easy and so far in any inquiry, as a good method. His governor should take pains to make him sensible of this, accustom him to order, and teach him method in all the applications of his thoughts; shew him wherein it lies, and the advantages of it; acquaint him with the several sorts of it either from general to particulars, or from particulars to what is more general, exercise him in both of them, and make him see in what cases each different method is most proper, and to what ends it best serves.'[2] His own general principle of method he states thus: 'He that hath found a way how to keep up a child's spirit easy, active and free, and yet at the same time to restrain him from many things he has a mind to, and to draw him to things that are uneasy to him; he, I say, that knows how to reconcile these seeming contradictions, has, in my opinion, got the true secret of education.'

Locke anticipated the play-way in education. 'Children

[1] R. Quick, *Some Thoughts Concerning Education by John Locke*, Appendix B.
[2] *Thoughts*, § 195. Cf. F. Bacon, *Advancement of Learning*, Bk II. 'For pedantical knowledge . . . whereunto appertain divers considerations of great fruits. As first, the turning and seasoning of knowledges as with what to initiate them, and from what for a time to refrain them. Secondly, the consideration where to begin with the easiest and so proceed to the more difficult, and on what courses to press the more difficult and then to turn them to the more easy. . . . A third is the application of learning according to the propriety of the wits for there is no defect in the faculties intellectual but seemeth to have a proper cure contained in some studies.'

should not have anything like work, or serious, laid on them; neither their minds nor their bodies will bear it.'[1] And 'were matters ordered right, learning anything they should be taught might be made as much a recreation to their play as their play is to their learning'. A condition of realising this fortunate state of affairs is that the task should be begun at the psychological moment, when the pupil is in the right mood for it — 'the favourable seasons of aptitude and inclinations be heedfully laid hold of'.[2] It should not be prolonged till exhaustion or aversion sets in : 'Care should be taken that what is of advantage to them they should always do with delight; and before they are wearied with one they should be timely diverted to some other useful employment'.[3] In the course of the task 'masters and teachers should raise no difficulties to their scholars but on the contrary should smooth their way and readily help them forwards where they find them stop'.[4] As constant attention is one of the hardest tasks that can be required of children, 'he that requires their application should endeavour to make what he proposes as grateful and agreeable as possible, at least he ought to take care not to join any displeasing or frightful idea with it'. 'The great skill of a teacher is to get and keep the attention of his scholar; whilst he has that, he is sure to advance as fast as the learner's abilities will carry him, and without that, all his hustle and pother will be to little or no purpose. To attain this he should make the child comprehend (as much as may be) the usefulness of what he teaches him, and let him see by what he has learnt that he can do something which he could not do before, something which gives him some power and real advantage above others who are ignorant of it. To this he should add sweetness in all his instructions, and by a certain tenderness in his whole carriage make the child sensible that he loves him and designs nothing

[1] *Thoughts*, § 149.   [2] Ibid., § 74.   [3] § 108.   [4] § 167.

but his good, the only way to beget love in the child which will make him hearken to his lessons and relish what he teaches him.'[1]

The aim should be to create in the pupil 'a liking and inclination to what you propose to them to be learned and that will engage their industry and application'.[2] This, Locke adds, should be no hard matter if children are handled as they should be. Children, too, are to be treated as rational creatures.[3] Locke explains what he means by reasoning with children :[4] 'I do not intend any other but such as is suited to the child's capacity and apprehension.'

A believer in teaching without tears, Locke held advanced views on child discipline. 'I am very apt to think that great severity of punishment does but very little good, nay, great harm in education; and I believe it will be found that *alteris paribus* those children who have been most chastised, seldom make the best men.'[5] He was strongly opposed to the use of the rod. 'The usual lazy and short way by chastisement and the rod which is the only instrument of government that tutors generally know, or ever think of, is the most unfit of any to be used in education.'[6] This sort of correction, he adds,[7] 'naturally breeds an aversion to that which 'tis the tutor's business to create a liking to'. If it needs be that offences come, then Locke offers advice[8] suggesting the employment of a Corrector after the manner of the Jesuits, but repeating : 'Beating is the worst and therefore the last means to be used in the correction of children and that only in cases of extremity after all gentle ways have been tried and proved unsuccessful.'

That Locke, rather than Rousseau, should be designated the father of the child-study movement can be justified by the exhortation :[9] 'He that is about children should

[1] § 167.   [2] § 72.   [3] § 54.   [4] § 81.   [5] § 43. Cf. § 52.
        [6] § 47.   [7] § 49.   [8] §§ 83–87.   [9] § 66.

well study their natures and aptitudes and see by often trials what turn they easily take and what becomes them; observe what their native stock is, how it may be improved, and what it is fit for; he should consider what they want, whether they be capable of having it wrought into them by industry and incorporated there by practice, and whether it be worth while to endeavour it. For in many cases all that we can do, or should aim at, is to make the best of what nature has given, to prevent the vices and faults to which such a constitution is most inclined, and give it all the advantages it is capable of. Everyone's natural genius should be carried as far as it could, but to attempt the putting another upon him, will be but labour in vain, and what is so plastered on will at best sit untowardly and have always hanging to it the ungracefulness of constraint and affectation.'[1]

But if the young gentleman is not to remain 'more ignorant than the clerk of our parish' he must learn to read and write. Various contrivances for learning his letters are described by Locke; after mastering these he is to proceed to reading, the general procedure advocated by Locke being: 'Let him never be driven to nor chid for; cheat him into it if you can, but make it not a business. 'Tis better it be a year later before he can read than that he should get an aversion to learning.'[2] After reading comes writing. In dealing with the acquisition of this skill Locke enunciates the principles that if one would do anything well he should not attempt to do two

[1] This exhortation has also been quoted in support of the contention that Locke was one of the first to express the guidance point of view. *Introduction to Testing and to the Use of Test Results*, by Margaret Selover, Agatha Townsend, Robert Jacobs, Arthur E. Traxler published by Educational Records Bureau, New York, 1950), p. 1. Cf., however, F. Bacon, *Of the Advancement of Learning*, Bk II: with regard to the 'application of learning according unto the propriety of the wits', Bacon observes that masters ought to attend to it for the guidance of the parents in choosing their son's course of life, and also because a man will advance so much faster in studies for which he has a natural aptitude than in any others.

[2] *Thoughts*, § 155.

parts of an action at the same time if they can be separated ;
learning to hold the pen must accordingly be taught independently of learning to form the letters.[1] Repre-
sentational drawing is added not for any aesthetic but
merely for its practical value, and at a later stage shorthand is mentioned as an optional subject.[2]

Although not mentioned in his treatise on education,
Locke advocated spelling reform. The following appears
in shorthand in his Journal (dated 15 August 1676) :
'*Spelling* . . . How little a lover so ever I am of fresh
fashions . . . considering that letters are but the lasting
marks of sounds, I think we would avoid much confusion
and great many needless difficulties if we would always
apply as near as we could the same characters to the
same pronunciation. [It would] perhaps look a little
strange and awkward at first to make a change all at
once, as in this paragraph, so much is custom able to
confirm us in love and admiration even of inconveniencies,
although it cannot but be acknowledged that it would be
much better if it were reformed, and nobody can deny
that it may be done by degrees and must have a beginning.
It would prevent a great many mistakes and make
languages of which we have so great a need and so
constant use much *easier* to be learnt, read and written by
all strangers, by the women and illiterate of the same
country.'[3]

Locke is a convinced believer in 'English for the
English'. Care is to be taken when the boy is learning
French and Latin, that his English is not neglected[4] . . .
'since 'tis English that an English gentleman will have
constant use of, that is the language he should chiefly
cultivate. . . . I am not here speaking against Greek and

[1] Ibid., § 160.
[2] § 161. Locke himself used a form of shorthand. Cf. M. Cranston, p. 80.
For shorthand in Roman times, see Marrou, pp. 312–13.
[3] M. Cranston, *John Locke : A Biography*, pp. 241–2, note.
[4] *Thoughts*, § 163.

Latin; I think they ought to be studied, and the Latin at least understood well by every gentleman. But whatever foreign languages a young gentleman meddles with (and the more he knows the better) that which he should critically study and labour to get a facility, clearness and elegancy to express himself in, should be his own; and to this purpose he should be daily exercised in it.'[1]

In spite of his general pragmatic standpoint Locke cannot evade the issue of the place of languages in the education of his pupil. After English, French is proposed, the reason for its priority over Latin being that it is a living language and can be acquired by the direct method.[2] Latin, too, Locke regards as absolutely necessary to a gentleman, but it should, like French be taught by the direct method and not after the traditional grammatical manner which Locke roundly condemns. No man can pass for a scholar that is ignorant of the Greek tongue, Locke admits,[3] but protests that he is not considering the education of a professed scholar, but of a gentleman to whom Latin and French are by everyone acknowledged to be necessary. While Latin is looked upon as necessary to a gentleman, it is ridiculous for a boy designed for a trade to spend time on a language for which he will never have any use.

To complete his curriculum Locke, unmindful perhaps of his previous warning regarding the extent of human knowledge and the limitation of the pupil's mind, adds arithmetic, astronomy, geometry, geography, chronology, history, ethics, law, natural philosophy. Other accomplishments include dancing and music, and wrestling is preferred to fencing. One more addition, which Locke recognises will evoke astonishment, is his recommendation

---

[1] *Thoughts*, § 189.   [2] Ibid., § 162.
[3] § 195. He evidently thought it was impossible to train both a scholar and a gentleman!

of a trade. 'And yet I cannot forbear to say I would have him learn a trade, a manual trade, nay two or three, but one more particular. . . . I should propose one, or rather both these, namely gardening or husbandry in general, and working in wood as a carpenter, joiner or turner, these being fit and healthy recreations for a man of study or business.'[1] After that Locke did not expect to meet the same opposition in advocating that a young gentleman should learn to keep accounts, 'though a science not likely to help a gentleman to get an estate, yet possibly there is not any thing of more use and efficacy to make him preserve the estate he has'.[2]

The young Englishman's education was rounded off with the Grand Tour, but Locke, regards the usual age, namely, from sixteen to twenty-one, as of all times the least suitable, preferring seven to fourteen as the best age to acquire the correct accent in foreign languages; at this age, too, a tutor's presence is not resented as it would be by an older pupil.

Two controversial issues emerge from Locke's reflections on education — the nature–nurture dilemma, and the validity of formal training. In justification of his intervention in embarking on the *Thoughts* he stresses the importance of education to the extent of declaring that education can accomplish everything, whereas in more philosophic mood in the *Second Treatise of Government* and in the *Conduct of the Understanding*, as we have seen, he acknowledges that nature sets limits to the efficacy of education. Thus in the opening sections of the *Thoughts*[3] he says that 'of all men we meet with, nine parts of ten are what they are, good or evil, useful or not, by their education. 'Tis that which makes the great difference in mankind.' And he repeats : 'That the difference to be found in the manners and abilities of men is owing more to their education than to anything else.' Later in the

---

[1] §§ 201, 204.   [2] § 210.   [3] § 32.

Thoughts he qualifies his statement[1] averring 'God has stamped certain characters upon men's minds which, like their shapes, may be a little mended, but can hardly be totally altered and transformed into the contrary'.

Most dispute has, however, arisen in the history of education on the issue whether Locke can be regarded as an upholder of the doctrine of formal training. As we have already seen, Plato cannot be acquitted of the charge of introducing the disciplinary conception of education or formal training. In Milton's tractate *Of Education* the term is definitely used : 'These are the studies wherein our noble and our gentle youth ought to bestow their time in a disciplinary way.' Locke cannot consequently be saddled with the responsibility for initiating the doctrine or for introducing the term. The question then resolves itself into whether he upholds the doctrine. His advocacy of certain Spartan practices in the physical upbringing of his young gentleman, and such a remark in regard to his moral training :[3] 'it seems plain to me that the principle of all virtue and excellency lies in the power of denying ourselves the satisfaction of our own desires', might seem to justify us in ascribing to him the disciplinary conception of education, but it is in the intellectual sphere that a decision must be taken. The warrant for attributing the disciplinary view to Locke is to be found in the *Thoughts*.[4] 'The studies which he [the tutor] sets him upon, are but as it were the exercise of his faculties and employment of his time, to keep him from sauntering and idleness, to teach him application and

---

[1] *Thoughts*, § 66. Laslett notes (p. 82): 'Locke is, perhaps, the least consistent of all great philosophers, and pointing out the contradictions either within any of his works or between them is no difficult task.' Also (p. 89): 'A great deal, perhaps too much, has been made of Locke's inconsistencies. But it must be remembered that all thinkers are inconsistent.'

[2] P. 17.

[3] *Thoughts*, § 38. In reply to Molyneux's objection to the severity of his educational method Locke suggested that Molyneux had taken his method to be more severe than it was. M. Cranston, p. 321.   [4] § 94.

accustom him to take pains, and to give him some little taste of what his own industry must perfect.'

The formal training of school subjects rests on the assumption that in the mind there are powers or faculties which can be improved by the teaching of such subjects. Locke's devastating criticism in *An Essay Concerning Human Understanding*, as we have seen, has effectively disposed of mental faculties, although even today the lesson has not been learnt by many educationists. In the *Thoughts*, written in a more popular strain, he says : 'I hear it is said that children should be employed in getting things by heart, to exercise and improve their memories. I could wish this were said with as much authority of reason as it is with forwardness of assurance, and that this practice were established upon good observation more than old custom ; for it is evident that strength of memory is owing to an happy constitution, and not to any habitual improvement got by exercise. 'Tis true, what the mind is intent upon, and, for fear of letting it slip, often imprints afresh on itself by frequent reflection, that it is apt to retain, but still according to its own natural strength of retention. But the learning pages of Latin by heart no more fits the memory for retention of anything else than the graving of one sentence in lead makes it the more capable of retaining firmly any other characters. If such a sort of exercise of the memory were able to give it strength, and improve our parts, players of all other people must needs have the best memories and be the best company. But whether the scraps that have got into their heads this way make them remember other things the better ; and whether their parts be improved proportionately to the pains they have taken in getting by heart others' sayings, experience will shew. Memory is so necessary to all parts and conditions of life, and so little is to be done without it, that we are not to fear it should grow dull and useless for want of exercise, if exercise

would make it grow stronger. But I fear this faculty of
the mind is not capable of much help and amendment
in general by any exercise or endeavour of ours, at
least not by that used upon this pretence in Grammar
Schools. . . .'

In regard to reasoning Locke likewise rejects what has
come to be known as transfer of training; in the *Conduct
of the Understanding*[1] he says: 'We see men frequently
dexterous and sharp enough in making a bargain who, if
you reason with them about matters of religion, appear
perfectly stupid.' And later he explains:[2] 'The mistake
is that he that is found reasonable in one thing is con-
cluded to be so in all, and to think or say otherwise is
thought so unjust an affront, and so senseless a censure,
that nobody ventures to do it.' Locke also suggests[3] that
there is no transfer between ability in Latin and in
English; in Latin 'the manner of expressing of one's self
is so very different from ours that to be perfect in that
would very little improve the purity and facility of his
English style'.

Locke's treatment of grammar may be regarded as a
'crucial instance' in deciding the question whether his
educational doctrine in the *Thoughts* is disciplinarian or
utilitarian, for no subject lends itself more readily to
justification on disciplinarian grounds. To the question
'To whom should grammar be taught?' Locke answers:[4]
'Men learn languages for the ordinary intercourse of
society and communication of thoughts in common life,
without any farther design in the use of them. And for
this purpose the original way of learning a language by
conversation not only serves well enough, but is to be
preferred as the most expedite, proper and natural.
Therefore, to this use of language one may answer
that grammar is not necessary. Others there are, the

[1] P. 15.   [2] *Conduct of the Understanding*, p. 20.
[3] *Thoughts*, § 172.   [4] Ibid., § 168.

greatest part of whose business in this world is to be done with their tongues and with their pens; and to these it is convenient, if not necessary, that they should speak properly and correctly, whereby they may let their thoughts into other men's minds the more easily, and with the greater impression. Upon this account it is, that any sort of speaking, so as will make him to be understood, is not thought enough for a gentleman. He ought to study grammar amongst the other helps of speaking well. . . . And to this purpose grammar is necessary; but it is the grammar only of their own proper tongues, and to those only who would take pains in cultivating their language, and in perfecting their styles.' 'There is a third sort of men, who apply themselves to two or three foreign, dead, and (which amongst us are called the) learned languages, make them their study, and pique themselves upon their skill in them. No doubt, those who propose to themselves the learning of any language with this view, and would be critically exact in it, ought carefully to study the grammar of it.' Grammar is throughout regarded purely as an instrumental subject and ancillary to language; its formal training value is ignored. Logic and rhetoric, frequently justified for their value as means of training the mind, are dismissed by Locke with but slight reference, the criterion applied being again the utilitarian — 'because of the little advantage young people receive from them'.[1]

Thus, as we have seen, in the *Thoughts* Locke maintains that practice in one phase of memory does not result in improvement in other aspects, that the learning of one language may adversely affect the learning of another, and that training in grammar does not improve the mind in general. In the *Conduct of the Understanding* a similar conclusion is deduced in respect of reasoning. The weight of evidence is accordingly against the charge that

[1] *Thoughts*, § 188.

F

Locke supports formal training and that he is a representative of the disciplinary view of education; the lapses which we have indicated are such as are likely to be encountered in a writer who does not specifically set himself to avoid the implications of the doctrine.

Although the *Thoughts* was directed to the upbringing of an ordinary gentleman's son, Locke was prepared, if called upon, to advise on the education of the young man's sister, as we should expect from the many expressions in his letters of tender solicitude for Elizabeth Clarke to whom, when little more than a year old, he speaks in playful terms as his 'little mistress' and a little later as 'his wife'. In a covering letter attached to a fair copy of the early draft of the *Thoughts* sent in 1684 to Edward Clarke, he evidently contemplated dealing with the education of girls, the last sentence running: 'Be therefore both you and your lady as severe as may be in examining these rules, doubt as much as you can of every one of them, and when upon a scrupulous review we have settled this part and supplied what possibly you may find wanting, I shall be ready to talk my mind as fully to Madame concerning her daughters, if she continue to be of the mind that may be worth her patience to hear it.'[1] And in the *Thoughts*[2] he explains: 'I have said *he* here because the principal aim of my discourse is how a young gentleman should be brought up from his infancy, which in all things will not so perfectly suit the education of daughters though where the difference of sex requires different treatment, 'twill be no hard matter to distinguish.'

[1] British Museum, Add. MS. 38777. See Rand, p. 25 note 1.
[2] *Thoughts*, § 6.

APPENDIX

List of works in Locke's library, supplied by Mr John Harrison of the University Library of Cambridge

Nos 1–9 were published before Locke's own work, so that only these books from his own library might be said to have any influence on Locke's *Some Thoughts concerning Education*. There may well be a good case for adding to the list the three works set out in the Appendix, depending upon the interpretation of education.—(J. H.)

1. BURGHLY (W. C., Baron), *Precepts*. 16°, London, 1636.
2. [NICOLE (P.)?], *De l'éducation des enfans et particulièrement de celle des princes*. 8°, Amsterdam, 1679.
3. DU FOUR (S.) *Instruction morale d'un père à son fils* . . . 12°, Paris, 1686.
4. FÉNELON (F. DE S. DE LA M.), *Éducation des filles*. 12°, Paris, 1687.
5. LE FEVRE (T.), *Méthode pour commencer l'humanité*. 12°, Saumur, 1672.
6. LA HOGUETTE (P.), *Testament, ou Conseils fidelles d'un bon père à ses enfants*. 7e éd. 12°, Paris, 1660.
7. OSBORNE (F.), *Advice to a Son* . . . 8°, Oxford, 1656.
8. RALEIGH (Sir W.), *Instructions to his sonne and to posterity*. 16°, London, 1636.
9. WALKER (O.), *Of Education, especially of Young Gentlemen*. 8°, Oxford, 1673.
10. AINSWORTH (R.), *The most natural and easie way of institution: containing proposals for making a domestic education less chargeable to parents*. 4°, London, 1698.
11. BORDELON (L.), *La Belle éducation*. 12°, Paris, 1693.
12. FLEETWOOD (W.), *A sermon of the education of children*. 4°, London, 1696.
13. *Instructions de l'empereur Charles V à Philippe II, roi d'Espagne* . . . 2° éd. 12°, La Haye, 1700.
14. *Knowledge [The] of the world or The art of well educating youth* . . ., vol. i. 8°, London, 1694.

15. LOCKE (J.), *Some Thoughts concerning Education*. 8º, London, 1693.
16. —— —— 3rd ed. 8º, London, 1695.
17. —— —— 4th ed. 8º, London, 1699.
18. —— *De l'éducation des enfants.* 12º, Amsterdam, 1695.
19. TILLOTSON (J.), *Six Sermons:* I. *Of Stedfastness in Religion.* II. *Of Family-religion.* III, IV, V. *Of Education of Children . . .,* 8º, London, 1694.

The three works referred to in Mr Harrison's note above :

1. BELGRADE (Abbé), *Réflections sur le ridicule et sur les moyens de l'éviter.* 12º, Paris, 1697.
2. LAMY (B.), *L'Art de parler.* 2ᵉ éd. 8º, Paris, 1676.
3. ORTIGUE DE VAUMORIÈRE (P.), *L'Art de plaire dans la conversation.* 12º, Paris, 1692.

CHAPTER VIII

ROUSSEAU[1]

ROUSSEAU is the most maligned and most misunderstood figure in the history of education, and for this he has himself largely to blame. The story of the heartless wretch who packed off his children to the Foundling Hospital as soon as they were born, although supported by his own *Confessions*, is doubtless a fabrication — a rationalisation to cloak what may be presumed to be his impotence. He had no children of his own,[2] no schooling and little or no experience of teaching. When towards the end of 1735 he was reprimanded by his father for his shiftless existence, he retorted by expressing his inclination to become a tutor: 'Finally, I might in a few years and with a little more experience become tutor to some young men of quality. . . . I confess frankly that that is the estate for which I feel some inclination.'[3]

Such an opportunity did present itself later, and although his experience of tutoring the two sons of M. de Mably, Provost of Lyons, revealed to Rousseau his

[1] 1712–78. F. C. Green, *Jean-Jacques Rousseau: A Critical Study of his Life and Writings* (Cambridge University Press, 1955).

For psychosomatic study of Rousseau see R. Grimsley, *Jean-Jacques Rousseau: A Study in Self-Awareness* (Cardiff: University of Wales Press, 1961).

[2] Frederika Macdonald, *Jean-Jacques Rousseau: A New Criticism* (London: Chapman & Hall, 1906), vol. i, p. 156. Grimsley nevertheless accepts the traditional view that Rousseau abandoned his children. Op. cit., pp. 77, 109, 154, 282, 306–7, 325. Also F. C. Green, pp. 37–38, but see p. 178, Mme de Luxembourg's search proved fruitless to trace the elder child through the records of the Foundlings' Hospital.

[3] A. L. Sells, *The Early Life and Adventures of J.-J. Rousseau* (Cambridge: Heffer & Sons, 1929), p. 103.

unfitness for the task,[1] it engaged his interest in education, and led him to prepare his first treatise on the subject, namely, the *Project for the Education of M. de Sainte-Marie*,[2] Sainte-Marie being the elder of the two boys. 'The end that one should set before oneself in the education of a young man', states Rousseau in the *Project*, 'is to form his heart, his judgment and his mind — in the order in which I have named them', thus echoing the precept in Locke's *Thoughts*: ''Tis virtue, then, direct virtue, which is the hard and valuable part to be aimed at in education.' In a few particulars, especially concerning the position and function of a tutor, we have in the *Project* anticipations of the *Émile*, but the great attention which in this treatise he devotes to the early social training of Sainte-Marie proves that Rousseau had not yet adopted his anti-social attitude which is characteristic of his later political and educational writings.

During his stay in Paris the announcement in the *Mercure de France* of the subject of the prize essay set by the Academy of Dijon in 1750[3] — 'Has the Restoration of the Arts and Sciences contributed to the Purification of Morals?' — gave Rousseau his opportunity, and the success attending his efforts marked the beginning of his literary fame and of his anti-social bias. This anti-social attitude was in no small measure temperamental, a defence mechanism against his gaucherie. His attempt to put the simple life into practice estranged the literary coterie with whom he was consorting, and this, added to his general

[1] Cf. *Émile*, Everyman translation, pp. 18, 86. In his *Confessions* (Bk VI) he says: 'I could only think of three methods to employ with them. They are always useless and frequently pernicious with children: sentiment, argument, anger.'—quoted Green, p. 67. After a similar experience, but extending over nine years, Kant likewise confessed there was hardly ever a tutor with a better theory or a worse practice. T. K. Abbott, *Kant's Critique of Practical Reason*, p. xvi.

[2] 1740. For English translation see W. Boyd, *The Minor Educational Writings of Jean-Jacques Rousseau* (London: Blackie & Sons, 1911).

[3] Doubtless inspired by Hume's essay 'On the Rise and Progress of the Arts and Sciences'. D. Hume, *Essays, Moral, Political and Literary* (1742).

introvertive tendencies, created the misunderstandings which embittered his life and caused it to be one of increasing misery.

Before considering the *Discourse on the Arts and Sciences* and others of Rousseau's *Discourses* it may be appropriate by reason of its educational bearings to interpolate an episode which created additional prejudice against Rousseau. Having come within the ambit of Madame d'Épinay's circle in 1747, he was provided by her with the Hermitage on the estate of d'Épinay at Montmorency which he occupied from April 1756 till December 1757. The Hermitage afforded Rousseau a happy interlude in his troubled life. Madame d'Épinay had conceived the idea of writing for the edification of her little son, then nine years old, a series of letters, and had submitted for his observations some of these to Rousseau, who approved of the idea but objected that the purpose, being too apparent, would defeat itself. Rousseau's replies have, according to Mrs Frederika Macdonald's researches,[1] been deliberately mutilated to discredit him; he is reported in the falsified version to have said that fathers and mothers are not made educators by nature nor are children made to be educated, and to have maintained the 'bizarre thesis' that no education is advisable. The true version according to the original manuscript, as contrasted with the published text of Madame d'Épinay's *Memoirs*, is as follows:

I have read, madame, with great attention your letters to your son; they are good, excellent; but entirely unsuited to him. Allow me to tell you this with all the sincerity I owe you. In spite of the tenderness and earnestness with which you adorn your counsel, the general tone of these letters is too serious. They show your purpose is to improve him — and if the purpose is to succeed, the child must not suspect it. I think the idea of writing to him a very happy one, that may

[1] Vol. i, pp. 222–7.

help to form his heart and mind; but two conditions are necessary for this; he should understand you; and he should be able to reply to you. These letters should be written for him alone — and these you have sent me would do for almost anyone but him! Believe me, keep them until he is older. Tell him stories and fables, that he can find out the moral of, and, above all, that he can apply to himself. Avoid generalities: *one only arrives at poor results, or at none at all, by putting maxims in the place of facts.* It is from what he has actually seen whether of right or of wrong, that you must start; when his ideas begin to form themselves, and when you have taught him to reflect, and to compare them, by degrees, you will change the tone of your letters, suiting it to his progress, and to the faculties of his mind. But if you tell your son now that your object is to form his heart and mind, and that you wish, whilst amusing him, to teach him the truth and his duties, he will be on his guard against everything you say: he will see a lesson in every word you utter, everything, even his top, will become an object of suspicion to him. Try to instruct him whilst amusing him, but keep the secret to yourself. . . . Here, Madame, you have it. I hope it may not vex you; for it is not possible for me to give you another. If I am not deceived in you, you will forgive my brutality; and you will begin your task over again with more courage, and more success than ever.[1]

The sentiments expressed in this reply coincide with those in the *Émile*, the phrasing in some cases being identical, and on this ground alone would support the contention that the account presented in Madame d'Épinay's published *Memoirs* is a later fabrication.

The *Discourse on the Arts and Sciences*[2] expresses Rousseau's anti-social doctrine or rather his protest against the artificial conventional standards which controlled current society. Rousseau's complaint is not modern; the book of Genesis records how it was through eating of the tree of knowledge that evil entered into the world, and

[1] Translation from Frederika Macdonald, vol. i, pp. 225–7.

[2] *The Social Contract and Discourses*, by Jean-Jacques Rousseau. Everyman, 'A Discourse on the Arts and Sciences', pp. 125–54.

Ecclesiastes, the preacher, proclaimed that he that increaseth knowledge increaseth sorrow. The early Stoic philosophers, repelled by the doctrine that happiness was to be attained through the search after pleasure, taught man to seek in his own soul the source of his satisfaction, that he was sufficient unto himself would be but to estimate at their true worth the externalities of life. This view finds expression in Seneca's *Ad Lucilium Epistulae Morales*, especially in that 'On the Part Played by Philosophy in the Progress of Man' from which Rousseau doubtless derived his *Discourse on the Arts and Sciences*.[1] Therein Seneca declares: 'Nature suffices for what she demands. Luxury has turned her back upon nature. A thatched roof once covered free men; under marble and gold dwells slavery.' In the *Discourse* Rousseau writes 'in praise of ignorance'. He assembles instances to prove that the decline and fall of ancient peoples coincided with the growth of knowledge among them. He argues that the days of their poverty, simplicity and ignorance were also the days of their strength, their happiness and their innocence, that, as Hegel later said, 'the owl of Minerva — the bird of wisdom, does not begin its flight till the evening shadows fall'. This argument is a defence of the supremacy of the moral life, for making virtue ruler. With Milton would he plead — 'Love virtue, she alone is free'.

The extravagances against which Rousseau inveighed in his *Discourse on the Arts and Sciences* he seeks to account for in his *Discourse on the Origin of Inequality*.[2] They are, in fact, the results of man's sense of possession and desire for private property; were he true to his own self there would be but few inequalities in social life. To sustain his contention Rousseau has to define the original nature of man, and it is this part of the *Discourse on Inequality* that has educational interest. Plato, it may be recalled, had

[1] See the writer's *The Philosophical Bases of Education*, pp. 121–3.
[2] 1755. *The Social Contract and Discourses*, Everyman, pp. 155–238.

F 2

postulated the existence of innate inequalities as the condition of even the most rudimentary form of social community: Rousseau emphasises the common nature of mankind.[1] For both Plato and Rousseau the question was mainly political. In modern times it takes a different form; the anthropologist now studies 'our contemporary ancestors' to deduce from their manners and customs the original nature of man; the psychologist attempts an analysis and classification of man's innate capacities, mainly in the interests of education. Rousseau, ignoring the comparative treatment, attacks directly the question of the nature of man; he frankly warns us that he is likewise not following the historical method — 'Let us begin then by laying facts aside, as they do not affect the question'. The plan he adopts is the hypothetical or conjectural. Wherein then lies the difference between the procedure of Rousseau and that of the modern psychologist? The latter generally accepts the biological standpoint, whereas Rousseau adopts what might be designated — the meta-biological. Even some modern geneticists recognise the total inadequacy of any explanation of man's life in terms of animal behaviour. Thus, H. S. Jennings declared:[2] 'There is no organism that differs so much from other organisms as do human beings. The things that are of most importance about children must be known from a study of children, rather than from a study of other organisms; and the same truth holds for human affairs in general.' This is Rousseau's position. Animal behaviour can be explained by the laws of mechanism, but man, according to Rousseau, is a free agent, and has some share in his own operations. Rousseau

[1] Cf. *Émile*, Bk I: 'If all human knowledge were divided into two parts, one common to all, the other peculiar to the learned, the latter would seem small compared with the former.'

[2] *Suggestions of Modern Science Concerning Education* — 'The Biology of Children in Relation to Education' (New York: The Macmillan Co., 1925), p. 6.

would even go the length of attributing ideas and intelligence to animals, allowing man in this respect to differ only in degree from them, but he adds that it is not so much the understanding that constitutes the specific difference between the man and the brute as the human quality of free agency. It is particularly in the consciousness of this liberty that, according to Rousseau, the spirituality of man's soul is displayed. In his analysis of human endowment Rousseau thus gives priority to the higher spiritual values, the existence of which modern psychologists are apt to ignore. To freedom he links progress, or self-improvement, anticipating Browning when he says that progress is man's distinctive mark alone, not God's, and not the beasts.

In *A Discourse on Political Economy*,[1] the subject being the principles of political obligation, Rousseau formulates the differences between public and domestic administration, also the principles of public education. His plan of public education is communistic, recalling the schemes set forth by Plato in the *Republic* and the *Laws*, and anticipating the communistic arrangement advanced by Fichte in *Address to the German Nation*. Reformers impatient to have their ideals realised, and depressed by the hopelessness of their task in the face of the forces of heredity — physical and social — would drastically dispose of the family and start afresh ; but if they thus dispose of the obstacles that obstruct their paths, they at the same time remove the supports which render progress possible. Plato had hoped, while destroying the family, to retain the family virtues, and Rousseau but reiterates the fallacy of composition whereby Plato's argument derived a certain plausibility, namely, that the love which each parent bore to his own child and the child to his parent would be intensified proportionally as all parents in common came to regard all the children of the state as

[1] 1755. *The Social Contract and Discourses*, Everyman, pp. 247–87.

their care. Aristotle in his *Politics* had indicated the fallacy
in Plato's proposals, but it is perhaps more clearly exposed by Kant's apt illustration that there would result a
harmony like that which a certain satirical poem depicts
as existing between a married couple bent on going to
ruin, 'O marvellous harmony, what he wishes, she wishes
also', or like what is said of the pledge of Francis I to the
Emperor Charles V, 'What my brother Charles wishes,
that I wish also (namely, Milan)'. But for the most
eloquent refutation of Rousseau's communistic views we
do not require to go outside Rousseau's own writings, for
in the *Émile*[1] he asks : 'Will the bonds of convention
hold firm without some foundation in nature? Can
devotion to the state exist apart from the love of those
near and dear to us? Can patriotism thrive except in the
soil of that miniature fatherland, the home? Is it not the
good son, the good husband, the good father, who makes
the good citizen?'

If we ignore the communistic aspect of the *Discourse on
Political Economy*, Rousseau's view of national education
accords with Greek theory and Spartan practice. He
agrees with Aristotle[2] who declares that since service to
the state as a whole has a single end, it is plain that the
education of all must be one and the same, and that the
supervision of this education must be public and not
private . . . public training is wanted in all things that
are of public interest. Rousseau echoes Aristotle, asserting :[3] 'Public education under regulations presented by
the government, and under magistrates established by the
Sovereign, is one of the fundamental rules of popular or
legitimate government.'

In his *Lettres à M. de Malesherbes*[4] Rousseau designates
the *first Discourse, the discourse* on Inequality and the treatise
on Education [*Émile*] his three principal works, and indi-

---

[1] Bk V.   [2] *Politics*, viii, 3.   [3] *Discourse*, p. 269.
[4] Edited by G. Kudler (London : The Scholartis Press, 1928), p. 34.

cates that they are inseparable and together constitute a complete whole. For his educational views it could equally well be said that three at least of his works should be consulted, namely, the *Nouvelle Héloïse*, the *Émile* and the *Considerations on the Government of Poland*.

In his *Considerations on the Government of Poland*[1] Rousseau applied his principles of national education, and although it is a departure from the historical order to consider it before the *Nouvelle Héloïse* and the *Émile*, it is a natural and logical order. The precedence thus accorded to it may help to counteract the popular belief that Rousseau was an individualist in education, as a cursory reading of the *Émile* might suggest.[2]

In the *Émile* Rousseau distinguishes three phases of education — the natural or negative; the social or moral; the civic or political. Only in dealing with Émile's experience of foreign travel does Rousseau refer in the *Émile* to the third aspect. In the *Considerations on the Government of Poland* he makes this civic aspect the chief aim; in it he preaches the most aggressive nationalism which, however necessary for the preservation of the national spirit of Poland at that time and for the later emancipation of that country, is now outmoded.

Rousseau recognises in this treatise the importance and recommends the inclusion of physical exercises, emphasising their moral value and the social training to be derived from participation in common games. He cites with approval an arrangement at Berne by which pupils acquire a training for the public duties which will later fall to their lot. Of intellectual studies there is practically

[1] 1772. See W. Boyd, *The Minor Educational Writings of Jean-Jacques Rousseau*, pp. 137–49.

[2] Cf. C. E. Vaughan, *The Political Writings of Jean-Jacques Rousseau* (Cambridge University Press, 1915), vol. i, p. 1: 'Strike out the *Discours sur l'inégalité* with the first few pages of the *Contrat Social* and the "individualism" of Rousseau will be seen to be nothing better than a myth.' Also p. 2: 'Rousseau, so far from supporting the individualistic theory, is its most powerful assailant.'

no mention, the whole scheme being planned to develop a national character. Education should be virtually free, and teaching should not be a profession but rather a civic duty undertaken at the outset of a career of public service. The administration of education was to be under the control of a council of magistrates, as advocated by Plato in the *Laws* and as earlier practised at Sparta. Throughout the *Considerations on the Government of Poland* Rousseau, as he repeatedly does in the *Émile*, reverts to the tradition of the ancients when he is required to give practical form to his proposals, for, as he maintains in the *Émile*, 'the ancients are nearer to nature and their genius is more distinct'.

Some time between the publication of the *Émile* and his flight from England, that is, between 1762 and 1767, Rousseau had prepared a *Comparison between Public and Private Education*.[1] Had this been preserved, it would have been appropriately treated here and would have facilitated the transition from the national or civic conception of education presented in *Considerations on the Government of Poland* to the private or domestic view of education expounded in the *Nouvelle Héloïse* and the *Émile*. Rousseau himself had recognised that such a comparison was requisite in any complete system of education and had intended to incorporate it in a revised edition of the *Émile*.

The private or domestic education presented in the *Nouvelle Héloïse*[2] is what we should call home education. Locke in the *Thoughts* had suggested, as stated above, that the principles determining physical upbringing 'might all be dispatched in this one short rule, namely, that gentlemen should use their children as the honest farmers and substantial yeomen do theirs'. This maxim Rousseau adopted and elaborated in the *Nouvelle Héloïse*,

---

[1] See C. E. Vaughan, *The Political Writings of Jean-Jacques Rousseau* (Cambridge University Press, 1915), vol. i, p. 234, and vol. ii, p. 142.
[2] 1761.

admitting as much when he says : 'Accustomed like the children of peasants to expose themselves to the heat and cold they grow as hardy ; are equally capable of bearing the inclemencies of the weather ; and become more robust as living more at their ease. This is the way to provide against the age of maturity, and the accidents of humanity.' The idyllic picture which in the *Nouvelle Héloïse* Rousseau delineates of the early education of her own two boys and her cousins' daughter at the hands of Madame de Wolmar served as the model for Pestalozzi's *Leonard and Gertrude*, Pestalozzi merely making of necessity a virtue and transposing Rousseau's conception into the terms of an underprivileged class.

In the *Émile* Rousseau distinguishes various stages in the pupil's development : (*i*) infancy characterised by habit and the training of the emotions ; (*ii*) childhood characterised by 'necessity' and the training of the senses ; (*iii*) boyhood characterised by 'utility' and the training of the intellect ; (*iv*) adolescence, the stage of 'morality', and of moral, aesthetic and social education. In the *Nouvelle Héloïse* he treats at greater length and in more detail of the childhood stage — 'till his understanding ripens', when the child will be placed under a tutor, as was Émile ; but up to the age of understanding, which he puts much earlier than in the *Émile*, namely, at six instead of at twelve years of age, Rousseau would in the *Nouvelle Héloïse* have the children educated at home by the mother, introducing even a girl cousin and approving of co-education till the boys are of age to come under the care of a tutor, when the girl would become the special care of her instructress and be thereafter educated on quite other lines.

The fundamental principles of education set forth in the *Nouvelle Héloïse* are identical with those of the *Émile*, the *Nouvelle Héloïse* for this reason being the natural and best introduction to the *Émile*. Rousseau regards the original nature of the child as good, and he assumes an initial equality among pupils, inequalities being the result of intercourse with a perverted society. Education, he contends, is necessary — 'the best disposition must be cultivated', and, like Plato, Rousseau believes that it cannot begin too early — 'the first and most important part of education, precisely that which all the world neglects, is that of preparing a child to receive education'. The aim of education is the liberty and happiness of the child, but Rousseau recognises that liberty and constraint are compatible, and does not attempt to minimise the influence of the 'heavy yoke of necessity' which nature lays upon the pupil at this stage. The education is an education through things, and it is a matter of indifference whether at twelve years of age or even at fifteen the pupil is totally ignorant of book knowledge. Throughout the whole work we have an eloquent plea for the predominance of environmental over hereditary influences.

Rousseau, if he was not conscious when he was writing *The Social Contract* that he was initiating a political revolution, was nevertheless under the impression, when penning the *Émile*,[1] that he was effecting a revolution in education. 'My thoughts are not those of others', he declares in the Author's Preface, and later in regard to method he counsels:[2] 'Reverse the usual practice and you will almost always do right.' In spite of these protests Rousseau owed much to the past and to earlier writers. His view of a rational principle governing the universe he derived from the Stoics, as he did also his anti-social views. His political ideas are developments of Locke's, and his early educational views also owe much to Locke.[3]

[1] References throughout to the *Émile* are to the Everyman translation by B. Foxley.   [2] Ibid., p. 58.
[3] Locke, *Two Treatises of Government*, i, ch. vi, § 58; Laslett, p. 201: 'He that will impartially survey the nations of the world will find so much of their governments, religions and manners brought in and continued amongst them by these means (Fashion, Custom) that he will have but

Rousseau counsels us to live according to nature,[1] and in education to follow the order of nature.[2] But the views of education according to nature usually attributed to Rousseau have, we suggest, not been derived from his writings but rather from a sentimentalism which finds expression in the poetic effusions of Wordsworth.

For Rousseau 'nature' has several connotations. When Rousseau says that 'education comes to us from nature from men or from things',[3] he is regarding nature as equivalent to 'endowment' — the inherited disposition and capacities of the individual. Before our innate tendencies are warped by our prejudices, they are what Rousseau terms 'nature'.[4] Nature in this sense, the sense in which the same term is used by Aristotle, is beyond our control : 'Now some hold that we become good by nature, some we become so by habit, and others that it is by teaching. As to nature, that is clearly not in our power ; it is something vouchsafed to the truly fortunate by some divine cause.'[5]

Education according to nature is frequently interpreted to mean nothing more than the spontaneous development of the innate dispositions of the child, nothing more than what modern psychologists term 'maturation'. Education according to nature, nature in the sense of endowment, leads to the non-interventionist policy in education, a hands-off procedure for which, however, there is no warrant in the *Émile*. Education Rousseau may regard as an evil, but it is a necessary evil. In fact, he specifically

little reverence for the practices which are in use and credit amongst men, and will have reason to think that the woods and forests where the irrational, untaught inhabitants keep right by following nature, are fitter to give us rules than cities and palaces where those that call themselves civil and rational, go out of their way, by the authority of example.'

Cf. also references to Locke in *Émile*, author's preface, also p. 53 of *Émile*, and elsewhere.

[1] Ibid., p. 46, also R. Grimsley, op. cit., p. 264. Cf. *Émile*, p. 39 : 'Brought up in all the rusticity of the country.'

[2] P. 49.   [3] P. 6.   [4] P. 7.   [5] Aristotle, *Ethics*, Bk X.

warns us against such a misconception : 'Things would be worse without this education. . . . Under existing conditions a man left to himself from birth would be more a monster than the rest.'[1] Later he says :[2] 'When I want to train a natural man, I do not want to make him a savage and to send him back to the woods, but that living in the whirl of social life it is enough that he should not let himself be carried away by the passions and prejudices of men ; let him see with his eyes and feel with his heart, let him own no sway but that of reason.' He repeats :[3] 'Émile is no savage to be banished to the desert, he is a savage who has to live in the town.' Rousseau's ideal is thus no Tarzan of the Apes.[4]

The view that Rousseau here rejects appears from time to time in literature. It is expressed thus by Bosanquet :[5] 'The impulse to look to the primitive for the type of perfection is natural and recurrent and is not without a certain rough justification. There are obvious obsessions of advancing civilisation from which all that is nearer to the primitive seems relatively free, and it is a natural suggestion that by pursuing a regressive inquiry we shall come upon a phase of experience which shall be single, utterly expressive and wholly free from alien preoccupation and from analytic thought.' Thorndike[6] nevertheless summarily dismisses this idyllic reversion with the comment : 'The result of such confidence in natural development alone can be predicted with surety. It would be no Eden of happy innocence and active intellectual advance but a return to the brutishness of the human race some hundred years ago.'

The second meaning attached to the term 'nature' in the *Émile* is a negative one, a consequence of Rousseau's

---

[1] *Émile*, p. 5.   [2] Ibid., p. 217.   [3] P. 167.
[4] Cf. p. 298 : 'We are not concerned with a savage of this sort.'
[5] B. Bosanquet, *Croce's Aesthetic* (Oxford University Press, 1920), p. 8.
[6] *Education*, p. 35.

adoption of the anti-social attitude. Society, for Rousseau, is not a natural, but an artificial, product, the outcome of a contract. And for Rousseau what is natural is good, and what is conventional or artificial is evil. Nature and society thus become opposed to each other; nature is accordingly defined negatively to society. A natural or a negative education does not mean no education; it signifies simply a non-social education. Rousseau's natural or negative education thus becomes what we should call a preventive education; it is not a preparation for life but rather a preparation against the social conditions in which, Rousseau fully realises, Émile must later play his part. Gradually and sadly does he seek to disillusion Émile as to the wicked world into which he is born.

> Full soon the soul shall have its earthly freight
> And custom lie upon thee with a weight
> Heavy as frost and deep almost as life.

Rousseau does not aim at producing an unsocial creature; he hopes to establish in Émile an ethical constancy before his inevitable entrance into society. The ultimate aim is nevertheless to reconcile the natural and the social training : 'If their teaching conflicts, the scholar is ill-educated and will never be at peace with himself; if their teaching agrees, he goes straight to his goal, he lives at peace with himself, he is well-educated.'[1]

The third meaning attached by Rousseau to the term 'nature' is a positive one, inherited from the Stoics who in turn derived it from Plato.[2] Nature or the universe is governed by a divine providence. To live 'according to nature' is to live in accordance with the rational principle

---

[1] *Émile*, p. 6.
[2] Nettleship in his essay 'The Theory of Education in the Republic of Plato' in *Hellenica*, p. 111, explains that for Plato 'the rational self in man is his most real self, and that life in accordance with the rational order of the world is his truest life'. For Locke the law of nature is also the law of reason — see above, p. 128.

of the universe, to live according to reason; 'he who obeys his conscience is following nature.'[1]   A divine will sets the universe in motion and gives life to nature; a divine intelligence exists 'not merely in the revolving heavens, not in the sun which gives us light, not in myself alone but in the sheep that grazes, the bird that flies, the stone that falls, and the leaf blown by the wind'.[2]

Not only is the ultimate principle of the universe spiritual, as idealism contends, but human nature is likewise spiritual and is not to be accounted for on mechanical or biological lines. 'For physics may explain', as Rousseau maintains in *The Origin of Inequality*,[3] 'in some measure the mechanism of the senses and the formation of ideas; but in the power of willing or rather of choosing, and in the feelings of this power, nothing is to be found but acts which are purely spiritual and wholly inexplicable by the laws of mechanism.'   And whereas instinct may govern man in a state of nature, that is, before morality has emerged and men are bound by social ties, thereafter the voice of duty takes the place of physical impulses, and reason must be consulted before he listens to his inclinations.[4]   Or, as Rousseau says in the *Émile*,[5] 'Distrust instinct as soon as you cease to rely altogether upon it. Instinct was good while he acted under its guidance only; now that he is in the midst of human institutions, instinct is not to be trusted; it must not be destroyed, it must be controlled which is perhaps a more difficult matter.'

Rousseau is almost universally regarded as a naturalist in philosophy, the result of a superficial rendering of 'living according to nature' whereas from the interpretation given above and from the articles of faith formulated

---

[1] *Émile*, p. 250.   [2] Ibid., pp. 236, 237.
[3] Everyman, p. 184.   [4] *The Social Contract*, Everyman, p. 18.
[5] *Émile*, p. 299.   Cf. for same view Pestalozzi's *Letters to Greaves on Infant Education*, p. 47.

in the 'Creed of a Savoyard Priest' he is manifestly an idealist. He serves as the bridge between the Stoics and Kant.[1] The *Émile* is likewise not a work on individual education, as might at first sight be inferred, but actually propounds a universal system. At the outset of the *Émile* he states[2] that education comes from nature, from men or from things, that is, the problem of education is the relationship of man to his physical and social environment. Emphasis may be laid either on the individual or on the social aspect of education. 'Two conflicting types of educational systems spring from these conflicting aims. One is public and common to many, the other private and domestic.'[3] If Rousseau refers the reader of the *Émile* to Plato's *Republic* for an account of public education, it is because he himself had evidently studied the *Republic* not without profit. In the *Émile*, however, he professes to restrict himself to 'the education of the home',[4] but the scheme he there presents is a scheme suited not to one individual only but to all; it is a universal scheme, and for this reason has become the fount of democratic education.[5] Many of the features nevertheless contribute to obscure this fact. The introduction of the individual pupil suggests the contrary interpretation, but it was merely the exigencies of exposition that compelled him to particularise and personify his principles in Émile; as Rousseau himself warns us: 'Lest my book should be

[1] Kant's formulation of the moral law follows Rousseau's statement 'every man is virtuous when his particular will is in all things conformable to the general will, and we voluntarily will what is willed by those whom we love' — *Discourse on Political Economy*, p. 262. Rousseau's 'general will' both in *The Social Contract* and here, is equivalent to a universal moral principle or law. Cf. C. E. Vaughan, *The Political Writings of Jean-Jacques Rousseau*, vol. ii, pp. 19–20.

[2] *Émile*, p. 6.   [3] Ibid., p. 8.   [4] P. 9.

[5] Cf. E. Caird, *The Critical Philosophy of Immanuel Kant* (Glasgow: James MacLehose & Sons, 1889), vol. ii, p. 356. 'Rousseau's primary conception of man is, in a sense, individualistic, that is, it is individualistic in the sense of the Stoics in which the claims of the individual are based on the fact that he is in himself a *universal*.'

unduly bulky I have been content to state those principles the truth of which is self-evident. But as to the rules which call for proof I have applied them to Émile or to others, and I have shown in very great detail how my theories may be put into practice. Such at least is my plan.'[1] And elaborating this literary technique he adds : 'At first I have said little about Émile, for my earliest maxims of education, though very different from those generally accepted, are so plain that it is hard for a man of sense to refuse to accept them, but as I advance, my scholar . . . appears upon the scene more frequently, and towards the end I never lose sight of him for a moment.' Rousseau maintains too that we must look at the general rather than the particular, and consider our scholar as man in the abstract ;[2] he further explains : 'I have discarded as artificial what belongs to one nation and not to another, to one rank and not to another ; and I have regarded as proper to mankind what was common to all, in any age, in any station, and in any nation whatsoever'.[3] He also believes in fitting a man's education to his real self, not to what is no part of him. That Rousseau is propounding a universal and not an individualist system is confirmed by his choice of a pupil : 'If I had my choice', he says,[4] 'I would take a child of ordinary mind. . . . It is ordinary people who have to be educated, and their education alone can serve as a pattern for the education of their fellows' ; he repeats : 'I assumed that my pupil had neither surpassing genius nor a defective understanding. I chose him of an ordinary mind to show what education can do for man.' Another assumption postulated in regard to the pupil for whom Rousseau proposes to prescribe an education, is that he should be 'a strong, well-made, healthy child'. Rousseau would not undertake the care of a feeble sickly pupil, for a healthy body is not only a condition of a healthy mind,

[1] *Émile*, p. 18.   [2] Ibid., p. 10.   [3] P. 217.   [4] P. 19.

but also the basis of moral character. The ideal of the superman of Plato, Quintilian and others gives place with Rousseau to the ideal of the common or natural man; the great souls, he believes, can find their way alone.[1]

Further difficulties are created by Rousseau's selection of Émile from among the rich and by his introduction of a tutor for Émile. Rousseau's apology for choosing his scholar from among the rich is — 'we shall have made another man; the poor may come to manhood without our help'. And if Émile comes of a good family so much the better — 'he will be another victim snatched from prejudice'. He proposes to give the sons of the rich a natural education that whatever might befall them in later life they would be independent of fate or fortune. A more penetrating interpretation is that the education which Rousseau proposed would be accepted as suitable for the poor, whereas by demonstrating that it was quite appropriate for the children of the rich Rousseau established that it was an education for all. It is necessary to emphasise this fact, that Rousseau is expounding a universal system of education, for frequently the *Émile* is regarded as an account of an individualistic scheme of education, and difficulty is thereby encountered in explaining how the democratic systems of Pestalozzi and others originated in the *Émile*.

Although the intervention of the tutor recalls Locke's procedure in the *Thoughts Concerning Education*, Rousseau disclaims any similarity in standpoint: 'I have not the honour of educating a young gentleman.'[2] The introduction of the tutor is indeed something more than a mere literary expedient; it is, in fact, a stroke of genius on the part of Rousseau. There must be only one voice if the scheme proposed is to be an integrated whole. It may be mistaken but it will at least be consistent, whereas when

[1] P. 19. Cf. p. 356: 'I cannot repeat too often that I am not dealing with prodigies.'　　　　　　　　　　[2] P. 321.

the child is subject to two parents his education may be both mistaken and inconsistent; in fact, as is now recognised, it is the dissensions and estrangements of parents that constitute one of the most serious obstacles in the upbringing of their children, and Rousseau obviates this by placing Émile under the sole charge of a tutor.

The anti-social bias of Rousseau first enunciated in the *Discourse on the Arts and Sciences* is reflected in the *Émile* and divides the work into two contrasting sections — the natural or negative education up to adolescence, and the moral or social thereafter. Aristotle had declared in the *Politics*[1] that man is by nature a social or political animal and that the state is a creation of nature. In the perfect state, too, the good man would also be the good citizen.[2] For Rousseau, however, nature and society are eternally at strife — 'Forced to combat either nature or society, you must make your choice between the man and the citizen, you cannot train both'.[3] Rousseau should nevertheless have added 'at the same time', for the *Émile* is an attempt first to train the man, then to train the citizen. 'Man's proper study', he explains,[4] 'is that of his relation to his environment. So long as he only knows that environment through his physical nature, he should study himself in relation to things; this is the business of childhood; when he begins to be aware of his moral nature, he should study himself in relation to his fellow men; this is the business of his whole life.' Again :[5] 'We are working in agreement with nature, and while she is shaping the physical man, we are striving to shape his moral being.' Thus the aim of education for Rousseau, as for Herbart later, was virtue or morality, the natural or physical education being but the preparatory stage.

The definite break, even direct opposition, between the natural or negative stage of education and the social or

---

[1] *Politics*, § 1253.   [2] § 1333.   [3] *Émile*, p. 7.
[4] Ibid., p. 175.   [5] P. 278.

positive stage is the extreme instance of Rousseau's
doctrine of the serial emergence of the faculties.[1]   That
it cannot be completely effected Rousseau is forced to
confess :[2] 'I think it impossible to train a child up to the
age of twelve in the midst of society without giving him
some idea of the relations between one man and another,
and of the morality of human actions.   It is enough to
delay the development of these ideas as long as possible,
and when they can no longer be avoided to limit them
to present needs, so that he may neither think himself
master of everything nor do harm to others without knowing or caring.'[3]   The impossibility of isolating Émile
entirely from the moral and social order should have led
Rousseau to revise his view of human development as
demarcated into well-pronounced stages, but its retention
is not without its compensations.

It necessitated the adoption of what has come to be
known as the psychological standpoint in education.
This is one of Rousseau's fundamental principles. 'My
method', he says,[4] 'does not depend on my examples ; it

---

[1] For criticism of the stratification view of human development as contrasted with the theory of concomitant development of the mental powers,
see Appendix III by Cyril Burt, to the report of the Consultative Committee on *The Primary School* (H.M. Stationery Office, 1931) :
'The traditional descriptions of mental growth divide the whole period
from birth to maturity into a series of sharply demarcated stages. . . .
But the one fact that modern investigations reveal most clearly is the
marked continuity of mental life.   There are no sudden breaks. . . . The
mental growth of the child is a fairly steady advance up an inclined plane,
not a jerky ascent from one level to another by a series of sudden steps ; and
the lines drawn between the successive stages of mental growth are more or
less artificial.'   [2] *Émile*, p. 61.
[3] In his *Philosophy of Right*, § 153, note, Hegel adds his criticism of
Rousseau's proposal : 'The attempts of speculative education to withdraw
people from their present social life and bring them up in the country, a
proposal made by Rousseau in *Émile*, have been vain because no one can
succeed in alienating man from the laws of the world.   Although the
education of young men must take place in solitude, we cannot believe
that the odour of the world of spirits does not in the end penetrate their
seclusion, or that the power of the spirit of the world is too feeble to take
possession of even the remotest corner.'   [4] *Émile*, p. 155.

depends on the amount of a man's powers at different ages and the choice of occupations adapted to these powers.' 'There is a time for every kind of teaching and we ought to recognise it, and each has its own dangers to be avoided.'[1] 'Every stage, every station in life, has a perfection of its own.'[2] 'Childhood has its own ways of seeking, thinking and feeling.'[3]

The principle is also expressed negatively. 'We know nothing of childhood; and with our mistaken notions the further we advance the further we go astray. The wisest writers devote themselves to what a man ought to know, without asking what a child is capable of learning. They are always looking for the man in the child, without considering what he is before he becomes a man.'[4] 'Nothing is useful and good for him which is unbefitting his age.'[5] 'Beware of anticipating teaching which demands more maturity of mind.'[6] 'Man's lessons are mostly premature.'[7] Émile 'should remain in complete ignorance of those ideas which are beyond his grasp. My whole book is one continued argument in support of this fundamental principle of education.'[8]

A consequence of the psychological standpoint was the acceptance of the 'participation' as opposed to the 'preparation' view of education.[9] Rousseau argued that the possibilities of each stage of life should be fully exploited before proceeding to the next stage, a principle assumed later by Froebel and Montessori, although generally associated with the name of Dewey. Thus Rousseau says:[10] 'What is to be thought of that cruel education

---

[1] *Émile*, p. 293   [2] Ibid., p. 122.   [3] P. 54.   [4] Author's Preface.
[5] P. 212.   [6] P. 165.   [7] P. 76.   [8] P. 141.
[9] There are three views:

	Recapitulation	Par icipation	Preparation
represented by	Stanley Hall	John Dewey	Herbert Spencer
denoting	past experience	present needs	future adult requirements

They might be combined in the statement that education is a rehearsal for life.   [10] *Émile*, p. 42.

which sacrifices the present to an uncertain future, that burdens a child with all sorts of restrictions and begins by making him miserable in order to prepare him for some far-off happiness which he may never enjoy?' Again :[1] 'What a poor sort of foresight to make a child wretched in the present with the more or less doubtful hope of making him happy at some future day.'[2]

The perfect adaptation to his capabilities of the tasks undertaken by the pupil creates interest, and Rousseau by providing for this anticipates Herbart's doctrine of interest[3] and its present-day equivalents — the Play Way and the Project Method. Thus Rousseau claims to be justified in saying of Émile :[4] 'Work or play are all one to him; his games are his work; he knows no difference.'

Education becomes for Rousseau a matter of guidance. In detailing the qualifications of the tutor he introduces the very term :[5] 'I prefer to call the man who has this knowledge master rather than teacher, since it is a question of guidance rather than instruction.' For the same reason Montessori later substitutes 'directress'. 'The art of teaching,' Rousseau further explains,[6] 'consists in making the pupil wish to learn.' Or negatively expressed :[7] 'We learn nothing from a lesson we detest.' He summarises his guidance programme for Émile in the statement :[8] 'Surround him with all the lessons you would have him learn without awaking his suspicions.'

'Mankind has its place in the sequence of things; childhood has its place in the sequence of human life; the man must be treated as a man and the child as a child. Give each his place.'[9] It was because Rousseau

---

[1] Ibid., p. 43.

[2] In *Virginibus Puerisque* R. L. Stevenson writes in similar terms in defence of youth.

[3] *Émile*, p. 41. 'Present interest, that is the motive power, the only motive power that takes us far and safely.'

[4] Ibid., p. 126. [5] P. 19. [6] P. 210.

[7] P. 209. [8] P. 85. [9] P. 44.

was the first to give the child his rightful place that the
Émile was characterised by Lord Morley as the charter of
youthful deliverance,[1] and that led Frederika Macdonald
to write :[2] 'Throughout Europe Rousseau's voice went
proclaiming with even more resistless eloquence than it
had proclaimed the *Rights of Man*, the *Rights of Childhood*.
Harsh systems, founded on the old medieval doctrine of
innate depravity, were overthrown. Before Pestalozzi,
before Froebel, the author of *Émile* laid the foundation of
our new theory of education, and taught the civilised
world remorse and shame for the needless suffering and
the quenched joy that throughout long ages had darkened
the dawn of childhood.' Rousseau's own panegyric on
childhood reads thus :[3] 'Love childhood, indulge its
sports, its pleasures, its delightful instincts. Who has not
sometimes regretted that age when laughter was ever on
the lips, and when the heart was ever at peace? Why
rob these innocents of the joys which pass so quickly, of
that precious gift which they cannot abuse? Why fill
with bitterness the fleeting days of early childhood, days
which will no more return for them than for you? Fathers,
can you tell when death will call your children to him?
Do not lay up sorrow for yourselves by robbing them of
the short span which nature has allotted to them. As
soon as they are aware of the joy of life, let them rejoice
in it, so that whenever God calls them they may not die
without having tasted the joy of life.'

What 'the delights of liberty' signify Rousseau explains
in the statement : 'That man is truly free who desires
what he is able to perform, and does what he desires.
This is my fundamental maxim. Apply it to childhood,
and all the rules of education spring from it.'[4] Rousseau's

---

[1] *Rousseau*, ii, p. 250.
[2] *Jean-Jacques Rousseau: A New Criticism*, vol. i, p. 181.   [3] *Émile*, p. 43.
[4] Ibid., p. 48. Cf. *Letters from the Mountain* : 'One must not confound
independence and liberty ; the two things are so different that they mutually
exclude each other. When every one does what pleases himself, he often

aim is 'a well-regulated liberty',[1] the same as Montessori later adopts. Rousseau is well aware of the distinction between liberty and licence, for he retorts to those who object to this aim : 'If such blundering thinkers fail to distinguish between liberty and licence, between a merry child and a spoilt darling, let them learn to discriminate'.[2] He would train his pupil to be 'as self-reliant as possible', whereas he contends that the ordinary educator 'teaches him everything except self-knowledge and self-control, the arts of life and happiness'.[3]

What simplifies the problem for Rousseau is his assumption of the innate goodness of the child. 'Man is by nature good', he says.[4] 'God makes all things good,'[5] and 'what is, is good.'[6] 'Our first impulses are always good.'[7] Locke had claimed that the mind instead of being by nature evil and desperately wicked was a clean slate. Rousseau goes further and maintains[8] 'that the first impulses of nature are always right; there is no original sin in the human heart, the how and the why of the entrance of every vice can be traced.' Dealing with the education of Sophy in Book V, he repeats[9] that all our natural inclinations are right. This doctrine of the innate goodness of the child is inherited by Fichte, Hegel and Froebel,[10] and contrasts oddly with the modern psycho-analytic view of human nature. Without the reforming influences of education the individual, according to the psycho-analysts,[11] 'would remain a selfish,

does what consists less in doing one's own will than in remaining un-compelled to obey the will of others; *it also consists* in being unable to compel others to do our will. . . . Whoever is a master is not free; to reign is to obey. . . . There is no liberty without laws, and no liberty when anyone is above the law.' Translation from Frederika Macdonald, vol. ii, p. 141.   [1] *Émile*, p. 56.

[2] Ibid., p. 43.   [3] P. 16.   [4] P. 198.   [5] P. 5.
[6] P. 334.   [7] P. 256.   [8] P. 56.   [9] P. 334.

[10] Kant maintains that in man there are only germs of good. Providence has not placed goodness ready formed in him. *On Education*, p. 15.

[11] Ernest Jones, *Papers on Psycho-Analysis* (London : Baillière, Tindall & Cox, 1913), p. 124.

jealous, impulsive, aggressive, dirty, immodest, cruel, ego-centric and conceited animal, inconsiderate of the needs of others, and unmindful of the complicated social and ethical standards that go to make a civilised society'.

If nevertheless we accept Rousseau's position and assume that our endowment is good and all our natural incli-nations are right, the task of education should be simple ; we have merely to fix the inborn propensities by habit, for, as Rousseau declares,[1] 'if the voice of instinct is not strengthened by habit, it soon dies'. Habit is all that is needed, as we have nature on our side, he says, speaking of Sophy's education.[2] Education, then, being but habit,[3] care must be taken to see that only right habits are estab-lished, and Rousseau issues his warning in the form of a paradox : 'The only habit', he says, 'the child should be allowed to contract is that of having no habits.'[4] Later he says of Émile :[5] 'No doubt he must submit to rules ; but the chief rule is this — be able to break the rule if necessary.'

Commentators, heedless of Rousseau's warning[6] — 'I must admit that my words are often contradictory, but I do not think there is any contradiction in my ideas',[7] have seized on Rousseau's apparently incompatible state-ments to score easy triumphs, but Rousseau's antinomy is resolved when we recognise that he distinguishes two types of habit, the natural and the social, and that while he advocates establishing natural habits — 'leave his body its natural habit' — he protests against making his pupil

[1] *Émile*, p. 14.

[2] Ibid., p. 333. Cf. Bacon, *Essays*, 'Of Custom and Education'. Educa-tion 'is, in effect, but an early custom'.

[3] *Émile*, p. 7. Cf. p. 271 : 'The habit of the bath, once established, should never be broken off.'

[4] Ibid., p. 30.

[5] P. 94.

[6] P. 72, note.

[7] In like manner he defends his use of paradox, preferring rather to fall into paradox than into prejudice (p. 57), and he does not hesitate to acknowledge exceptions to his own rules (p. 207).

'a mere slave of public opinion'.[1] Thus he explains :[2]
'Always distinguish between natural and acquired tendencies', and again :[3] 'The only useful habit for children
is to be accustomed to submit without difficulty to necessity, and the only useful habit for man is to submit without
difficulty to the rule of reason. Every other habit is a vice.'

To attain liberty education must act both negatively
and positively. The negative training consists in restricting the child's desires, the positive in supplying the pupil
with the strength he lacks so far as it is required for
freedom, not for power.[4] Rousseau effects the former by
keeping the child dependent on things. 'Keep the child
dependent on things only' is his prescription. 'By this
course of education you will have followed the order of
nature.' 'There are two kinds of dependence ; dependence on things which is the work of nature and dependence on men which is the work of society. Dependence
on things, being non-moral, does no injury to liberty, and
begets no vices, dependence on men, being out of order,
gives rise to every kind of vice.'

Keeping the child dependent on things has two aspects
— intellectual and moral. The intellectual aspect is the
basis of Pestalozzi's *Anschauung* — the direct awareness
of objects or the immediate experience of situations.
Negatively it implies the postponement of book knowledge. 'Give your scholar no verbal lessons ; he should
be taught by experience alone.'[5] 'Reading is the curse
of childhood. . . . When I thus get rid of children's
lessons I get rid of the chief cause of their sorrow.'[6] 'I
hate books ; they only teach us to talk about things we
know nothing about.'[7] 'I am pretty sure Émile will
learn to read and write before he is ten, just because I care
very little whether he can do so before he is fifteen.'[8]

[1] P. 163.   [2] P. 130.   All habits are, however, socially initiated.
[3] P. 125, note.   [4] P. 49.   [5] P. 56.   [6] P. 80.
[7] P. 147.   [8] P. 81.

Languages he dismisses as among the useless lumber of education ;[1] geography is only learning the map ;[2] as a real knowledge of events cannot exist, apart from the knowledge of their causes and effects, history is beyond their grasp. And more generally he says :[3] 'I do not like verbal explanations. Young people pay little heed to them, nor do they remember them. Things! Things! I cannot repeat it too often. We lay too much stress upon words; we teachers babble, and our scholars follow our example.'[4] And he sums up :[5] 'Never substitute the symbol for the thing signified unless it is impossible to show the thing itself.'

The moral aspect of Rousseau's negative education consists not in teaching virtue or truth, but in preserving the heart from vice and from the spirit of error,[6] and takes the form of 'the discipline by natural consequences'. 'Children should never receive punishment as such,' recommends Rousseau,[7] 'it should always come as the natural consequence of their fault.' 'He must never act from obedience, but from necessity.'[8] Having removed Émile from parental care without conferring on the tutor the necessary authority for his pupil's conduct the only control that could be exercised, left to Rousseau, was the discipline by natural consequences. Nature and reason are for Rousseau, as they were for Locke, equivalent, but Rousseau failed to recognise, what Locke did, that it was only when he reached the age of reason and could understand the workings of nature and the conventions of society that the child could be allowed to govern himself. Dewey agrees with Locke rather than with Rousseau

---

[1] *Émile*, p. 73.   [2] Ibid., p. 74.   [3] P. 143.
[4] Cf. Locke, *On the Human Understanding*, Bk III, ch. x, § 14: 'Another great abuse of words is the taking them for things.' Also cf. the *Conduct of the Understanding*, § xxix.
[5] *Émile*, p. 133.   [6] Ibid., p. 57.   [7] P. 65.
[8] P. 53. Herbert Spencer, ignorant of Rousseau's treatment, reiterated the same argument in his chapter on 'Moral Education' in his *Education: Intellectual, Moral and Physical*.

maintaining :[1] 'If a person cannot foresee the con-
sequencees of his act, and is not capable of understanding
what he is told about its outcome by those with more
experience it is impossible for him to act intelligently.'

Not only are there to be no direct moral lessons but
there are to be no indirect moral lessons. Thus in contrast
to Plato, who advocated beginning with the false first,
Rousseau protests against young children learning fables.
'Men may be taught by fables; children require the
naked truth.'[2] The reason he adds is that the child is
attracted by what is false and misses the truth, and the
means adopted to make the teaching pleasant, prevent
him profiting by it. Rousseau does not, however, propose
to proscribe fables altogether; he would merely postpone
their introduction till such time as they could be properly
understood and applied, that is, till the adolescent stage;
'the time of faults is the time for fables. When we blame
the guilty under the cover of a story we instruct without
offending him, and he then understands that the story is
not untrue by means of the truth he finds in its application.'[3]

The importance of the negative aspect of education may
be inferred from the statement that 'the most dangerous
period in human life lies between birth and the age of
twelve'[4] and from the attention Rousseau devotes to it.

The positive education of the childhood period comprises physical[5] and sensory[6] training. The physical
education is modelled on that of Sparta. 'This was the
education of the Spartans; they were not taught to stick
to their books, they were taught to steal their dinners.
Were they any the worse for it in after life? Ever ready
for victory, they crushed their foes in every kind of warfare, and the prating Athenians were as much afraid of

---

[1] Cf. *Democracy and Education*, pp. 32–33. For fuller discussion of the
discipline by natural consequences see the writer's *The Philosophical Bases
of Education* (The University of London Press, 1956), pp. 55–59.

[2] *Émile*, p. 77.   [3] Ibid., p. 210.   [4] P. 57.

[5] Pp. 82–97.   [6] Pp. 97–122.

G

their words as of their blows.'[1] But for a temporary reinstatement by some of the early humanists this reversion
to Greek practice initiated in Europe a new development
in physical culture which had suffered from the mediaeval
doctrine of the mortification of the flesh.

The importance of physical condition for the moral
and mental training of the child is frequently insisted on
by Rousseau. It is, as with Plato, 'the body for the sake
of the soul'. Rousseau remarks :[2] 'A feeble body makes
a feeble mind.' 'All wickedness comes from weakness.'
'The weaker the body, the more imperious its demands ;
the stronger it is, the better it obeys.' 'Would you cultivate your pupil's intelligence, cultivate the strength it
is meant to control? Give his body constant exercise,
make it strong and healthy, in order to make him good
and wise ; let him work, let him do things, let him run
and shout, let him be always on the go ; make a man of
him in strength, and he will soon be a man of reason.'
'As he grows in health and strength he grows in wisdom
and discernment. This is the way to attain to what is
generally incompatible, strength of body and strength of
mind, the reason of the philosopher and the vigour of the
athlete.'[3]

The other aspect of the positive education during the
age of childhood is the training of the senses. Man's first
reason is, in Rousseau's opinion, a reason of sense experience. Our first teachers are our feet, hands and eyes.
'To substitute books for them does not teach us to reason,
it teaches us to use the reason of others rather than our
own ; it teaches us to believe much and know little.'[4]
Training the senses does not, however, for Rousseau consist in practising formal exercises ; it implies judgment by

---

[1] *Émile*, p. 84.   [2] Ibid., pp. 21, 33, 21, 82, 84.
[3] Cf. Plato, *Timaeus*, § 86. 'No man is voluntarily bad ; but the bad
become bad by reason of an ill disposition of the body, and bad education.'
[4] *Émile*, p. 90.

their means in concrete situations encountered in life, and is accordingly not open to the objections which have been urged on psychological grounds against some doctrines of sensory training. Thus he proposes such tasks as determining whether a ladder is big enough to reach the cherries on a tree, whether a plank is long enough to bridge a stream, the length of line required for fishing or how much rope to construct a swing. In running races the distances are made unequal, and Émile has to estimate their length so that he may choose the shortest.

The main concern of earlier educators was to assist pupils to acquire the contents of a prescribed course of study. The outstanding feature of the *Émile* is the complete abandonment of a predetermined curriculum. Émile was to be educated entirely through activities and by first-hand experience. Kant[1] claimed that he was effecting a Copernican revolution in metaphysics by assuming not that knowledge should conform to objects, but that objects should conform to our method of knowing. Rousseau's attempt to shift the centre of gravity from the curriculum to the child may be regarded as a parallel revolution in education. This new standpoint has been adopted by later writers, for example, by Nunn:[2] 'The school must be thought of primarily not as a place where certain knowledge is learnt, but as a place where the young are disciplined in certain forms of activity, namely, those that are of greatest and most permanent significance in the wider world.' The Consultative Committee's Report on *The Primary School*[3] repeats: 'the curriculum is to be thought of in terms of activity and experience rather than of knowledge to be acquired and facts to be stored'.

Another surprising feature of the *Émile* is the prolongation of childhood up to twelve years of age. The long

[1] *Critique of Pure Reason*, Preface to second edition, 1787.
[2] T. P. Nunn, *Education: Its Data and First Principles* (London: Edward Arnold & Co. Revised edition, 1930), p. 242.
[3] Board of Education, H.M. Stationery Office, 1931, p. 93.

preparatory period recalls Greek education, and could hardly be justified in a more complex age. Rousseau keeps protesting that he is not educating Émile but merely preparing him for education.[1] The art of teaching, at this stage, 'is to lose time and save it'.[2] 'Give nature time to work', he advises,[3] 'before you take over her business, lest you interfere with her dealings. You assert that you know the value of time and are afraid to waste it. You fail to perceive that it is a greater waste of time to use it ill than to do nothing, and that a child ill-taught is further from virtue than a child who has learnt nothing at all. . . . Do not be afraid, therefore, of this so-called idleness. What would you think of a man who refused to sleep lest he should waste part of his life? You would say, "He is mad; he is not enjoying his life, he is robbing himself of part of it; to avoid sleep he is hastening to his death." Remember that these two cases are alike, and that childhood is the sleep of reason.' The result that Rousseau expects from this course he formulates thus :[4] 'His ideas are few but precise, he knows nothing by rote but much by experience. If he reads our books worse than other children, he reads far better in the book of nature; his thoughts are not in his tongue but in his brain; he has less memory and more judgment; he can only speak one language, but he understands what he is saying, and if his speech is not so good as that of other children his deeds are better.' 'He has reached the perfection of childhood; he has lived the life of a child; his progress has not been bought at the price of his happiness; he has gained both.'

During the years of transition between childhood and adolescence, the boyhood stage between twelve and fifteen, the lost ground must be recovered and education accordingly speeded up. 'Time was long during early childhood; we only tried to pass our time for fear of using

[1] *Émile*, p. 297.   [2] Ibid., p. 106.   [3] P. 71.   [4] Pp. 124–5, 126.

it ill; now it is the other way; we have not time enough
for all that would be of use.'[1] Rousseau is accordingly
compelled to restrict Émile's training to what is useful.
'What is the use of that? This is the sacred formula.'[2]
'This is the time for work, instruction and inquiry. And
note that this is no arbitrary choice of mine, it is the way
of nature herself.' The experiences must likewise be pre-
selected and are not quite haphazard: 'Take care that
all the experiments are connected together by a chain of
reasoning, so that they may follow an orderly sequence in
the mind.'[3]

The occupations rejected at the previous stage must
now be reviewed in the light of the principle of utility
and to those that stand the test Émile is to be introduced.
They comprise practical science, geography and manual
work. Rousseau accordingly plies Émile with concrete
problems and engineers him into situations which challenge explanation. These satisfy the definition of the
project — a practical problem in its natural setting. The
aim is not 'to teach him the various sciences, but to give
him a taste for them and methods of learning them
when this taste is more mature'.[4] Against the formalism
of abstract science Rousseau protests: 'The scientific
atmosphere destroys science,'[5] 'among the many short
cuts to science we badly need someone to teach us
the art of learning with difficulty.' The apparatus
Émile uses in his investigations is to be self-invented:
We should make all our apparatus ourselves. . . . I
would rather our apparatus was somewhat clumsy and
imperfect, but our ideas clear as to what the apparatus
ought to be, and the results to be obtained by means of
it.'

The method which Rousseau recommends is commonly
identified with the heuristic method. Rousseau's heurism

[1] P. 134.   [2] P. 142.   [3] P. 140.
        [4] P. 135.   [5] P. 139.

nevertheless is not strictly a heuristic method; it is a
method of discovery, but it does not necessitate following
the order of the original discoverers. It is more akin to
Dewey's experimental procedure. It is formulated thus :[1]
'Let him know nothing because you have told him, but
because he has learnt it for himself.' 'You have not got
to teach him truths so much as to show him how to set
about discovering them for himself.'

Geography[2] is to be learnt by observation of natural
phenomena. 'His geography will begin with the town he
lives in and his father's country house, then the places
between them, the rivers near them, and then the sun's
aspect and how to find one's way by its aid. Let him
make his own map, at first containing only two places;
others may be added from time to time, as he is able to
estimate their distance and position. You see at once
what a good start we have given him by making his eye
his compass.'

Like Locke, although for quite different reasons, Rousseau would prescribe a trade for his pupil. Locke[3] had
proposed gardening or husbandry in general, and working in wood as carpenter, joiner or turner, these being
fit and healthy recreations for a man of study or business.
Rousseau requires Émile to learn a trade that with any
change of fortune he might be independent economically,
for its social value in recognising the dignity of labour,
in helping him to overcome the prejudices which otherwise he would acquire, and to aid generally in training
the mind. 'In society', Rousseau maintains,[4] 'a man
either lives at the cost of others or he owes them in labour
the cost of his keep; there is no exception to this rule. . . .
Man in society is bound to work; rich or poor, weak or
strong, every idler is a thief.' 'Remember,' Rousseau
counsels,[5] 'I demand no talent, only a trade, a genuine

---

[1] *Émile*, pp. 131, 168.   [2] Ibid., pp. 131–4.   [3] *Thoughts*, § 204.
[4] *Émile*, p. 158.   [5] Ibid., p. 159.

trade, a mere mechanical art, in which the hands work harder than the head, a trade which does not lead to fortune but makes you independent of her.' The trade which most completely satisfies Rousseau's demands is that of the carpenter : 'It is clean and useful ; it may be carried on at home ; it gives enough exercise ; it calls for skill and industry, and while fashioning articles for everyday use, there is scope for elegance and taste.'[1] Not content with this, Rousseau contends that technical training has a transfer value :[2] 'If instead of making a child stick to his books I employ him in a workshop, his hands work for the development of his mind. While he fancies himself a workman, he is becoming a philosopher.' 'He must work like a peasant and think like a philosopher, if he is not to be as idle as a savage. The great secret of education is to use exercise of mind and body as relaxation one to another.'

The general principle governing Émile's education during these transition years is that of learning by doing. 'Teach by doing whenever you can, and only fall back upon words when doing is out of the question.' 'Let all the lessons of young people take the form of doing rather than talking ; let them learn nothing from books which they can learn from experience.'[3]

There is nevertheless a significant exception, the one book which to Rousseau's thinking 'supplies the best treatise on an education according to nature'. It is *Robinson Crusoe*. 'This is the first book Émile will read ; for a long time it will form his whole library and it will always retain an honoured place. It will be the text to which all talks about natural science are but the commentary.'[4]

Émile's knowledge is still restricted to nature and things : 'The very name of history is unknown to him, along with metaphysics and morals. He knows the

[1] P. 163.   [2] Pp. 140, 165.   [3] Pp. 144, 214.   [4] P. 147.

essential relations between men and things, but nothing of the moral relations between man and man.'[1] The résumé of his training up to fifteen runs thus : 'Having entered into possession of himself our child is now ready to cease to be a child. He is more than ever conscious of the necessity which makes him dependent on things. After exercising his body and his senses you have exercised his mind and his judgment. Finally we have joined together the use of his limbs and his faculties. We have made him a worker and a thinker ; we have now to make him loving and tender-hearted, to perfect reason through feeling.'

To adolescence, 'the crown and coping-stone of education', Rousseau was doubtless the first great educator to devote special attention ; he complains :[2] 'Works on education are crammed with wordy and unnecessary accounts of the imaginary duties of children ; but there is not a word about the most important and most difficult part of their education, the crisis which forms the bridge between the child and the man'. The period when education is usually finished is, he insists, just the time to begin ; it is our second birth, for 'we are born so to speak twice over ; born into existence, and born a man.'[3]

Adolescent education is designed to prepare Émile for the moral and social order in which he must play his part. Instead of studying himself in relation to things he must now study himself in relation to his fellow-men :[4] 'As there is a fitting age for the study of the sciences, so there is a fitting age for the study of the ways of the world.'[5] 'We have reached the moral order at last ; we have just taken the second step towards manhood.'[6] 'What then is required for the proper study of men? A great wish to know men, great impartiality of judgment, a heart sufficiently sensitive to understand every human passion,

[1] *Émile*, p. 170.   [2] Ibid., p. 278.   [3] P. 172.
[4] P. 175.   [5] P. 292.   [6] P. 196.

and calm enough to be free from passion. If there is any time in our life when this study is likely to be appreciated, it is this that I have chosen for Émile; before this time men would have been strangers to him; later on, he would have been like them.'[1]

Émile's earlier social contacts were restricted to casual encounters with village boys; there was occasionaly co-operation with other youths, but no opportunity for companionship with boys of his own social class. There were visits to hospitals which would create disgust in Émile at mankind. The early education was largely a preparation against the hazards of life. It demanded estrangement from society. Émile was in the social order, but not of it. Rousseau had condemned Plato's communistic scheme, contending that the home was the best training ground for governing the state; he should have recognised that companionship with other boys of his own age would have been Émile's best preparation for associating with them in later manhood. Any social training Émile received was like learning to swim without going into the water, with the same result, as Dewey tells, to the youth so taught.[2]

Even the social training to which Rousseau would introduce Émile at the adolescent stage is to be acquired second-hand, through the experiences of others, in contrast with the early education which was to be first-hand. The hazards involved in participation are too great; people cannot be left to learn the laws by breaking them. In the moral sphere there may be no second chance; one mistake may only lead to another, not to its elimination; social training must be given in advance of the situation, for example, in matters of sex. Instruction before experience is the order here. 'We must take the opposite way

[1] P. 206.
[2] Asked what he did when he got into the water he laconically replied: 'Sank'.

G 2

from that hitherto followed and instruct the youth rather through the experience of others than through our own.'[1] The attitude Rousseau would have Émile adopt, reads: 'I would have you so choose the company of a youth that he should think well of those among whom he lives, and I would have you so teach him to know the world that he should think ill of all that takes place in it. Let him know that man is by nature good, let him feel it, let him judge his neighbour by himself; but let him see how men are depraved and perverted by society; let him find the sources of all their vices in their preconceived opinions; let him be disposed to respect the individual, but to despise the multitude; let him see that all men wear almost the same mask, but let him also know that some faces are fairer than the mask that conceals them.'[2]

The moral training was not only to be at second-hand, but it was also to be indirect, through history, fables, etc. The studies which Rousseau had previously dismissed as premature and inappropriate are now reinstated; for the realistic subjects of the transition years the humanistic subjects are now substituted. There is, in fact, a complete inversion of the earlier education just as Plato's higher education necessitated the conversion of the soul from the sensible to the intelligible aspects of the world.

This is accordingly the time to introduce the pupil to history: 'With its help he will read the hearts of men without any lessons in philosophy; with its help he will view them as a mere spectator, dispassionate and without prejudice; he will view them as their judge, not as their accomplice or their accuser.'[3]

Of the difficulties in turning history to moral account Rousseau is fully conscious. The first is that history records the evil rather than the good: 'It is revolutions and catastrophes that make history interesting; so long as a nation grows and prospers quietly in the tranquillity

[1] *Émile*, p. 198.　　　　[2] Ibid., p. 193.　　　　[3] P. 199.

of a peaceful government, history says nothing. . . .
History only makes them famous when they are on the
downward path. . . . We only hear what is bad; the
good is scarcely mentioned. Only the wicked become
famous, the good are forgotten or laughed to scorn, and
thus history, like philosophy, is for ever slandering mankind.'[1] In 'Crabbed Age and Youth' R. L. Stevenson
echoes with a quite unfeigned satisfaction the same
complaint.

A further difficulty which Rousseau recognises is that
'history shows us actions rather than men, because she
only seizes men at certain chosen times in full dress; she
only portrays the statesman when he is prepared to be
seen; she does not follow him to his home, to his study,
among his family and his friends; she only shows him
in state; it is his clothes rather than himself that she
describes.'[2]

Against the use of the figures of history as moral
examples for the instruction of youth Morley has protested in the following terms: 'The subject of history is
not the heart of man but the movements of society.
Moreover the oracles of history are entirely dumb to one
who seeks from them maxims for the shaping of daily
conduct, or living instruction as to the motives, aims,
caprices, capacities of self-restraint, self-sacrifice of those
with whom the occasions of life bring us into contact.'
Even this objection was foreseen by Rousseau: 'History
in general is lacking because it only takes note of striking
and clearly marked facts which may be fixed by names,
places and dates; but the slow evolution of these facts,
which cannot be noted in this way, still remains unknown.
We often find in some battle, lost or won, the ostensible
cause of a revolution which was inevitable before this
battle took place. War only makes manifest events already

[1] Pp. 199–200.
[2] P. 202. Cf. Thackeray's introduction to *Esmond*.

determined by moral causes, which few historians can perceive.'[1]

The dilemma with which we are confronted in attempting to exploit history as a means of moral instruction is that the more scientifically history is treated the more is it regarded as a history of great movements and general tendencies, a matter of principles rather than of personalities, and consequently the less adapted does it become to provide moral examples; whereas, even assuming that the historical heroes are worthy moral examples, to secure biographical material for moral lessons we are compelled to distort the presentation of history. The choice is therefore between the incompatible alternatives, history or moral instruction.

These difficulties limit the field of choice, and Rousseau is reduced to commending the ancient writers of historical biographies, especially Plutarch, the modern biographies being too conventional.[2] The spectacles of history portrayed in such biographies are to serve the pupil sometimes as warnings, sometimes as forms of 'catharsis', as the vicarious expression of his own passions; thus 'the play of every human passion offers lessons to anyone who will study history to make himself wise and good at the expense of those who went before.'[3] The examples of history are thus not to be regarded as models for imitation, 'for he who begins to regard himself as a stranger will soon forget himself altogether'.[4]

In spite of all the care exercised on the training of the pupil it must needs be that offences come. Their correction, Rousseau suggests, should be secured indirectly. 'The time of faults is the time for fables';[5] for 'when we blame the guilty under the cover of a story we instruct without offending him'. The moral of the fable should accordingly not be formulated. 'Nothing is so foolish and unwise as the moral at the end of most fables; as if the moral was not, or ought not to be, so clear in the fable itself that the reader cannot fail to perceive it.'

Till now Émile has scarcely heard the name of God;[1] 'at fifteen he will not even know that he has a soul, at eighteen even he may not be ready to learn about it.'[2] Some instruction is now inevitable, Rousseau recognises, and this he formulates in the 'Creed of a Savoyard Priest'. Rousseau does not explain why a creed is advisable. It may be, as a modern writer puts it:[3] 'Definitions, formulae (some would add, creeds) have their use in any society, in that they restrain the ordinary intellectual man from making himself a public nuisance with his private opinions.'

The 'Creed of a Savoyard Priest' makes no pretext to be the theoretical formulation of the tenets of revealed religion, and the title is unfortunate. After relating the obstacles in the way of accepting any theological dogma Rousseau turns back to the book of nature. Rousseau's aim was to refute the materialistic philosophy of his age,[4] to re-establish the validity of the concepts, God, freedom and immortality, and to reaffirm the principles of right conduct. The materialists regarded matter as inert and lifeless; they postulated motion without accounting for its origin. Rousseau rejecting the idea of self-initiated or self-perpetuating motion contended that voluntary action was the only type of motion of which we had direct

---

[1] P. 216.   [2] P. 220.

[3] A. T. Quiller-Couch, *On the Art of Writing* (Cambridge University Press, 1916), p. 15

[4] Rousseau refers to the materialist as one 'who prefers to say that stones have feelings rather than that men have souls' (*Émile*, p. 242). He likewise rejects the naturalist's contention that there is no difference between intelligent behaviour on the perceptual level and the abstract reasoning of which only men are capable: 'It is not in my power to believe that passive and dead matter can have brought forth living and feeling beings, that blind chance has brought forth intelligent beings, that that which does not think has brought forth thinking beings' (ibid., p. 239). For relation of Rousseau's theology to Christianity see R. Grimsley, op. cit., pp. 324–30.

experience, hence the first article of his creed : 'There is a will which sets the universe in motion and gives life to nature.'[1]   As the universe is an orderly system, he is led to infer the second article of his creed — the proof of God's existence from the well-known argument from design : 'If matter in motion points me to a will, matter in motion according to fixed law points me to an intelligence.'[2]   And he adds :[3] 'This being who wills and can perform his will, this being active through his own powers, this being who moves the universe and orders all things, is what I call God.'

As man's will is determined by his judgment, and his judgment by his intelligence, the determining cause of action is in himself and he is accordingly free.   Freedom, for Rousseau, is thus self-determinism.   The third article of his creed is : Man is therefore free to act, and as such he is animated by an immaterial substance.[4]

Justice and goodness are inseparable, Rousseau claims,[5] for that love of order which creates order we call goodness, and that love of order which preserves order we call justice.   To redress the apparent disparity between justice and goodness in this life an infinite time is required ; such is Rousseau's argument for the immortality of the soul. 'Had I no other proof of the nature of the soul, the triumph of the wicked and the oppression of the righteous in this world would be enough to convince me.'[6]

In support of his objections to innate ideas Locke cites instances to illustrate the diversity of human behaviour ;

---

[1] *Émile*, p. 236.   [2] Ibid., p. 237.   [3] P. 239.

[4] P. 243.   Rousseau adds that it is not the word 'freedom' that is meaningless, but the word 'necessity'.   Kant assigned necessity to the phenomenal or scientific sphere and freedom to the moral order.   Hegel regards freedom as 'the truth of necessity'.

Kant's *Critique of Practical Reason* might be regarded as little more than a metaphysical formulation of Rousseau's 'Creed of a Savoyard Priest'.

[5] *Émile*, p. 245.   Rousseau does not derive these rules from the principles of the higher philosophy ; he finds them in the depth of his heart (p. 249).

[6] In the *Critique of Practical Reason* Kant employs the same argument to equate happiness with virtue.

Rousseau condemns this procedure, assailing those writers who venturing to reject the clear and universal agreement of all peoples, and, setting aside this striking unanimity in the judgment of mankind, seek out some obscure exception known to them alone.[1] He challenges Montaigne to tell him if there is any country upon earth where it is a crime to keep one's plighted word, to be merciful, helpful and generous, where the good man is scorned and the traitor held to honour. Contrariwise, Rousseau emphasises the universality of the principles of good conduct and assumes an innate principle of goodness: 'Do you think there is anyone upon earth so depraved that he has never yielded to the temptation of well-doing?'[2]

The ultimate sanction of the moral laws[3] is to be found in religion, but after eloquently recounting the obstacles in the way of accepting any definite religious belief Rousseau turns again to the book of nature:[4] 'In this good and great volume I learn to serve and adore its Author. There is no excuse for not reading this book, for it speaks to all in a language they can understand.' Such is the method to be adopted in reasoning with Émile on religion. 'So long as we yield nothing to human authority nor to the prejudices of our native land, the light of reason alone, in a state of nature, can lead us no further than to natural religion; and this is as far as I should go with Émile. If he must have any other religion, I have no right to be his guide; he must choose for himself.'[5]

The 'Creed of a Savoyard Priest' is frequently regarded as an unwarranted interpolation in the *Émile*, but a review of Rousseau's religious doctrines as expressed in this section of his work is necessary to make intelligible, or to justify, the postponement of religious instruction till the adolescent stage. If it is necessary for Émile to

---

[1] *Émile*, p. 252.   [2] Ibid., p. 254.   [3] P. 278, note.
[4] P. 270.   [5] P. 278.

have an intelligent appreciation of the proofs of God's existence, of freedom and of immortality, then it is not to be wondered at that at fifteen he need not have heard the name of God nor even known that he had a soul. Rousseau has evidently ignored the fact that he is legislating for the ordinary man who takes his creed on trust and does not usually trouble to justify it on rational grounds.

In addition to instruction in ethics and religion, Rousseau would prescribe for the adolescent the study of aesthetics, the philosophy of the principles of taste. Rousseau's account of these principles is somewhat vague ; but this is not surprising when we remember the state of the development of the science of the beautiful at the time he wrote. The simplicity of taste which goes straight to the heart is, in Rousseau's opinion, only to be found in the classics,[1] and these Rousseau would employ for purposes of instruction in aesthetics as he previously had recommended them for instruction in morals.

During the critical period of adolescence Émile's physical training is not neglected. He is required to engage in an occupation which keeps him busy, diligent and hard at work, an occupation which he may become passionately fond of, one to which he will devote himself entirely. For this purpose Rousseau recommends the chase,[2] although he does not even profess to justify the cruel passion of killing ; it is enough that it serves to delay a more dangerous passion.

Rousseau believes it necessary to prescribe for Émile direct moral exhortation on chastity, although he admits that he has had to abandon the task of giving examples of the form which the lessons should take. The general plan of sexual instruction he outlines in the following passage :[3] 'If instead of the empty precepts which are prematurely dinned into the ears of children, only to be

[1] *Émile*, p. 309.   [2] Ibid., p. 285.   [3] P. 289.

scoffed at when the time comes when they might prove useful, if instead of this we bide our time, if we prepare the way for a hearing, if we then show him the laws of nature in all their truth, if we show him the sanction of these laws in the physical and moral evils which overtake those who neglect them, if while we speak to him of this great mystery of generation, we join to the idea of the pleasure which the author of nature has given to this act the idea of the duties of faithfulness and modesty which surround it, and redouble its charm while fulfilling its purpose; if we paint to him marriage, not only as the sweetest form of society, but also as the most sacred and inviolable of contracts, if we tell him plainly all the reasons which lead men to respect this sacred bond, and to pour hatred and curses upon him who dares to dishonour it; if we give him a true and terrible picture of the horrors of debauch, of its stupid brutality, of the downward road by which a first act of misconduct leads from bad to worse, and at last drags the sinner to his ruin; if, I say, we give him proofs that on a desire for chastity depend health, strength, courage, virtue, love itself, and all that is truly good for man — I maintain that this chastity will be so dear and so desirable in his eyes, that his mind will be ready to receive our teaching as to the way to preserve it; for so long as we are chaste we respect chastity; it is only when we have lost this virtue that we scorn it.'

The sexual instinct must be sublimated by redirecting it to the affection for an ideal of true womanhood which Rousseau would picture for Émile with all the eloquence and emotion he could compass, and this ideal he would personify and assign to it a name, the name Sophy. Before, however, introducing Émile to Sophy, Rousseau considers it necessary to describe the education in accordance with which the wife of Émile should be trained.

Émile's education is not even yet complete. Between

his betrothal to Sophy and his marriage he is required to travel, the object being that he should get to know mankind in general.[1]

The education of woman had by most early educators been treated much after the manner of Locke who in his *Thoughts* wrote : ' I have said *he* here because the principal aim of my discourse is how a young gentleman should be brought up from his infancy which in all things will not so perfectly suit the education of daughters though where the difference of sex requires different treatment, 'twill be no hard matter to distinguish.' Rousseau, however, at least paid woman the compliment of realising that her education demands independent treatment, and for this alone must be forgiven much.

Rousseau was congenitally even more unfitted than most other men to understand woman, and his views are accordingly even more contradictory. In his earliest writings his belief was that the hand that rocks the cradle rules the world ; thus in the *Discourse on the Arts and Sciences* he maintains that men will always be what women choose to make them, and, in the *Discourse on the Origin of Inequality*, addressing 'the amiable and virtuous daughters of Geneva' he repeats : ' It will always be the lot of your sex to govern ours. . . . Continue, therefore, always to be what you are, the chaste guardians of our morals, and the sweet security for our peace.' Disillusioned, nevertheless, by his somewhat unfortunate experience of the sex, he came to modify his views and in the *Nouvelle Héloïse* and the *Émile* to emphasise the training of the heart rather than of the head ; the aim of woman's life as expressed in these works might be summed up in the popular precept, slightly modified : be good, sweet maid, and let who will, be clever. And for the place of woman in the scheme of things Rousseau might have quoted Milton to the effect that God made woman for marriage

---

[1] *Émile*, p. 415.

but marriage for man.[1] Thus in the *Nouvelle Héloïse*[2] Rousseau explains : 'I have still the same difficulty in supposing that there can be but one common model of perfection for two beings so essentially different. Attack and defence, the assurance of the men and modesty of the women, are by no means effects of the same cause, as the philosophers have imagined, but are natural institutions which may be easily accounted for and from which may be deduced every other moral distinction. Besides, the designs of nature being different in each, their inclinations, their perceptions ought necessarily to be directed according to their different views ; to till the ground and to nourish children require very opposite tastes and constitutions. A higher stature, stronger voice and features, seem indeed to be no indispensable marks of distinction ; but this external difference evidently indicates the intention of the Creator in the modification of the mind. The souls of a perfect woman and a perfect man ought to be no more alike than their faces.' And again : 'Husband and wife were designed to live together but not to live in the same manner. They ought to act in concert, but not to do the same things. The kind of life which would delight the one would be insupportable to the other ; the inclinations which nature has given them are as different as the occupations she has assigned them ; they differ in their amusements as much as in their duties. In a word, each contributes to the common good by different ways, and the proper distribution of their several cares and employment is the strongest tie that cements their union.' In the *Émile* he repeats :[3] 'The

---

[1] Rousseau adopts Aristotle's view of woman rather than Plato's. Cf. *Politics*, i. 13, § 9 : 'The courage of a man is shown in commanding, of a woman in obeying. And this holds of all other virtues.' Hegel, *Philosophy of Rights*, § 166, addition, repeats Rousseau's later views. M. Fénelon in his *Instructions for the Education of Daughters* (1687) advises : 'Begin early thus to harden her for disappointments, to moderate her desires and affections, and to render her easy to bear refusals.'

[2] Letters XLVI and CXXIX.   [3] P. 339.

man should be strong and active; the woman should be weak and passive.' 'A man seeks to serve, a woman seeks to please; the one needs knowledge, the other taste'; '"what will people think" is the grave of a man's virtue and the throne of a woman's', and even goes the length of affirming that woman is made for man's delight.[1] He wavers once, and admits the frailty of the male when he concedes: What is most wanted in a woman is gentleness; formed to obey a creature so imperfect as man, she should early learn to submit to injustice and to suffer the wrongs inflicted on her by her husband without complaint; she must be gentle for her own sake, not his.[2]

As men and women have different vocations, their education must be different: 'When once it is proved that men and women are and ought to be unlike in constitution and in temperament, it follows that their education must be different.'[3] Women's education is to be planned in relation to, and to be made subservient to, that of man. Its aim is: 'To be pleasing in his sight, to win his respect and love, to train him in childhood, to tend him in manhood, to counsel and console, to make his life pleasant and happy, these are the duties of women for all time, and that is what she should be taught while she is young.'[4] The woman's education is also conditioned by the fact that she never attains the age of reason; hers is a case of arrested development! 'If women could discover principles and if men had as good heads for detail, they would be mutually independent.'[5] 'The search for abstract and speculative truths, for principles and axioms in science, for all that tends to wide generalisation, is beyond a woman's grasp; their studies should be thoroughly practical. It is their business to apply the principles discovered by men, it is their place to make

[1] *Émile*, p. 332   [2] Ibid., p. 333.   [3] P. 326.
[4] P. 328.   [5] P. 340.

the observations which lead men to discover those principles.'[1] 'Speaking generally if it is desirable to restrict a man's studies to what is useful, this is even more necessary for women, whose life, though less laborious, should be even more industrious and more uniformly employed in a variety of duties, so that one talent should not be encouraged at the expense of others.'

That Sophy's physical training should be different from that of Émile is understandable, the one aiming at grace, the other at strength,[2] but it is inexcusable to infer that since little boys should not learn to read, still less should little girls, and most ungallant to add the reason — most of them make a bad use of the fateful knowledge. As there is nothing so obviously useful, nothing which needs so much practice or gives so much opportunity for error as cyphering, it should precede reading.[3] The general principle to be followed in the education of girls is : 'Show the sense of the tasks you set your little girls, but keep them busy.'

The antithesis between the training of *Émile* and that of Sophy is strikingly illustrated in regard to religion. As Émile was considered incapable of forming any true idea of religion till adolescence, that was regarded as sufficient justification for the postponement of his religious teaching till this late stage; from the same premise Rousseau infers that we cannot speak of religion too soon to little girls, 'for if we wait till they are ready for a serious discussion of these deep subjects, we should be in danger of never speaking of religion at all'.[4] And he adds :[5] 'When you teach religion to little girls never make it gloomy or tiresome, never make it a task or a duty, and therefore never give them anything to learn by heart, not even their prayers. . . . It does not matter that a girl should learn her religion young, but it does matter that

[1] P. 349.   [2] P. 329.   [3] P. 332.
          [4] P. 340.   [5] P. 341.

she should learn it thoroughly, and still more that she should learn to love it.'

Sophy's religion is to be reasonable and simple, with few doctrines and fewer observances,[1] and the confession of faith which Rousseau formulates for her is simpler and more appropriate than that of the Savoyard Priest prescribed for Émile : 'There is a judge of human fate, that we are all His children, that He bids us all be just, He bids us love one another, He bids us be kindly and merciful, He bids us keep our word with all men, even with our enemies and His ; we must know that the apparent happiness of this world is naught; that there is another life to come in which this Supreme Being will be the rewarder of the just and judge of the unjust.'

Two contrasted and almost contradictory schemes of education have been presented by Rousseau for Émile and for Sophy, but for individuals with similar natural endowment who, although their functions in society may be different, must nevertheless abide each other, some compromise would be necessary ; the rational system of training Émile would have to be tempered by the somewhat conventional training of Sophy, if they were ever to live happily together.

Rousseau's influence on his contemporaries may be assessed by Kant's confession.[2] 'I am by disposition an inquirer. I feel the consuming thirst for knowledge, the eager unrest to advance ever further, and the delights of discovery. There was a time when I believed that this is what confers real dignity upon human life, and I despised the common people who knew nothing. Rousseau has set me right. This imagined advantage vanishes. I learn to honour men, and should regard myself as of much less use than the common labourer, if I did not

---

[1] *Émile*, p. 359.

[2] *Fragmente aus dem Nachlasse*, quoted by N. Kemp Smith. *A Commentary to Kant's Critique of Pure Reason* (London: Macmillan & Co., 1918), p. lvii.

believe that my philosophy will restore to all men the common rights of humanity.' And the arresting impression made on the intelligentsia of Rousseau's own day by the publication of the *Émile* may be inferred from the incident that only once did Kant miss his daily constitutional, namely, on the day when the *Émile* arrived; the work so engrossed him that he read it to the end without a break.[1] The popular reception accorded it was just the reverse — it was condemned by the Archbishop of Paris immediately after publication as an irreligious work and ordered to be torn and burnt in Paris by the Public Executioner. Such a contradiction is only paralleled by Rousseau's own writings and in his life. Rousseau nevertheless stands to modern education as Plato to ancient education; the heading of almost every chapter in *The Schools of To-morrow*[2] is a quotation from Rousseau.

[1] E. Cassirer, *Rousseau, Kant, Goethe* (Princeton University Press, 1945). H. Heine, *Religion and Philosophy in Germany*, English translation, p. 108, gives the following account of Kant's routine: The history of Immanuel Kant's life is difficult to portray, for he had neither life nor history. He led a mechanical, regular, almost abstract bachelor existence in a little retired street of Königsberg. I do not believe that the great clock of the cathedral performed in a more passionless and methodical manner its daily routine than did its townsman, Immanuel Kant. Rising in the morning, coffee-drinking, writing, reading lectures, dining, walking, everything had its appointed time, and the neighbours knew that it was exactly half-past three o'clock when Immanuel Kant stepped forth from his house in his grey tight-fitting coat, with his Spanish cane in his hand, and betook himself to the little linden avenue called after him to this day, the Philosopher's Walk.

[2] By John Dewey and Evelyn Dewey (London: J. M. Dent, 1915).

CHAPTER IX

PESTALOZZI[1]

AMONG the great educators Pestalozzi cuts a sorry figure; he appears a man afflicted with new ideas which he found himself unable to formulate or to put effectively into practice. This he was himself the first to confess. In his *Swansong* (1826) he admits:[2] 'My lofty ideals were pre-eminently the product of a kind, well-meaning soul, inadequately endowed with the intellectual and practical capacity which might have helped considerably to further my heartfelt desire. It was the product of an extremely vivid imagination which in the stress of my daily life proved unable to produce any important results.' Pestalozzi was a simple and sensitive soul who arrived at his principles mostly by intuition; a worse expounder of his own doctrines could hardly be imagined. In one work he describes his educational ideal in the form of a romance; in another, he is, as Herbart says,[3] meta-morphosed into a pedantic drillmaster in arithmetic pleased with himself for having filled a thick book with the multiplication table. It was nevertheless fortunate that his reputation attracted philosophers like Fichte and Herbart, who not only critically examined his system but also published their versions of it. In fact, no great

[1] J. H. Pestalozzi, 1746–1827. For life, see Kate Silber, *Pestalozzi: The Man and his Work* (London: Routledge & Kegan Paul, 1960). This supersedes all previous works in English on Pestalozzi.

[2] *Pestalozzi's Educational Writings*, edited by J. A. Green (London: Edward Arnold, 1912), p. 228.

[3] Herbart, *ABC of Sense Perception and Minor Pedagogical Works*. Translated by W. J. Eckoff (New York: D. Appleton & Co., 1903, p. 52.) Hereafter referred to as Herbart's *Minor Pedagogical Works*.

European educator has ever had such a succession of distinguished visitors to his schools, and from their reports we can reconstruct a picture of the man and his work.[1]

Pestalozzi's aim in life was to ameliorate the lot of the poor. As Herbart commented :[2] 'The welfare of the people is Pestalozzi's aim. . . . He did not seek the wreath of merit in your mansions but in their hovels.' His humanitarianism was reinforced in early youth by his reading of Rousseau's works. While this aim restricted his outlook, it compelled him to concentrate on the fundamentals of education, for, as Herbart remarks, 'the most pressing needs are the more universal'.[3] Pestalozzi was thus forced to formulate a practical scheme of education suitable for all, and, in spite of himself, to lay the foundation of our elementary school system. Of this he became dimly conscious towards the end of his days, for in the *Letters to Greaves* he states :[4] 'It [the end held out as the highest object of all man's efforts] must embrace all mankind, it must be applicable to all, without distinction of zones, or nations in which they may be born. It must acknowledge the rights of man in the fullest sense of the word. . . . They embrace the rightful claims of all classes to a general diffusion of useful knowledge, a careful development of the intellect, and judicious attention

---

[1] Visited at Richterswil on Lake Zürich by Fichte (1793).
Visited at Burgdorf by Herbart twice (1797–9).
Visited at Yverdon by Froebel (1805, 1808).
Visitors from Britain and Ireland included Dr. Mayo, Greaves — to whom *Hints to Mothers on Early Infant Education* was addressed, Mrs. Hamilton, Miss Edgeworth, Synge, Pullen, Owen, Dr. Andrew Bell, Lord Brougham. See also K. Silber, *Pestalozzi: The Man and his Work*, Appendix I, pp. 278–315, 'Pestalozzianism in Britain and the United States'.

[2] Herbart, *Minor Pedagogical Works*, pp. 36–37.

[3] P. 36.

[4] *Letters on Early Education*. Addressed to J. P. Greaves, Esq., by Pestalozzi. Translated from the German manuscript (London : Sherwood, Gilbert & Piper, 1827), p. 88. Cf. *Evening Hours of a Hermit* : 'All mankind are fundamentally alike, and for the satisfaction of their needs there is one and the same way.'

to all the faculties of man — physical, intellectual and moral.'

Echoing Rousseau's dictum 'Life is the trade I would teach him',[1] Pestalozzi maintains[2] that the ultimate end of education is not a perfection in the accomplishments of the school but fitness for life, and in *How Gertrude Teaches Her Children*[3] he elaborates: 'We have spelling schools, writing schools, catechism schools, and we want — men's schools'.

Pestalozzi's efforts to realise his aim were a succession of failures. He had been intended for the ministry, then for the law, but his advanced social views precluded the possibility of a public career, and he decided to become a farmer. He settled at Neuhof in 1774 and introduced a number of beggar children and waifs into his house to rescue them from their degraded condition, hoping to restore their self-respect and manhood — to educate the poor for poverty — but the scheme failed and the institution was closed in 1779. In his *Ansichten und Erfahrungen*[4] he explains that he not only tried to find work for the poor children, but also wished to warm their hearts and to develop their minds, and through self-instruction to elevate them to a sense of the inner dignity and worth of their nature; he also acknowledges his failure, admitting that he took upon his own shoulders a burden which he could not bear and which he should have left to others, and thereby exhausted himself, plunged himself into domestic confusion and brought indescribable suffering on himself.

After the failure at Neuhof a literary interlude ensued,

---

[1] *Émile*, p. 9.   [2] *Letters to Greaves*, p. 85.

[3] *How Gertrude Teaches Her Children*, by J. H. Pestalozzi. Translated by Lucy E. Holland and Francis C. Turner (London: Swan Sonnenschein & Co., 1907), p. 178. Also J. A. Green, *Pestalozzi's Educational Writings* (London: Edward Arnold, 1912), pp. 85–153.

[4] *Ansichten und Erfahrungen* (Views and Experiences concerning the idea of Elementary Training), published in 1807.

the most important productions of this period being *The Evening Hours of a Hermit* and *Leonard and Gertrude: A Book for the People*, both appearing in 1780. The former, according to Pestalozzi himself, was to serve as a preface to all that he should write in the future. In it he warns parents not to hurry their children into working at things remote from their immediate interests, and after the manner of Rousseau, not to anticipate the regular course of their development. The danger lies in children's lessons dealing with words before they have encountered the actual things. Here Pestalozzi gives expression to a suspicion of verbolatry as pronounced as that of Rousseau, also to his doctrine of *Anschauung*, the equivalent of Rousseau's dependence on things. Hermann Krüsi, one of Pestalozzi's coadjutors, in *My Educational Recollections*,[1] writes how before his meeting with Pestalozzi at Burgdorf he held the system in high estimation which by dexterous questions could elicit answers from the children. He continues: 'Having read in educational writings that Socrates had possessed this faculty in a high degree, the term "to Socratize" presented to me an almost magic charm. When I communicated my views on this subject to Pestalozzi he could not refrain from a knowing smile. "This art," he then said quite earnestly, "when applied at the proper time and place, has its own value, but it is utterly worthless for teachers and children in the public schools. Socrates was surrounded by young men who had a background in the knowledge of words and things. If you take pains to give your children first this background, then the necessary questions about things within their own observation will be naturally suggested. Without this background every attempt to elicit proper

---

[1] Translated by his son Hermann Krüsi in *Studies in Education*, edited by Earl Barnes (Philadelphia, 1903), vol. i, second edition, p. 273. Cf. *How Gertrude Teaches Her Children*, Second Letter. J. A. Green, *Pestalozzi's Educational Writings*, p. 94.

answers from the children by artfully put questions is merely thrashing of straw, and leads to sore deception or discouragement which may even deprive you of faith in yourself." [1]

Leonard and Gertrude describes how, mainly by means of education, the regeneration of a small community was effected by the noble efforts of a pious woman, the wife of a village mason in humble circumstances. In the village of Bonnal, the home of Leonard becomes the model educational institution, and Gertrude, the mother of the children, the ideal educator. This home-education represents Pestalozzi's ideal,[2] and it was only the circumstances in which he laboured that compelled him in practice to adopt class-teaching methods. These he regarded as a necessary but temporary expedient till mothers in sufficient numbers should be adequately educated to superintend the instruction of their own children.

As yet there was no formal analysis of *Anschauung*, but the 'contact with realities' for which Pestalozzi pleaded in his *Evening Hours of a Hermit* is exemplified in the procedure of Gertrude. 'Yet she never adopted the tone of instructor toward her children; she did not say to them: "Child, this is your head, your nose, your hand, your finger"; or "Where is your eye, your ear?" but instead she would say: "Come here, child, I will wash your little hands", "I will comb your hair", or "I will cut your finger nails". Her verbal instruction seemed to vanish in the spirit of her real activity, in which it always

---

[1] Cf. *Kant on Education*, English translation, p. 81 : 'In the culture of *reason* we must proceed according to the Socratic method. . . . The Socratic method should form, then, the rule for the catechetical method. True, it is somewhat slow, and it is difficult to manage so that in drawing ideas out of the child, the others shall also learn something.'

[2] Cf. *Leonard and Gertrude*: 'The school ought really to stand in closest connection with the life of the home.' *Evening Hours of a Hermit*: 'The home should be the foundation of any natural scheme of education. Home is the great school of character and of citizenship.'

had its source. The result of her system was that each child was skilful, intelligent, and active to the full extent that his age and development allowed.

'The instruction she gave them in the rudiments of arithmetic was intimately connected with the realities of life. She taught them to count the number of steps from one end of the room to the other, and two of the rows of five panes each, in one of the windows, gave her an opportunity to unfold the decimal relations of numbers. She also made them count their threads while spinning, and the number of turns on the reel, when they wound the yard into skeins. Above all, in every occupation of life she taught them an accurate and intelligent observation of common objects and the forces of nature.'

Between December 1798 and June 1799 another opportunity, likewise foredoomed to failure, presented itself to Pestalozzi to put his ideas into practice, this time at Stanz. About eighty children, left destitute after the village had been reduced to ashes by the French troops, were put in Pestalozzi's charge, but the population being Catholic were naturally more hostile to a protestant representative of a government which had brought ruin upon them. The retreating French forces commandeered the convent where Pestalozzi was established, and ended the experiment. Nevertheless some measure of success attended his efforts, and illustrated the truth of his view that education should be based on love. 'Even before the spring sun had melted the snows from our mountains, my children were no longer recognisable.' The great human sympathy for children with which Pestalozzi was endowed in a singular degree had prevailed. But affection, even when it is reciprocal, is not enough ; the pupil must be trained to independence. As Herbart insists :[1] something more than a love for a subject is required of the youth ; a well balanced, many-sided interest is demanded.

[1] *Minor Pedagogical Works*, pp. 74–76.

Pestalozzi's next venture was at Burgdorf (1799–1804) and it was here that he developed and formulated his teaching technique.[1] The Burgdorf period produced *How Gertrude Teaches Her Children* or *Letters to Gessner* (1801) — Pestalozzi's most important treatise on educational method. Reviewing this work, Herbart states :[2] 'It is his intention to place in the hands of wholly ignorant teachers and parents such writings as they need only to cause the children to read off and learn by heart, without adding anything of their own. What he believed could be carried into effect most immediately he preferred ; he must have his levers sturdy enough not to break even in clumsy hands. The book in which, under the form of letters to a friend, he describes the outlines of such a plan, belongs really in the hands of such men as have influence on the organisation of the lowest schools and upon parents of the lowest social ranks. Such men would be able to spread his actual school books, which are to be published in the future. What is faulty in the whole publication therefore is, perhaps, its title, which brings it immediately into the hands of women, of mothers.'

Pestalozzi's intention, as he himself conceived it,[3] was to discover the nature of teaching itself, to found popular instruction on psychological principles, to produce a general methodology of instruction based on a psychologically ordered sequence.

Although the title and the form of Pestalozzi's chief

[1] A personal impression of Pestalozzi at this stage by one of his collaborators, Hermann Krüsi, is given in *My Educational Recollections* (see above).

[2] *Minor Pedagogical Works*, pp. 37–38. Cf. p. 183. Also *How Gertrude Teaches Her Children*, p. 41 : 'I believe it is not possible for common popular instruction to advance a step, so long as formulas of instruction are not found which make the teacher, at least in the elementary stages of knowledge, merely the mechanical tool of a method, the result of which springs from the nature of the formulas and not from the skill of the man who uses it.'   [3] Ibid., pp. 139, 19, 25.

work are unfortunate, it is nevertheless the main source of his contributions to the psychology, sociology and philosophy of education. Of the Pestalozzian method Herbart says :[1] 'Its peculiar merit consists in having laid hold more boldly and more zealously than any former method of the duty of building up the child's mind, of constructing in it a definite experience in the light of clear sense-perception, not acting as if the child had already an experience but taking care that he gets one. . . . The Pestalozzian method, therefore, is by no means qualified to crowd out any other method but to prepare the way for it. It takes care of the earliest age that is capable of receiving instruction.' Herbart here refers to Pestalozzi's conception of *Anschauung*, a term for which there is no precise English equivalent, and the early translations of which seriously prejudiced the acceptance of Pestalozzi's doctrines in this country.[2] By *Anschauung* is to be understood the immediate experience of objects or situations. Terms used by English and American writers to convey the same idea include : mere awareness, immediate apprehension, direct acquaintance, spontaneous appreciation, concrete experience, personal contact, first-hand impressions, face-to-face encounter, the direct impact of things and persons.

Anschauung is the basis of all knowledge and experience. Kant remarks : 'All thought . . . must directly or indirectly go back to *Anschauungen*,' and 'Whatever the process and the means may be by which knowledge refers to its objects, there is one that refers to them directly and forms the ultimate material of all thought, namely, *die Anschauungen*'.[3] *Anschauung* is not, however, restricted to mere awareness of objects ; it comprises also

---

[1] *Minor Pedagogical Works*, p. 61.
[2] Cf. title of pamphlet published in Dublin in 1815, 'A Sketch of Pestalozzi's Intuitive System'.
[3] *Critique of Pure Reason* — The Elements of Transcendentalism.

spontaneous appreciation of moral actions and direct realisation of situations. It emphasises the immediacy of the experience, but does not imply simplicity in the process; negatively it excludes the intervention of any object or process between the subject and his experience. Its primary purpose, for Pestalozzi, was to further the converse of man with his world.[1]

For Kant the forms of *Anschauung* were space and time. In his *Letters to Greaves*[2] Pestalozzi accepts Kant's classification. 'The relations and proportions of number and form constitute the natural measure of all those impressions which the mind receives from without. They are the measures, and comprehend the qualities of the material world; form being the measure of space and number the measure of time.' Earlier, and generally, he distinguished three aspects of *Anschauung*, namely, form, number and name. How he arrived at this division he records as follows:[3] 'Living, but vague, ideas of the elements of instruction whirled about in my mind for a long time. . . . At last, like a *Deus ex machina*, came the thought — the means of making clear all knowledge gained by sense-impression comes from number, form and language. It suddenly seemed to throw a new light on what I was trying to do.

'Now, after my long struggle, or rather my wandering reverie, I aimed wholly and simply at finding out how a cultivated man behaves, and must behave, when he wishes to distinguish any object which appears misty and confused to his eyes, and gradually to make it clear to himself.

'In this case he will observe three things :

(*i*) How many, and what kinds of objects are before him.

(*ii*) Their appearance, form or outline.

---

[1] Herbart, *Minor Pedagogical Works*, p. 46. [2] P. 134.
[3] *How Gertrude Teaches Her Children*, pp. 86–88. Cf. pp. 33, 51–52.

(*iii*) Their names ; how he may represent each of them by a sound or word.

'The result of this action in such a man manifestly presupposes the following ready-formed powers :

(*i*) The power of recognising unlike objects, according to the outline, and of representing to oneself what is contained within it.

(*ii*) That of stating the number of these objects, and representing them to himself as one or many.

(*iii*) That of representing objects, their number and form by speech, and making them unforgettable.

'I also thought number, form and language are, together, the elementary means of instruction, because the whole sum of the external properties of any object is comprised in its outline and its number, and is brought home to my consciousness through language. It must then be an immutable law of the technique of instruction to start from and work within this threefold principle :

(*i*) To teach children to look upon every object that is brought before them as a unit, that is, as separated from those with which it is connected.

(ii) To teach them the form of every object, that is, its size and proportions.

(*iii*) As soon as possible to make them acquainted with all the words and names descriptive of objects known to them.

'And as the instruction of children should proceed from these three elementary points, it is evident that the first efforts of the technique of instruction should be directed to the primary faculties of counting, measuring, and speaking, which lie at the basis of all accurate knowledge of objects of sense. We should cultivate them with strictest psychological technique of instruction, endeavour to strengthen and make them strong and to bring them,

H

as a means of development and culture, to the highest
pitch of simplicity, consistency and harmony.'

On Pestalozzi's analysis of *Anschauung* much criticism
has been expended.[1]   One of Herbart's earliest essays on
education was devoted to a consideration of it — *Pestalozzi's
Idee eines ABC der Anschauung* (1802),[2] and Fichte dealt at
some length with it in the ninth of his *Addresses to the
German Nation* on 'The Starting Point that Actually
Exists for the New National Education' (1807–8),[3]
Herbart objecting mainly to Pestalozzi's treatment of
form, preferring the triangle to the quadrilateral as the
basic geometrical figure, Fichte to the treatment of
language, and both to some of the applications of the
Pestalozzian method.   To the objection that colour is a
primary datum of *Anschauung* and should have equal recognition with form, Herbart replies[4] that the cardinal
fault of uneducated sight consists in adherence to colour.
'More exactly speaking, it consists in being immersed in
the pre-eminent colour, in losing weaker colours at the
instance of the stronger.   Correctness of sense-perception
which is opposed to this fault, consists in synthetically
connecting everything that pertains to the form of the
thing.   It is attention to form to which our vision requires
to be especially educated.'

Apprehension of form was developed by Pestalozzi
mainly through drawing, on the ground that children are
ready at an earlier age for knowledge of proportion and

[1] Dealing with Locke's conception of 'substance', D. J. O'Connor (*John
Locke*, Penguin Books, 1952, pp. 84–85) enumerates as follows the conditions
which determine the application of the term : 'Qualities should be (*i*)
manifested in the same spatio-temporal neighbourhood, (*ii*) associated in
this way during a certain minimum of time, (*iii*) should change when they
do so, jointly and in coordination, (*iv*) physical objects must be public and
neutral, (*v*) should contain both visual and tactual components.'

[2] See Herbart, *Minor Pedagogical Works*, pp. 28–49, 57–61.

[3] J. G. Fichte, *Reden an die deutsche Nation*.   A translation by R. F. Jones
and G. H. Turnbull was published by The Open Court Publishing Company, Chicago and London, 1922.

[4] *Minor Pedagogical Works*, p. 135.

for the guidance of the slate-pencil than for guiding the pen and making tiny letters.[1]

Pestalozzi, in fact, built all power of doing, even the power of clear representation of all real objects, upon the early development of the ability to draw lines, angles, rectangles and curves.[2] Thus he states[3] that 'by exercises in lines, angles and curves, a readiness in gaining sense-impressions of all kinds is produced in the children, as well as skill of hand, of which the effect will be to make everything that comes within the sphere of their observation gradually clear and plain.' Against the tendency for the means to obscure the aim, and for drawing to become an end in itself, Pestalozzi protested,[4] saying 'Nature gives the child no lines, she only gives him things, and lines must be given him only in order that he may perceive things rightly. The things must not be taken from him in order that he may see only lines.' And concerning the danger of rejecting Nature for the sake of lines, on another occasion he angrily exclaimed:[5] 'God forbid that I should overwhelm the human mind and harden it against natural sense-impressions, for the sake of these lines and of the technique of instruction, as idolatrous priests have overwhelmed it with superstitious teaching, and hardened it against natural sense-impressions.'

By basing writing on drawing, separating the acquisition of the forms from the command of the writing instrument, and using the skill acquired in writing for the expression of significant ideas[6] Pestalozzi anticipated in many points the Montessori method of teaching writing.

[1] *How Gertrude Teaches Her Children*, p. 35. Cf. p. 84: 'I found in the effort to teach writing, the need of subordinating this art to that of drawing, and in the efforts to teach drawing the combination with, and subordination of this art to, that of measurement.'

[2] P. 60. [3] P. 51.

[4] P. 69. [5] P. 69.

[6] Cf. p. 129: 'As writing, considered as form, appears in connection with measuring and drawing, so it appears again as a special kind of learning to talk.'

The defect of his method, as in language teaching, is that he carried his analysis to its ultimate limits, whereas what is psychologically simple to the child is not necessarily what remains when analysis cannot be carried further; in writing, the unit is the word or the letter, not the so-called element of the letter.

Scope for the application of Pestalozzi's principle of concreteness was readily found in arithmetic. Reviewing Krüsi's development as a teacher, Pestalozzi writes: 'For instance, when he asked in arithmetic, How many times is seven contained in sixty-three? the child had no real background for his answer, and must with great trouble dig it out of his memory. Now, by the plan of putting nine times seven objects before his eyes, and letting him count them as nine sevens standing together, he has not to think any more about this question; he knows from what he has already learnt, although he is asked for the first time, that seven is contained nine times in sixty-three. So it is in other departments of the method.'[1] The general principle of *Anschauung* as applied to arithmetic Pestalozzi formulated in these terms:[2] 'That by exercising children beginning to count with real objects, or at least with dots representing them, we lay the foundation of the whole of the science of arithmetic, and secure their future progress from error and confusion.'

Whereas experiment has demonstrated that the apprehension of number-forms can be facilitated by modifications of the arrangement of the units proposed by Pestalozzi, and objection has been taken to the various devices based on the Pestalozzian number pattern on the ground that they involve counting,[3] experience has but confirmed the general principle that the concrete repre-

[1] *How Gertrude Teaches Her Children*, p. 54.

[2] P. 51. Vertical strokes were usually adopted by Pestalozzi to represent the units.

[3] Catherine Stern, *Children Discover Arithmetic* (New York: Harper & Brothers, 1949), p. 19.

sentation of number is indispensable to the beginnings of the teaching of arithmetic.

With the language aspect of *Anschauung* Pestalozzi concerned himself more particularly, although he did not quite regard the name as co-ordinate in rank with form and number.[1] Fichte complains[2] that acquaintance with the word-sign adds nothing to the knowledge of an object but simply brings it within the sphere of what can be communicated to others. Herbart nevertheless comes again to the defence of Pestalozzi contending[3] that to young children a word, a name, is not as to us merely the sign of a thing. The word itself is the thing. They linger upon the sound. Not until the latter has become commonplace to them do they learn to forget it in attention to the thing itself. Pestalozzi reasoned that the child must learn to talk before he can be taught to read,[4] and recognised the child's need for a full and facile vocabulary. Thus he affirms :[5] 'The advantage of a fluent and early nomenclature is invaluable to children. The firm impression of names makes the things unforgettable, as soon as they are brought to their knowledge ; and the stringing together of names in an order based upon reality and truth develops and maintains in them a consciousness of the real relation of things to each other. Certain it is that when a child has made the greater part of a scientific nomenclature his own, he enjoys through it at least the advantage that a child enjoys who in his own, a great house of business, daily becomes acquainted from his

[1] Cf. *How Gertrude Teaches Her Children*, p. 150.

[2] *Addresses to the German Nation*, English translation, p. 166.

[3] *Minor Pedagogical Writings*, p. 38. Froebel in *The Education of Man* repeats that the word and the thing are to the child one and the same.

[4] *How Gertrude Teaches Her Children*, p. 36 : 'The child must learn to talk before he can be reasonably taught to read'; p. 84: 'Thus I found, in teaching to read, the necessity of its subordination to the power of talking.'

[5] P. 33. Cf. p. 51 : 'Through a well-arranged nomenclature, indelibly impressed, a general foundation for all kinds of knowledge can be laid, by which children and teacher, together, as well as separately, may rise gradually, but with safe steps, to clear ideas in all branches of knowledge.'

cradle upwards with the names of countless objects.'
Pestalozzi does not propose that the child should acquire
a stock of names merely for their own sake but as a means
to the mastery of things, a function which the name has
had from the earliest times. He complained[1] that in the
lower schools for more than a century there had been
given to empty words a weight in the human mind that
not only hindered attention to the impressions of nature,
but even destroyed man's inner susceptibility to these
impressions. His own method, he explains,[2] was 'like
Nature with the savage, I always put the picture before
the eye, and then sought for a word for the picture'.

Pestalozzi's insistence upon the need of a training in
language as an indispensable preliminary to an adequate
education moved Herbart to ask :[3] 'What stands so long
and universally in the way of human education as lack
of language? Who is more surely excluded from the
benefits of instruction conferred in human conversation
than he who neither knows how to choose the appropriate
expression nor how to appreciate the force of an expression well invented? Does even the educated man
ever come to the end of the study of language, the
creatress of all conversation, all society?'

Pestalozzi reduced language to words or names, and
the latter he resolved into sounds. For each stage he
constructed formal exercises, beginning with syllables
which he regarded as the irreducible elements. The first
exercises took the form, for example, a — ab — bab, etc.,
much after the manner of the present-day phonic methods
of teaching to read. Lists of names of the most important
objects in all divisions of the kingdom of nature, history,
geography, human callings and relations he required to
be memorised, and lastly sentences had to be formed in
various ways. Pestalozzi's analysis was carried to extremes

---

[1] *How Gertrude Teaches Her Children,* p. 113.   [2] Ibid., p. 55.
[3] *Minor Pedagogical Works,* pp. 43–44.

and evoked censure; the redeeming feature of his method
was nevertheless that it based reading on sounds and not
on spelling, and thereby prepared the way for modern
methods. On the ground of content, too, it was condemned both by Fichte[1] and by Herbart[2] for, in *The
Mother's Book*,[3] Pestalozzi was misled into beginning with
the child's body, arguing that the first object of the
child's knowledge must be the child himself.

Notwithstanding such objections the value of *Anschauung* as the basis of instruction remains unimpaired.
Anschauungsunterricht became an established element in the
German school curriculum; in an emasculated form it
functioned in nineteenth-century English education as the
object lesson.

Immediate experience is generally confused and must
be made definite; it must likewise be generalised. This
requirement was expressed by Kant in the oft-quoted
statement: 'Gedanken ohne Inhalt sind leer, Anschauungen ohne Begriffe sind blind' — 'Thoughts without content are empty, *Anschauungen* without concepts are
blind.'[4] And Kant adds: 'Therefore it is equally necessary to make our concepts sensuous [that is, to add to
them the object of immediate experience] as to make
our immediate experiences intelligible [*sich verständlich*],
that is, to bring them under concepts.' In his *Letters to
Greaves*[5] Pestalozzi explains: 'But if a mother is to teach
by things, she must recollect also that to the formation
of an idea more is requisite than bringing the object
before the senses. Its qualities must be explained; its
origin must be accounted for; its parts must be described,
and their relation to the whole ascertained; its use, its
effects or consequences must be stated. All this must be

[1] *Addresses to the German Nation*, English translation, p. 164.
[2] *Minor Pedagogical Works*, pp. 54, 60.
[3] See *How Gertrude Teaches Her Children*, pp. 231–3.
[4] *Critique of Pure Reason*. The Transcendental Logic. Introduction.
[5] P. 123.

done, at least, in a manner sufficiently clear and comprehensible to enable the child to distinguish the object from other objects, and to account for the distinction which is made.' More technically expressed : *Anschauungen* must be made distinct by analysis according to form, number and name ; they must then be made clear, and, for Pestalozzi, they are clear when they can be described. The final stage is to make them definite, that is, able to be defined, for, as Pestalozzi explains, the power of describing usually precedes that of defining which formally implies referring an object to its genus or species.

In this progressive development no step must be missed. There must be no gaps in instruction. This is Pestalozzi's principle of the sequential organisation of knowledge, second in significance only to his doctrine of *Anschauung*. It was this feature of his teaching that appealed to and was championed by Herbart :[1] 'I had long held this feeling of a clear apprehension to be the sole and genuine spice of instruction, and a regularity of sequence perfect and adequate in all respects was to me the grand ideal in which I saw the thorough-going means for securing to all instruction its rightful effect. The main endeavour of Pestalozzi, as I was given to understand, was exactly the same ; namely, to find this sequence, this arrangement and combination of all things which must be taught either simultaneously or successively. On the supposition that he had found it, or at least that he was on the right way thither, every unessential addition, every adventitious aid would be an injury. It would be reprehensible, because it would distract attention from the main point. If he has not found that sequence, it still remains to be found, or at least to be amended and continued. But even in that case his method is correct ; at least to the extent of throwing out the injurious additions. Its laconic brevity

[1] *Minor Pedagogical Works*, pp. 34–35. Programmed learning is based on this principle.

is its essential merit. Not a useless word is heard in his school; the train of apperception is never interrupted. The teacher pronounces for the children constantly. Every faulty letter is expunged from the slate immediately. The child never dwells on its mistakes. The right track is never departed from; hence every moment marks progress.'

Although *How Gertrude Teaches Her Children* is mainly concerned with the nature and development of knowledge, Pestalozzi would not have it thought that this is the aim of education, for he says: 'To have knowledge without practical power, to have insight, and yet to be incapable of applying it in everyday life, what more dreadful fate could an unfriendly spirit devise for us.'[1] And Fichte adds:[2] 'All this part of education is but a means and a preliminary exercise for the second essential part, the civic and religious education.' Reviewing *How Gertrude Teaches Her Children*, Herbart observes:[3] 'Without doubt the most necessary instruction must be that which teaches man what he most needs to know. Now what is needful to us is needful either to our physical or our moral nature. We need it either as sensuous beings to enable us to live or we need it as beings in the social relations of citizenship, family life, and so forth, in order that we may know and do our duty. Agriculture, manufacturing, commerce and all other gainful art and science pertain to the first class; religion, ethics, notions of civic right and obligations belong to the second.' Herbart's classification might be said to represent the main aspects of education in Pestalozzi's earlier efforts, the ideal education comprising for him a general introduction to the various forms of handicraft and to simple social relations. In his later work he was nevertheless inclined to regard the

---

[1] *How Gertrude Teaches Her Children*, p. 173.
[2] *Addresses to the German Nation*, English translation, p. 169.
[3] *Minor Pedagogical Works*, p. 36.

H 2

requirements of education as three in number — the training of the hand, the head and the heart.

Of the threefold division of the educational process — the physical, the intellectual, the moral-religious — the first comprises not merely physical culture but also artistic skill and technical dexterity since all involve the physical organs. Fichte approves[1] of the inclusion by Pestalozzi of the development of the pupil's bodily powers, quoting a passage from *How Gertrude Teaches Her Children*,[2] but complains that Pestalozzi has failed to supply a graduated scheme of physical exercises, an omission Pestalozzi had himself deplored. While mental development in general consists in the inner organisation of impressions received from without, art reverses the process in so far as it modifies the external world by means of inner impulses and tendencies. The basis of all art is partly internal, partly external; partly mental, partly physical. Artistic skill comprises the effort to embody the products of the human mind, to give expression to the impulses of the human heart, to exercise the dexterities required in domestic and social life. Such is Pestalozzi's view of art as expounded in the *Swansong*.[3] The development of technical skill follows the same laws as the development of knowledge.[4]

Although Pestalozzi, following Rousseau, believes that the child is born good,[5] we must nevertheless take his education out of the hands of blind nature,[6] as the world

[1] *Addresses to the German Nation*, English translation, p. 167.

[2] Pp. 177–8. Cf. *Letters to Greaves*, pp. 89–98.

[3] Theodor Wiget, *Grundlinien der Erziehungslehre Pestalozzis* (Leipzig: K. F. Koehler, 1914), pp. 94–95.

[4] *How Gertrude Teaches Her Children*, p. 173.   [5] P. 75.

[6] P. 160. 'Man can only become man through his inner and spiritual nature. He becomes through it independent, free and contented. Mere physical nature leads him not hither. She is in her very nature blind; her ways are ways of darkness and death. Therefore, the education and training of our race must be taken out of the hands of blind sensuous Nature and the influence of her darkness and death, and put into the hands of our moral and spiritual being and its divine, eternal, inner light and truth.'

he enters is a world spoilt alike for the innocent enjoyment of the senses and for the feelings of his inner nature.[1] The moral faculty is present in infancy. 'God has given the child a spiritual nature, that is to say, He has implanted in him the voice of conscience ; and He has done more, He has given him the faculty of attending to this voice.'[2] The moral virtues originate in the relations existing between the child and his mother. In them too lies the whole essence of the natural germ of that state of mind which is peculiar to human dependence on the Author of our being.[3] An ABC of *Anschauung*, but a special type of *Anschauung*, an analogous or inner *Anschauung* is necessary, as is also a perfect gradation of methods for developing the soul and feelings, 'the essential purpose of which should be to use the advantage of instruction and its mechanism for the preservation of moral perfection, to prevent the selfishness of the reason by preserving the purity of the heart from error and one-sidedness ; and, above all, to subordinate my sense-impressions to my convictions, my eagerness to my benevolence, and my benevolence to my righteous will.'[4]

In his earlier writings Pestalozzi stressed the equality rather than the correlation of his three main divisions of education — the physical, the intellectual and the ethico-religious, or to elaborate these — the physical, the technical, the aesthetic, the intellectual, the moral and the religious aspects of personality. In his later writings he insists that the three aspects should be co-ordinated by one spiritual principle. Thus in the *Swansong* he definitely characterises the relationship between them as one of harmony. 'The education of all three sides of our nature proceeds on common lines in equal measure, as is necessary if the unity of our nature and the equilibrium of our

---

[1] P. 187   [2] *Letters to Greaves*, p. 19.
[3] *How Gertrude Teaches Her Children*, p. 184.   [4] P. 189.

powers are to be recognised from the outset.'[1] And in the *Letters to Greaves*:[2] 'The powers of man must be so cultivated that no one shall predominate at the expense of another, but each be excited to the true standard of activity; and this standard is the spiritual nature of man.'

Earlier in *How Gertrude Teaches Her Children* the idea of harmonious development was mentioned:[3] 'The aim of all instruction is, and can be, nothing but the development of human nature, by the harmonious cultivation of its powers and talents, and the promotion of manliness of life.' Emphasis on harmonious development or on well-balanced training, it need hardly be remarked in the case of Pestalozzi, should not blind us to the fact that education while suppressing idiosyncrasy should respect individuality. In the *Swansong* Pestalozzi — in opposition to Rousseau, who believed that the great souls could find their way alone — advises: 'Unusual capacity should be given every possible chance, and, above all, it should be rightly guided.' A further danger in the quotation from *How Gertrude Teaches Her Children*, from which Pestalozzi was delivered by reason of the poverty of his pupils, is that it may be interpreted to support a mere training of the mental faculties without regard to the social value of the training and the social situations which the pupil will later encounter.

In 1805 Pestalozzi transferred from Burgdorf to Yverdon, where he remained till 1827, He had by now acquired international fame; princes visited his institution. But the days of his astonishing popularity were also the days of his greatest mental distress; dissension persisted among his staff with which, by reason of his administrative incapacity, he was unable to cope. This explains

---

[1] J. A. Green, *Pestalozzi's Educational Writings*, p. 281.   [2] P. 18.

[3] Pp. 156–7. Also in *Views and Experiences*: 'The sole aim of education is the harmonious development of the powers and dispositions which make up personality.'

why Froebel's estimate of Pestalozzi's work is so much at variance with that of Herbart. It was the earlier efforts of Pestalozzi in the adverse circumstances at Burgdorf,[1] where any measure of success was commendable, that Herbart approved, whereas Froebel later encountered the more ambitious enterprise at Yverdon only to have his great expectations disappointed.[2] Writing of his first visit,[3] Froebel says: 'What I saw was to me at once elevating and depressing, arousing and also bewildering. . . . The disappointing side of the teaching plan, against which I intuitively rebelled, although my own tendencies on the subject were as yet so vague and dim, lay, in my opinion, in its incompleteness and one-sidedness. Several subjects of teaching and education highly important to the all-round harmonious development of a man seemed to me thrust far too much into the background, treated in stepmotherly fashion, and superficially worked out.' This conviction was but confirmed by Froebel's second visit to Yverdon.[4] 'The powerful, indefinable, stirring and uplifting effect produced by Pestalozzi when he spoke, set one's soul on fire for a higher, nobler life,' writes Froebel, 'although he had not made clear or sure the exact way towards it, nor indicated the means whereby to attain it. Thus did the power and many-sidedness of the educational effort make up for the deficiency in unity and comprehensiveness; and the love, the warmth, the stir of the whole, the human kindness and benevolence of it replaced the want of clearness, depth, thoroughness, extent, perseverance, and steadiness. . . . On the whole I passed a glorious time at Yverdon, elevated in tone, and critically decisive for my after life. At its close, however, I felt more clearly than ever the deficiency of inner

[1] Herbart's visit to Burgdorf took place in 1797-9.

[2] Froebel in his *Autobiography* admits: 'There was no educational problem whose resolution I did not firmly expect to find there.'

[3] The first visit lasted a fortnight, Froebel leaving Yverdon mid-October 1805.   [4] 1808-10.

unity and interdependence, as well as of outward comprehensiveness and thoroughness in the teaching there.'

Pestalozzi's efforts in education were tentative, and although lacking the scientific precision demanded today, they were in the broader sense of the term experimental.[1] His results had not that consistency which obtains in a purely *a priori* scheme of education, nor did they command that respect which attaches to the conclusion of a philosophical theory;[2] as the products of hard-won experience they nevertheless possess a reliability which many other more pretentious systems do not. With Pestalozzi it may truly be said that necessity was the mother of invention, and this he himself recognised when he prayed:[3] 'God, I thank Thee for my necessity.' It was this necessity that constrained him to make *Anschauung* the common starting-point of all instruction, to insist that teaching should follow an orderly sequence, to formulate a general method based on psychological principles, to recognise the practical and emotional aspects of personality, to lay the basis of our elementary-school system and to reinforce the democratic tradition in education.

[1] Pestalozzi frequently referred to his own methods as experimental. Cf. *How Gertrude Teaches Her Children*, pp. 154, 166, 172.
[2] Cf. *How Gertrude Teaches Her Children*, p. 83: 'Since my twentieth year, I have been incapable of philosophic thought, in the true sense of the word.'
[3] P. 18.

CHAPTER X

HERBART[1]

'PEDAGOGY as a science', says Herbart,[2] 'is based on ethics and on psychology. The former points out the aim of culture, the latter the way, the means and the obstacles.' Likewise in *The Application of Psychology to the Science of Education* : 'Education is related to ethics by the conception of the aim which the educator has in view. By the consideration of means and obstacles it is forced back on psychology.'[3] In *Observations of a Pedagogical Essay* he further explains : 'I have for twenty years employed metaphysics, mathematics, and side by side with them self-observation, experience and experiments, merely to find the foundations of true psychological insight. And the motive for these not entirely effortless investigations has been, and is, in the main my conviction that a large part of the enormous gaps in our pedagogical knowledge results from lack of psychology.'[4]

As the negative or critical aspect of Herbart's psychology is better known in educational circles than the positive or constructive, we shall deal with it first.

Locke, as we have indicated in a previous chapter, had

[1] 1776–1841.

[2] J. F. Herbart, *Umriss pädagogischer Vorlesungen*, translated by A. F. Lange under title of *Outlines of Educational Doctrine* (New York: The Macmillan Co., 1904), § 2.

[3] *Briefe über die Anwendung der Psychologie auf die Pädagogik*, translated by B. C. Mullinger (London : Swan Sonnenschein, 1898), Letter I.

[4] *Bemerkungen über einen pädagogischen Aufsatz* (1814). J. F. Herbart's *Kleinere philosophischen Schriften* (Leipzig : G. Hartenstein, 1842), vol. ii, pp. 15–28. Included in *ABC of Sense Perception and Minor Pedagogical Works*, translated by W. J. Eckoff (New York: D. Appleton, 1903), p. 72. The *ABC*, etc., is later throughout referred to simply as *Minor Pedagogical Works*.

not only refuted the doctrine of innate ideas but had also challenged the existence of mental faculties. Herbart agreed in discarding mental faculties, and quite definitely rejected formal training. Stout[1] regarded Herbart's uncompromising polemic against innate faculties, activities and predispositions as the most striking negative feature of his psychology. 'The soul', says Herbart,[2] 'has no innate tendencies nor faculties.' Again,[3] 'it is an error, indeed, to look upon the human soul as an aggregate of all sorts of faculties.' Commenting on this rejection of the faculties Stout remarks : 'The human mind has always been prone to mistake abstractions for realities, even when the corresponding concretes stand out in clear and definite detail. This propensity becomes almost irresistible in a case in which concrete details are shadowy and evasive. Hence we find that the faculty psychologists, unable to make legitimate use of their generalisations in the explanation of particular phenomena, treated them as if they were real forces producing these phenomena. Thus in their hands psychology became transformed into a kind of mythology which was none the less mischievous because scarcely anyone overtly and explicitly professed to believe in it.'

On the training of the faculties Herbart in his *Brief Encyclopaedia of Practical Philosophy*[4] remarks : 'Those, however, who have no proper insight seldom grasp anything about the rules of education. They cling to the old idea that there are certain powers or faculties in the soul

---

[1] G. F. Stout, *Mind*, vol. xiii (1888), pp. 321–38, 473–98, 'The Herbartian Psychology'; vol. xiv (1889), pp. 1–26, 'Herbart compared with the English Psychologists and with Beneke'; pp. 353–68, 'The Psychological Work of Herbart's Disciples'.

[2] *Lehrbuch zur Psychologie* (first edition 1816), translated by Margaret K. Smith under title *Textbook of Psychology* (New York : D. Appleton & Co., 1891). Vol. iv of Herbart's *Collected Works* in German (Langensala, 1891), pp. 205–436, contains the fuller second edition with sections differently numbered.   [3] *Outlines of Educational Doctrine*, § 20.

[4] *Kurze Encyclopädie der Philosophie*, § 107.

which have to be exercised, and it does not matter what
they are exercised on. The exercises might well belong
to the same category as gymnastic exercises, because men
have only one kind of muscle, and by gymnastics the
muscles of the body become strong and pliable. In actual
fact every apperceptive system comprises elements of imagination, memory and reason, though naturally not all
in equal proportions. In one and the same person there
can quite easily be, and usually is, an apperceptive system
composed predominantly of intellectual elements while
another is rich in imagination, while in a third memory
plays the greatest part. Intense feeling may colour
one apperceptive system, whereas apathy characterises
another. What educators call formal training is accordingly a complete chimera, since it presupposes the exercise
of powers existing only in the imagination of those who
hold such views on psychology.' And in the *Textbook of
Psychology* he illustrates :[1] 'Memory and imagination agree
in this, that in every man their special strength is limited
to certain classes of subjects. For him who wishes geometrical imagination, exercises in the so-called art of
poetry would be quite useless ; and he who retains without
any trouble the technical terms of a science which interests
him, has often a bad memory for village gossip.'

Herbart is frequently accused not only of disposing of
mental faculties but even of presenting us with 'a psychology without a soul'. Herbart could admit the
charge, but would plead in extenuation that this was
merely a methodological expedient. The soul was a
metaphysical necessity, but it was only as it entertains
presentations[2] and thereby becomes mind that psychology
can profitably deal with it ; 'we may regard the mind as
the soul endowed with the power of presentation,'[3] he

[1] § 93. Cf. also § 122.
[2] Herbart's term *Vorstellung* is rendered throughout by 'presentation'
and is virtually equivalent to Locke's term 'idea'.
[3] *Textbook of Psychology*, § 162.

says, and,[1] 'so far as it possesses presentations or conceives, the soul is called mind; so far as it feels or desires it is called the heart'. At the outset of the *Textbook of Psychology* Herbart had explained: 'the treatise of psychology may very well be allowed to precede that on metaphysics, and in this way the metaphysical idea of the soul (the substance of the mind) may be dispensed with at first. By this, the beginner lightens his task, partly because he can tarry longer in the circle of experience, and partly because the manifold relations of psychology to morals, pedagogy, politics, philosophy of history and of art, heighten the interest in the study.' Stout,[2] however, notes that the incompatibility of the soul as a simple unitary entity and the mind as a concrete multiplicity escaped Herbart: 'in Herbart's procedure there is one — and only one — fundamental incoherence. His metaphysical speculation conducted him to the doctrine that the soul is an absolutely simple being; for psychological purposes he substituted, instead of the conception of simplicity, that of systematic totality. In doing so he was inconsistent, but the inconsistency was necessary and praiseworthy. Without it no psychology would have been possible for him.'

A further charge levelled against Herbart is the intellectualism of his psychology, ideas and their relation to one another being, it is said,[3] the sole origin of all other mental activities such as feeling and will. In his *Textbook of Psychology* Herbart nevertheless devotes a chapter to the 'Faculty of Feeling'.[4] There he explains that if we restrict our account of mental processes to presentations and their origin we are by no means able to indicate all that goes on in our minds; we must also consider feeling and desire. 'Feeling', he tells us,[5] 'is not a

---

[1] *Textbook of Psychology*, § 33.   [2] *Mind*, vol. xiv, p. 363.

[3] R. Ulich, *History of Educational Thought* (New York: The American Book Co., 1945), p. 275.   [4] §§ 95–106.

[5] *Application of Psychology*, Letter XVI, also *Textbook*, §§ 32, 36, 37.

separate, independent faculty of the soul, but only a consequence of the mutual interaction of ideas.' In the mental life when a presentation in process of realising itself is inhibited by another presentation, an unpleasant feeling is aroused, but if its realisation is facilitated, pleasure ensues. Herbart distinguishes feelings from emotions, pointing out that the latter have a physical component, and, as he adds, act upon the body with remarkable, often dangerous, power; thus courage and timidity are very often dependent upon health and sickness.

Herbart's view of the dependence of feeling and emotion on ideas has important consequences educationally. There can be no education of the feelings *per se*.[1] Herbart would accordingly not be content to rely for moral training on the emotionalism of Rousseau or the sentimentalism of Pestalozzi. He demands a surer foundation, and, as we shall see, finds it in 'the circle of thought'; as he himself puts it:[2] 'The disposition of the heart has its source in the mind.'

The intellectualism of Herbart's psychology is intensified by the ambiguity of the term *Empfindung* to signify both sensation and feeling. Thus in the Introduction to *The Science of Education*[3] he says that out of thoughts arise feelings (*Empfindungen*), and, from these, principles and modes of action. Professor Rein of Jena (1847–1929), the last of the great German Herbartians, explained the statement thus:[4] 'It is to be regretted that

---

[1] Cf. Sir W. Le Gros Clark, 'The Humanity of Man', Presidential Address to the British Association, 1961 : 'The conception at one time current in psychology that mental experience can be separated into the rather sharply contrasted categories termed "cognitive" and "affective" has long since been recognised as misleading, for intellectual and emotional factors are so closely interlocked in any form of behaviour that they cannot be dissociated — even arbitrarily.'   [2] *Textbook of Psychology*, § 33.

[3] *Allgemeine Pädagogik aus dem Zweck der Erziehung abgeleitet*, translated by H. M. and E. Felkin under title *The Science of Education* (London : Swan Sonnenschein, 1904).   [4] In a reply to the author.

we Germans unfortunately employ the term *Empfindung* in two senses. First, we understand by it *Gefühl*, i.e. feeling — we speak of a man with fine *Empfindungen* (sensibility) and mean thereby a man with fine feelings. On the other hand we understand by *Empfindung* the mental reaction to an external stimulus, what the Englishman understands by sensation. Herbart here by *Empfindungen* was thinking of *Gefühl* (feeling) which can be so intimately and so vitally associated with presentations (*Vorstellungen*) that out of them arise volitional acts which, by reason of their comprehensiveness and worth, rank as principles or moral ideas. The circle of thought is, according to Herbart, no mere intellectual structure but is interwoven throughout with feelings and volitional impulses. The task of educative instruction is to anchor in the youth's soul this circle of thought.'

Herbart's positive contribution to psychology lies in the emphasis placed on the subjective factors in the mind, in the recognition of activities, not themselves in consciousness which form an integral functional part of mind.[1] Herbart's view of mind and his method differ from that of his English associationist predecessors. They regard mind as a succession of mutually exclusive mental states, and their method is the introspective. Herbart holds that mental states, while each has its own intrinsic quality, act and react on one another in manifold ways and constitute a single concrete system.

The English associationists also sought to formulate in a few simple laws — similarity, contrast, contiguity, the conditions under which certain mental experiences were revived or recalled : Herbart, on the other hand, sought to account for the disappearance of presentations from consciousness instead of their reinstatement in consciousness. He posed the problem in these terms :[2] 'Our

[1] See G. F. Stout, *Mind*, vol. xiii, 'The Herbartian Psychology'.
[2] *Textbook of Psychology*, 1st ed., § 89, 2nd ed., § 47.

presentations recede from consciousness and return again. For which shall we seek explanation — the receding or the returning? The question must first be directed towards the former although in the past it is usual to discuss only the latter.' Herbart explains the disappearance of presentations from consciousness after this fashion.[1] To preserve his metaphysical concept of the soul as a unity Herbart concludes that contrary presentations of the same sensory modality, e.g. red and blue, sour and sweet, conflict and tend to suppress each other. The presentation that is repressed[2] is not annihilated, otherwise it could not later be recalled. What happens is that it is transmuted into a force,[3] becoming a tendency in the subconscious, the special feature of which is its constant striving to reassert itself in consciousness as a presentation. This is a condition of the reproduction of ideas. It should be added that a presentation once produced is never quite lost.[4]

Only antithetical presentations suffer eclipse and are resolved into subconscious mental activities. The reciprocal arrest does not arise with presentations of different sensory modalities, for example, with a tone and a colour, nor with presentations of different quality but compatible with one another, for example, with the several attributes which together constitute an object. Such a unity Herbart terms a 'complex', a term reintroduced later by Jung to characterise a constellation of ideas in the unconscious. Herbart's significant contribution

---

[1] *Textbook of Psychology*, 2nd ed., §§ 124, 125.

[2] The term 'repression' plays a prominent role in psycho-analysis. Ernest Jones in *Siggmund Freud: Life and Work* (London: The Hogarth Press, 1953), pp. 309, 408, acknowledges its prior use by Herbart. Note that 'repression' with Herbart as with Freud results from conflict. It may be added that in his *Textbook of Psychology* Herbart has a section on dreams (2nd ed., § 216 — German edition of Collected Works, vol. iv, pp. 411–12).

[3] The title of the Second Part of the *Textbook of Psychology* is: Von den Vorstellungen als Kräften.

[4] *Textbook of Psychology*, 1st ed., § 127, 2nd ed., § 87.

to psychology is accordingly the recognition of a system of forces operating in the subconscious, in addition to presentations in the mind. Stout[1] designates the two spheres 'presentative activities' and 'presented content'.

Another conception which Herbart finds necessary to introduce is the threshold of consciousness (*Schwelle des Bewusstseins*). A presentation which is in consciousness is said to be *above* the threshold; if the arresting forces are just sufficient and no more than to secure eclipse, it is said to be *on* the threshold; if the forces of repression are sufficient to secure total eclipse, the presentation is said to be *below* the threshold. Herbart further distinguishes[2] the static threshold (*die statische Schwelle*) from the dynamical (*mechanische*) threshold. With the former the conditions of equilibrium of presentations are established and presentations below the static threshold are without influence on conscious processes: with the latter, equilibrium is not established, and presentations below the dynamical threshold operate as important factors in determining the course of events within consciousness. These two thresholds Ernest Jones claims correspond topographically with the position of Freud's two censorships; the former where an inhibited idea is robbed of its activity and can enter consciousness only when the inhibition is lifted; it is therefore not unlike a suppressed idea in the preconscious;[3] the latter type of threshold is where wholly repressed ideas are still in a state of rebellious activity and succeed in producing, e.g., feelings of oppression.

Presentations related together in the past tend to cohere and form what Herbart calls 'an apperception mass'. Such an organised system of presentations

[1] *Mind*, vol. xiv (1889), p. 3.
[2] *Textbook of Psychology*, 1st ed., § 127.
[3] E. Jones, op. cit., p. 442: 'Freud took care never to use the term *unterbewusst*, subconscious, which he regarded as misleading; it suggests merely something that is slightly less conscious.'

exercises a selective function, facilitating the assimilation of congruent ideas while reacting to exclude incompatible ideas. As Stout explains:[1] 'Attention and apperception reciprocally determine each other. It is through apperception that a presentation acquires the significance and interest which enables it to attract attention. On the other hand the heightened intensity which accrues to it as an object of attention enables it to react with increased energy upon the mental system to which it belongs.' The modern psychologist[2] adds that the environment for intellectual growth that the child encounters is also in part conditioned by the inner organisation of the child's mind. Thus what we notice depends not so much on the strength of the external stimulus or on the susceptibility of the subject as on the context, the mental system[3] dominant at the time. This accounts for the fact that different people, or the same person at different times, have different perceptions under the same external conditions. As Herbart remarks of *Anschauung*:[4] even in the same surroundings every man has his own world. In literature the principle finds expression in various forms. Carlyle says: The eye sees what it brings the power to see; and Browning: Tis the taught already that profit by teaching.

---

[1] *Mind*, vol. xvi, p. 23.

[2] J. McV. Hunt, *Intelligence and Experience* (New York: The Ronald Press, 1961), p. 357.

[3] An alternative term for 'apperception mass' is 'mental background', J. Adams, *Exposition and Illustration*, ch. iv (the whole chapter deals with 'Mental Backgrounds'); in *The Humanities Chart Their Course* (Stanford University Press, California, 1945), p. 19, Max Radin in 'The Search for the Major Premise' says: 'I have preferred the metaphor of a cultural "matrix" to the more usual one of a background, because we think of a background as something fixed and dead and we picture living reality moving in front of it, to be sure, but quite detachable.' 'The concept "frame of reference" has been substituted and defined as the functionally related factors, both past and present, which operate at the moment to determine perception, judgment and affectivity.' *The Journal of Personality*, vol. xviii, p. 370, June 1949, quoting M. Sherif and H. Cantril, *The Psychology of Ego Involvement* (New York: John Wiley & Son).

[4] *Lehrbuch*, § 213.

Apperception thus emphasises the significant part that old knowledge plays in the acquisition of the new, how new knowledge should always be a development of previous knowledge. Stout[1] regards it as the main principle which psychology lends to the theory of education as its starting point. James, on the other hand, in his *Talks to Teachers*,[2] to discount the exaggerated significance attributed to the principle at one time in American educational circles, contends that it means nothing more than the act of taking a thing into the mind, but how children take a thing into their minds is just what teachers would like to know.

Following the precedent set by Herbart himself,[3] we shall deal with his educational doctrines before considering his ethics or 'practical' philosophy. Both were dependent on his psychology, and precedence of publication was accorded to the *Allgemeine Pädagogik* since it suffered less from the lack of psychology.

Although psychology provides the means, philosophy dictates the end of education. While Herbart confesses that education has no time to make holiday till philosophical questions are once for all cleared up,[4] in the same work[5] he admits : 'To teach completely how life is determined by its two rulers, Speculation and Taste, we must seek for a system of philosophy, the keystone of instruction,' and he also claims[6] that the true perfection of education is philosophy.

In the opening sentences of *Abhandlung über die ästhetische Darstellung der Welt als das Hauptgeschäft der Erziehung* (Dissertation on the presentation of the world from the aesthetic standpoint as the main task of education)[7] he

---

[1] *Analytic Psychology*, vol. ii, pp. 137–8.   [2] P. 157.
[3] *Minor Pedagogical Works*, pp. 285–6.   [4] *The Science of Education*, p. 108.
[5] P. 195.   [6] *Minor Pedagogical Works*, p. 151.
[7] Translated by Eckoff in Herbart, *ABC of Sense Perception and Minor Pedagogical Works*, pp. 92–120, under the title 'The Aesthetic Presentation of the Universe, the Chief Office of Education', and by H. M. and E.

affirms : 'The one and the whole work of education may be summed up in the concept — morality.' But he goes on to explain that while morality is the *highest* aim, to set up morality as the *whole* aim of humanity and education an expansion of the concept is required, as is also a proof of its necessary presuppositions and the conditions of its actual possibility. And in the *Allgemeine Pädagogik* he repeats :[1] 'I therefore believe that the mode of consideration which places morality at the head is the most important, but not the only and all-embracing standpoint of education'. The aesthetic coherence of the world may also be regarded as the ideal of education.[2]

Neither ethics nor aesthetics can, however, determine fully the end of education. This Herbart admitted, although his admission has usually been ignored, both by his critics and by his expositors. Education must inlcude the ideals of truth and of righteousness as well as of goodness and beauty. Intellectual inquiry and religious reverence are as natural to man and as necessary to him for the full realisation of his personality as are ethical endeavour and aesthetic enjoyment; and the aim of education as of life itself cannot be formulated in any more succinct phrase than that of Eucken, namely, to exalt personality.

Felkin in *The Science of Education*, pp. 57–77, under the title 'On the Aesthetic Revelation of the World as the Chief Work of Education'.

[1] *The Science of Education*, p. 108.

[2] *Minor Pedagogical Works*, p. 16. In early Greek thought there was no separation between ethics and aesthetics. Ward in his *Encyclopaedia Britannica* article on 'Herbart' (eleventh edition, 1911, p. 337; fourteenth edition, 1929, p. 447) explains the relationship between Aesthetics and Ethics thus : 'Aesthetics elaborates the "ideas" involved in the expression of taste called forth by those relations of objects which acquire for them the attribute of beauty or the reverse. The beautiful is predicated absolutely and involuntarily by all who have attained the right standpoint. Ethics, the chief branch of Aesthetics deals with such relations among volitions as thus unconditionally please or displease.'

C. Burt in *The Young Delinquent*, p. 480, regards the relationship thus : 'The so-called moral sense is in part an aesthetic sense, a nice fastidious taste in matters of social behaviour.'

Herbart is sometimes accused of ignoring the individuality of the pupil. In the *Umriss*[1] he nevertheless affirms that we need not go further than experience to see that there is a great diversity in intellectual talents, and in the Introduction to that work declares that the assumption of unlimited plasticity is inadmissible and that the educability of the child is limited by his individuality. In the *Minor Pedagogical Works*[2] he says it is a chief requisite of a good pedagogical plan that it be flexible enough to fit the various capacities. What Herbart, however, seeks to avoid is that individuality should develop into eccentricity. Where this occurs, a state of society results in which 'each brags of his own individuality, and no one understands his fellows'.[3] It should also be noted that he does not, as did T. Percy Nunn[4] later, make the development of individuality the aim of education. Individuality is one of the data of education, not the end. It has to be fashioned into personality, and this is achieved through the development of a variety of interests and their integration.

Human activity, for Herbart, has two main aspects: many-sided interest and moral character. Many-sided interest is further qualified by 'well balanced' — *gleich-schwebende Vielseitigkeit*.[5] This is equivalent to the popular statement — the harmonious expansion of all the powers of the individual. Many-sidedness is opposed not only to one-sidedness but also to versatility,[6] it must be distinguished, Herbart says in the *Allegmeine Pädagogik*,[7] from its exaggeration — dabbling in many things.

Interest in its turn has two aspects — a subjective or psychological, and an objective. The objective comprises the various activities in which the individual participates

---

[1] § 60.   [2] P. 181.   [3] *The Science of Education*, p. 142.
[4] *Education: Its Data and First Principles* (London: Edward Arnold & Co., 1930).   [5] *The Science of Education*, p. 111.
[6] *Umriss*, § 65.   [7] *The Science of Education*, p. 111; also p. 119.

or the different aspects of the environment, physical and social, to which he reacts; it consists of the two main divisions (*i*) knowledge and (*ii*) social responsiveness, or what Dewey and other term socialty.

Knowledge he divides into (*i*) actual phenomena, (*ii*) scientific laws, (*iii*) aesthetic relations (or the empirical, the speculative and the aesthetic), representing different attitudes to our natural environment or different aspects of experience; and sociality into (*i*) individual, (*ii*) civil and (*iii*) religious, representing different attitudes in human interaction or different aspects of our spiritual environment. These constitute the six facets of a many-sided interest, and when properly exploited provide a liberal training or an all-round education.

Existing mental contents originate from two main sources — experience and social intercourse.[2] Through experience we acquire knowledge, and through intercourse we develop social responsiveness. While we cannot dispense with experience and intercourse we must realise how limited are the opportunities which circumstances afford. They must be supplemented by instruction, for, as Herbart claims,[3] experience seems, as it were, to expect that instruction will follow to analyse the material amassed and to collect and arrange the scattered and formless fragments. He thus sums up: 'Interest arises from interesting objects and occupations. Many-sided interest originates in the profusion of these. To create and develop this interest is the task of instruction which carries on and completes the preparation begun by intercourse and experience.'[4] Instruction alone, he adds,[5] can lay claim to cultivate a well-balanced, all-embracing

---

[1] Ibid., p. 133. Cf. *Minor Works*, p. 39. 'What is needful to us is needful either to our physical or our moral nature. We need it either as sensuous beings to enable us to live or we need it as beings in the social relations of citizenship, family life and so forth, in order that we may know and do our duty.' [2] *Umriss*, § 36.

[3] *The Science of Education*, p. 138. [4] Ibid., p. 120. [5] P. 141.

many-sidedness. It is for this reason that Herbart keeps reiterating that he has no conception of education without instruction; conversely, he does not acknowledge any instruction which does not educate.[1]

Instruction thus acquires the place of first importance in Herbart's educational theory. 'The chief means of positive education lies in instruction taken in its widest sense', he claims.[2] In *How Gertrude Teaches Her Children* Pestalozzi lamented that men do not apply their skill to found education upon principles and to bring instruction and education into harmony. The latter task is what Herbart, if anyone, has achieved. For Locke instruction was the least part of education : for Herbart it was the chief.

Not all instruction is, however, educative ; the types of instruction which in Herbart's opinion[3] are not educative are those which afford only temporary excitement or light entertainment, and such studies as remain isolated and inert.

Instruction may take two main forms — synthetic and analytic.[4] The child's experience may be augmented through the teacher's description of events or activities; this is narrative instruction and, according to Herbart,[5] has but one law — to describe in such a way that the pupil believes he sees what is described. Or the teacher may avail himself of the pupil's experience eliciting the facts which he requires for his exposition. These facts may have to be supplemented, but whether supplied by the teacher or the pupil they require to be organised according to the purpose the teacher has in view. Both these forms of exposition — narrative and developmental

---

[1] *The Science of Education*, p. 84.   [2] *Aphorismen*, XXI.   [3] *Umriss*, § 126.
[4] In the *Textbook of Psychology* Herbart explains the distinction between analytic and synthetic instruction thus : 'The former occurs through reproduction for a purpose ; the latter seeks to produce a combination of new concepts in conformity with a purpose.'
[5] *The Science of Education*, p. 155.

— are classed by Herbart as synthetic. The pupil's experience may not only be inadequate; it may even be erroneous, in which case the teacher must dissect it to utilise the elements in a new systematic whole; this Herbart terms analytic instruction, and he adds :[1] 'The pupil ought properly to provide the material for analytic instruction, especially in later years.' The various forms of presentation or exposition are not mutually exclusive, but may be combined as occasion requires in the same lesson.[2]

Herbart in his *Allgemeine Pädagogik*[3] illustrates how the analytic and synthetic types of instruction may be employed in the respective fields of interest already enumerated — empirical, scientific, aesthetic, human, social and religious, but his treatment, he acknowledges, is too general to provide a curriculum which must arrange the opportunities provided in accordance with the needs of the pupils and the talents of the individual teacher. Earlier,[4] Herbart had suggested as a guide to the organisation of teaching material the principle of recapitulation, a doctrine which, common to many educators from Plato to Montessori and Dewey, plays a prominent part in Herbartian literature : 'If pupils would continue the work of their forefathers they must have travelled the same way ; above all, they must have learned to recognise these forefathers as their own from their early years.'

The interests which constitute the main divisions of education Herbart[5] reminds us are interests of one person, and he warns us : 'Do not forget interest among interesting things.' It is with the doctrine of interest in this sense,

[1] Ibid., p. 187.
[2] W. Rein, in his *Outlines of Pedagogics*, English translation, p. 153, distinguishes narrative presentation (*erzählend darstellend*) from progressively developing presentation (*entwickelnd darstellend*) which would include both Herbart's purely synthetic and analytic forms. J. Adams, *Exposition and Illustration*, pp. 57–63, follows Herbart more closely.
[3] *The Science of Education*, pp. 170–86.
[4] Ibid., p. 165.   [5] P. 132.

although it occupies only a minor place in his writings, rather than with the doctrine of instruction that Herbart's name has come to be associated in Britain and in America mainly through its exposition by Adams in his *Herbartian Psychology Applied to Education* and by Dewey in his early essay, 'Interest in relation to Training of the Will'. Even the aim of the project method, Kilpatrick admits,[1] is to reaffirm the old doctrine of interest.

The doctrine of interest is implied in a passage in Plato's *Republic*[2] quoted earlier. Rousseau in the *Émile* had declared : 'Present interest, that is the motive power, the only motive power that takes us far and safely.' And in one of his *Letters to Greaves*,[3] Pestalozzi explains : 'This interest in study is the first thing which a teacher . . . should endeavour to keep alive. There are scarcely any circumstances in which a want of application in children does not proceed from a want of interest; and there are, perhaps, none under which a want of application in children does not originate in the mode of treatment adopted by the teacher. I would go so far as to lay it down as a rule that whenever children are inattentive and are apparently taking no interest in a lesson, the teacher should always first look to himself for the reason.' Herbart sums up Pestalozzi's complaint in the dictum that weariness is the cardinal sin of instruction,[4] and explains[5] — 'The word interest stands in general for that kind of mental activity which it is the business of instruction to create. Mere information does not suffice ; for this we think of as a supply or store of facts which a person might possess or lack, and still remain the same being. But he who lays hold of his information, and reaches out for more, takes an interest in it.'

Interest is thus a concomitant of mental activity.

[1] W. H. Kilpatrick, *Remaking the Curriculum*, p. 48.
[2] See above, p. 19.   [3] XXX.
[4] *The Science of Education*, p. 138.   [5] *Umriss*, § 62.

Herbart is, however, no advocate of 'activity for activity's sake' even though it is mental activity, nor of 'activity leading to further activity'. 'Interest', he says,[1] 'means self-activity. But not all self-activity, only the right degree of the right kind is desirable, else lively children might very well be left to themselves. There would be no need of educating or controlling them. It is the purpose of instruction to give the right *direction* to their thoughts and impulses, to incline these toward the morally good and the true.' Interest he opposes to apathy. It displays a preference over mere perception for certain objects by arousing in the mind analogous presentations and involuntarily suppressing others. It differs from certain other mental processes by depending on its object and referring to the present.[2]

By requiring that interest should be a result of instruction we do not, as is popularly supposed, emasculate education; interest is not to be confused with amusement, and it is not for lack of warning by Herbart that their identification has gained currency. 'The teacher', he says,[3] 'should not be misled into turning instruction into play, nor designedly into work; he sees before him a serious business and tries to forward it with gentle but steady hand.' 'That which is too simple', he repeats,[4] 'must be avoided'; and again,[5] 'Instruction must be comprehensible and yet difficult rather than easy, otherwise it causes *ennui*', or, as his British expositor explains,[6] 'we find that so far from enervating the pupil, the principle of interest braces him up to endure all manner of drudgery and hard work. . . . The theory of interest does not propose to banish drudgery but only to make drudgery tolerable by giving it a meaning.'

[1] Ibid., § 71. [2] *The Science of Education*, pp. 128–9.
[3] Ibid., p. 192. [4] *Umriss*, § 77, note.
[5] *The Science of Education*, p. 238.
[6] J. Adams, *Herbartian Psychology*, pp. 262, 263.

'Interest depends partly on native capacity which the school cannot create; but it depends also on the subject-matter of instruction.'[1] Not only, however, on the selection of the appropriate subject-matter, but also on its arrangement. We must know both what we are teaching and how to teach it.

When presentations arise spontaneously in the pupil's mind, the pupils are said to be attentive and the instruction has an interest for them.[2] When attention has to be enforced, it is doubtful whether an interest in the subject can ever be evoked. Or, as A. N. Whitehead says in *The Aims of Education*:[3] 'In training a child to activity of thought, above all things we must beware of what I will call "inert ideas" — that is to say, ideas that are merely received into the mind without being utilised, or tested, or thrown into fresh combinations'. The distinction between 'animate' as against what might be called 'inanimate' knowledge is not absolute, for the knowledge generally regarded as inanimate can become animate if the teacher relates it to some topic that has real significance for the pupil; as Herbart explains:[4] 'Presentations that must by effort be raised into consciousness because they do not rise spontaneously, may become spontaneous by gradual strengthening. But this development we cannot count on, unless instruction, advancing step by step, brings it about.'

Knowledge is likewise likely to be inanimate if it remains detached or dissociated from a general system of ideas. In his *Umriss* Herbart warns us — 'If the facts of knowledge are allowed to fall asunder . . . instruction endangers the whole of education'.[5] And Whitehead elaborates:[6] 'The results of teaching small parts of a large number of subjects is the passive reception of disconnected ideas, not illuminated with any spark of vitality.

[1] *Umriss*, § 125. [2] Ibid., § 72. [3] P. 1.
[4] *Umriss*, § 71. [5] Ibid., § 268. [6] *The Aims of Education*, p. 2.

Let the main ideas which are introduced into a child's education be few and important, and let them be thrown into every combination possible.' As whatever remains isolated has little significance, Herbart emphasises the correlation of studies.[1]

No matter what subject-matter is selected or what method of exposition — analytic or synthetic, is adopted, the same sequence must be followed in instruction if interest is to ensue. Herbart insisted that teaching procedure should be adapted to the stages discernible in the learning process. He first distinguished two phases — an intensive and an extensive. *Vertiefung* — concentration on, or to be engrossed in, a subject, and *Besinnung* — integration and organisation of the results of *Vertiefung*.[2] In one of his *Aphorisms*[3] he explains that *Vertiefung*, concentration, occurs when a thought so dominates the mind that it suppresses the usual contents of consciousness, and *Besinnung*, organisation, when the usual contents assert themselves and incorporate the new; integration is essential not only to organise the effects of concentration but also to prevent a lopsided development.

As these two concepts are too general for practical purposes Herbart finds it necessary to subdivide concentration into clearness and association, and organisation into system and method. Clearness, association, system and method thus become Herbart's formal steps in teaching.[4]

'In order always to maintain the mind's coherence', he contends,[5] 'instruction must follow the rule of giving equal weight in every smallest possible group of its objects to concentration and reflection; that is to say, it must care equally and in regular succession for clearness

[1] *Umriss*, § 58, note.
[2] *The Science of Education*, pp. 123–8. Also *Textbook of Psychology*, § 210.
[3] *Aphorismen*, I.
[4] *The Science of Education*, p. 126; *Umriss*, §§ 68–69.
[5] *The Science of Education*, pp. 144–5.

I

of every particular, for association of the manifold, for organising what is associated, and for a certain practice in expansion through this arrangement. Upon this depends the distinctness which must rule in all that is taught.'

Under clearness Herbart includes the analysis and synthesis of the given. It is equivalent to the so-called Herbartian step of presentation. Through association the new knowledge presented to the pupil is connected with the old; and association accordingly implies the apperceptive process and is analogous to the preparation stage of the Herbartian five formal steps. Its purpose is to secure a proper orientation of the subject to be taught. 'For association', Herbart tells us,[1] 'the best mode of procedure is informal conversation, because it gives the pupil an opportunity to test and to change the accidental union of his thoughts, to multiply the links of connection, and to assimilate, after his own fashion, what he has learned. It enables him, besides, to do at least a part of all this in any way that happens to be the easiest and most convenient.' Association prepares the way for system, which is 'the perfect order of a copious co-ordination'. 'By exhibiting and emphasising the leading principles', Herbart adds, 'system impresses upon the minds of pupils the value of organised knowledge.'[2] In the Herbartian tradition system is termed generalisation. Furthermore, a system is not to be learned merely, it is to be used, applied, and often needs to be supplemented by additions inserted at appropriate places.[3] This application Herbart terms 'method' whereas by his successors the self-explanatory term 'application' has been appropriated to denote the extension of the formulated principle.

These various steps are believed by Herbart to be requisite, one by one, in the order given for every section

[1] *Umriss*, § 69.   [2] Ibid., § 69.   [3] § 68.

small or large, of subjects to be taught.[1] While various
educationists have attempted to substantiate this claim,[2]
the procedure can be said to be valid only for that form
of instruction which Herbart had mainly in view, the
aim of which is the acquisition of knowledge ; when the
aim of the lesson is the development of skill, a different
procedure will doubtless be found to be more appropriate.

Herbart's formal steps apply to method-wholes, in-
structional units or centres of interest, not to individual
lessons ; that is, they are stages in the exposition of a
topic which has a unity and completeness in itself. It
was the mechanical application of the formal steps in
each and every lesson that brought the Herbartian
method into discredit, and for this formalism there was
no warrant in the writings of Herbart.

In introducing the concept of many-sidedness of interest
Herbart had intimated that one aspect of human activity
was being neglected ; namely, action, and, what immediately impels thereto — desire.[3] The two spheres of
human activity are accordingly interest and desire, knowing and willing. They are nevertheless not unconnected,
being linked through instruction.[4] Just as instruction
creates a many-sided interest, so it has also the task of
developing what from the standpoint of character training Herbart now calls 'the circle of thought'. The
section dealing with the influence of the circle of thought
on character[5] is the central point of the *Allgemeine*

[1] § 68. Cf. § 70.
[2] E.g. J. J. Findlay, *Principles of Class Teaching* (London : Macmillan &
Co., 1907).
[3] *The Science of Education*, p. 129. G. F. Stout, *Mind*, vol. xiii, p. 490 :
'Desire is, according to Herbart, a composite mode of consciousness belonging on the one hand to the region of feeling, on the other to that of presented content. It has no unique character by which it can be marked off
from both.'
[4] Cf. Descartes, *Meditations*, IV : 'It is accordingly a dictate of the
natural light that the knowledge of the understanding ought always to
precede the determination of the will.'
[5] *The Science of Education*, pp. 209–10.

Pädagogik; it is, in Herbart's own words,[1] the vantage point from which the whole should be viewed.

Herbart's firm conviction is that the chief seat of the cultivation of character lies in the circle of thought and that in the formation of the circle of thought the main business of education consists.[2] Character training, he claims,[3] is unable to accomplish its work unless in conjunction with instruction. 'It will be seen when the task of setting forth the whole of virtue is renewed in its completeness that the main things are accomplished by instruction.'[4] In the Introduction to the *Allgemeine Pädagogik* he affirms:[5] 'Those only wield the full power of education who know how to cultivate in the youthful soul a large circle of thought closely connected in all its parts, possessing the power of overcoming what is unfavourable in the environment, and of dissolving and absorbing into itself all that is favourable.' In his reply to Jackmann's review he repeats : 'Instruction will above all form the circle of thought and education the character. The latter is nothing without the former — herein is contained the whole sum of my pedagogy' ; and in his *Brief Encyclopaedia*[6] he takes credit for introducing the term 'an educative instruction'. This principle of the determination of the inner aspect of character by means of instruction is Herbart's chief contribution to educational thought, and proves how futile it is from his standpoint to oppose education or the training of character to instruction. 'Moral education', he sums up,[7] 'is not separable from education as a whole.'

While instruction is thus the central theme of Herbart's doctrine he never allows us to forget that man's

---

[1] *Replik gegen Jackmanns Recension der Allgemeinen Pädagogik.*
[2] *The Science of Education*, pp. 220, 214.   [3] *Umriss*, § 150.
[4] *Replik gegen Jackmanns Recension.*
[5] *The Science of Education*, p. 92.
[6] Also in *Application of Psychology*, Letter II.
[7] *The Science of Education*, p. 108.

worth lies not in his knowing but in his willing.[1] Before, however, proceeding with the task of harmonising the ethical endowment of the pupil with the moral ideal Herbart disposes of a conception which, though he sometimes does not even regard it as a part of education, is a precondition of it, namely, *Regierung* (orderliness or teacher's control of pupil's behaviour). This is one of the three chief concepts, *Regierung* (orderliness), *Unterricht* (instruction), *Zucht* (character training or self-discipline), according to which his whole doctrine is treated.[2] 'It may be doubted', he explains,[3] 'whether the treatment of discipline in the sense of keeping order belongs to pedagogy or should not more appropriately be appended to those parts of practical philosophy which treat of authority in general.' He adds in the *Umriss*[4] that moral improvement is not brought about by the enforcement of authority, and that education can only begin after order has been restored.[5] Later on in the *Allgemeine Pädagogik* he nevertheless concedes[6] that orderliness may have both an indirect and a direct bearing on character; it partly helps to make that instruction possible which will influence the subsequent formation of character, and it serves to create through action or inaction a beginning of character. The separation of the concepts, as Herbart observes,[7] serves to aid the reflection of the educator who ought rather to know what he is about than make a perceptible difference between them in practice.

The distinction between *Regierung* and *Zucht* can be presented in a series of antitheses. The former serves primarily the needs of the teacher, the latter those of the pupil. 'To maintain quiet and order in the lessons, to banish every trace of disrespect to the teacher is the

[1] *Umriss*, § 58.
[2] *Replik gegen Jackmanns Recension.*
[3] *The Science of Education*, p. 94.
[4] Ibid., § 189.
[5] P. 99.
[6] Pp. 230–1.
[7] *Umriss*, § 43.

business of *Regierung*; direct action on the temperament of youth with a view to character training is *Zucht*.'[1] *Regierung* secures merely external conformity, whereas the work of *Zucht* is not to secure a certain mode of external behaviour but rather to develop insight and the appropriate volition in the mind of the pupil.[2] '*Regierung* takes into account the results of actions, later on *Zucht* must look to unexecuted intentions.'[3] *Regierung* is intermittent, whereas *Zucht* is persistent, lasting, slowly insinuating and only abating gradually.[4] The aim of *Regierung* lies in the present, whereas *Zucht* has in view the future adult.[5]

Discipline need not be repressive, and Herbart reviews the various means of maintaining order — supervision, the threat of punishment, compulsion; and concludes : When the environment is so arranged that childish activity can spontaneously discover the road to the useful and expend itself thereon, then discipline is most successful,[6] and in the *Umriss*[7] he sums up : The foundation of control consists in keeping children employed.

Regierung – control or restraint, is, as Herbart from his own experience as a tutor was forced to recognise,[8] a necessary evil, doubtless better than anarchy, but its defect is that it weakens while education seeks to strengthen. It is negative and inhibitive, whereas education should be positive and purposive. Although Herbart's main contribution to the history of school discipline in Britain and America has been through his doctrine of interest, his distinction between *Regierung* and *Zucht*, between good behaviour secured by administrative regulations and gentlemanly conduct exercised by voluntary self-restraint has significance in education, since the term 'discipline' is in English generally employed to convey what was by

---

[1] *The Science of Education*, pp. 238, 239.
[2] Ibid., p. 111.   [3] P. 233.   [4] P. 234.
[5] *Umriss*, § 42. Cf. § 126.   [6] *The Science of Education*, p. 101.
[7] § 46.   [8] *Berichte an Herrn von Steiger*, iii.

Herbart characterised as *Regierung*. A 'well-disciplined' school may be the worst possible institution for the development of character, since it may leave no opportunities for the practice of such actions as are initiated by the pupils' own motives nor afford occasion for the exercise of self-discovery and self-imposed discipline. It does not train the pupils to the right use of such freedom as they will later enjoy; it secures an immediate appearance of docility by paralysing the pupils' power of initiative, and it invites an equally violent reaction that destroys any unity of character that the pupils might otherwise develop. Discipline in Herbart's sense of *Zucht*, not in the sense of *Regierung*, should be the aim of every teacher who desires to play his part in the formation of character.

Before dealing with character training Herbart has to dispel a confusion regarding transcendental freedom. Kant aimed at formulating a metaphysics of ethics; he sought to determine the conditions of the possibility of the moral life, not to trace its actual development. 'Transcendental' was employed by Kant to designate what is a necessary condition of the possibility of experience; but it came to be identified with 'transcendent', that is, what is beyond the limits of experience. Herbart accepted transcendental freedom in Kant's sense, but not in the popular sense. While apparently disagreeing with Kant generally, he was at one with him on fundamentals.

Both Herbart and Kant recognised that morality was the highest aim of mankind, and, accordingly, of education. Freedom is, however, the indispensable postulate of morality. For Kant the only principle that could determine the will without infringing its freedom was pure respect for the law. Any external influence, inclination or desire entering into the motive would deprive the moral law of its sanctity. If therefore pure respect for the law is the only valid motive in morality, the teacher's efforts to influence the character of his pupils would be stultified, for they would import into his pupils' decisions those empirical elements which Kant was at pains to exclude.

This was the dilemma that confronted Herbart. He rebutted it by distinguishing between, and retaining, both the metaphysical and the genetic views of freedom. He supports Kant's metaphysical justification of freedom :[1] Kant's axiom remains externally true — no practical (moral) principle must require the actuality of any object whatever. Kant who strictly opposes the empirical to pure reason, is, he says, right. In the *Allgemeine Pädagogik* he adds :[2] 'It was certainly a mistake to *begin* ethics with this categorical imperative. The purely positive must here take precedence, and many things be unfolded in their relation and sequence which Kant had not thought of. But they who forget themselves so far as to desire the release of mankind from the categorical imperative make a still graver mistake.' The educator must adopt a different standpoint from that of the critical philosopher — for the teacher morality is an occurrence[3] — as Kant himself recognised in his lectures *On Education*.

Herbart rejected the transcendental freedom which implies the possibility of action without motives — 'the will that wills naught would be a self-contradiction',[4] for this would make the pupil's choice arbitrary and wholly indifferent to the influence which education or environment might exert, and render futile all moral training : 'Not the slightest breath of transcendental freedom may blow through any cranny into the domain of character.'[5] But he did this without denying true freedom of the will for he declares :[6] 'Freedom is of the utmost direct importance to the formation of character, provided it issues in

---

[1] 'Aesthetische Darstellung', *The Science of Education*, pp. 63–64.
[2] *The Science of Education*, p. 206.
[3] 'Aesthetische Darstellung', *The Science of Education*, p. 54.
[4] *Minor Pedagogical Works*, p. 99.
[5] Ibid., p. 96.   [6] *Umriss*, § 152.

well-weighed and successful action.' Education, he also states,[1] would be tyranny if it did not lead to freedom. He concludes :[2] 'I must beg some readers not to identify *inner* freedom with *transcendental* freedom.'

The great paradox for Herbart, as for all educators, is to determine the child to the free choice of the good, to render freedom and discipline compatible. The educator is in this sense, as Herbart admits,[3] unavoidably a determinist. Kant in his lectures *On Education* recognised this difficulty : 'One of the great problems of education is how to unite submission to the necessary restraint with the child's capability of exercising his freewill — for restraint is necessary.' And Herbart confesses :[4] 'The author believes he will never be understood by those to whom the coexistence of determinism and morality is still a riddle.' The problem has been formulated by a modern French philosopher :[5] 'The task of the educator is a strange one : to act on mind and conscience in such a way as to render them capable of thinking and judging, of themselves, to determine initiative, arouse spontaneity, and fashion human beings into freedom.'

Just as there was an objective and a subjective aspect of the many-sided interest, so, for Herbart, there is an objective and a subjective side of moral character — that which determines, and that by which it suffers itself to be determined. But, as Herbart reminds us,[6] both what determines and what is determinable have their origin in the circle of thought.

The objective aspect, that which determines the character, comprises the 'practical' or moral ideas. Instead of six types of interests, there are five moral ideas. These

[1] *Berichte an Herrn von Steiger*, i.
[2] *The Science of Education*, p. 263, note.   [3] *Aphorismen*, XIX.
[4] 'Aesthetische Darstellung', *The Science of Education*, p. 77.
[5] E. Boutroux, *Education and Ethics*. English translation by F. Rothwell (London: Williams & Norgate, 1913), p. x.
[6] *The Science of Education*, p. 209.

are (*i*) *Innere Freiheit* (inner freedom), (*ii*) *Vollkommenheit* (perfection or proficiency), (*iii*) *Wohlwollen* (benevolence), (*iv*) *Recht* (justice), (*v*) *Billigkeit* (equity or retribution). The first two deal only with the form and not with the content of moral action ; the other three lie at the base of social order. Distinguishing between inner freedom and transcendental freedom in *The Science of Education*[1] Herbart explains that we are conscious of the former whenever we force ourselves to do our duty against our inclinations. The idea of perfection, he states,[2] implies a high regard for both body and mind and their systematic cultivation ; perfection nevertheless does not connote the complete realisation of the moral ideal but merely the proficiency with which the will is obeyed. Benevolence implies consideration of, or sensitiveness to, others. The idea of justice demands that the pupils abstain from contention, and the idea of equity is especially involved in cases where the pupil has merited punishment as requital for the intentional infliction of pain. The motto of right is 'To every man his own' ; of equity, 'To every man what he deserves',[3] Virtue is the perfect conformity of the will to the moral ideas ; duty is enjoined to overcome hindrances in the attainment of virtue. The moral ideal is, for Herbart, as it was for Plato, not a single virtue but a system of virtues, as the blanket term 'justice' might suggest.

Corresponding to the four formal steps in intellectual instruction are the four stages for training in corporate life ; these are *Merken* (to imprint), *Erwarten* (to antici-

---

[1] P. 263 note.   [2] *Outlines of Educational Doctrine*, § 10.
[3] *The Science of Education*, p. 260.

J. Ruskin in *Unto This Last* interprets Justice by Righteousness, and distinguishes Justice from Equity as follows : The word 'righteousness' properly refers to the justice of rule, or right, as distinguished from 'equity' which refers to the justice of balance. More broadly Righteousness is King's justice ; and Equity Judge's justice : the King guiding or ruling all, the Judge dividing or discerning between opposites (therefore, the double question 'Man, who made me a ruler [δικαστής] or a divider [μεριστής] over you?').

pate), *Fordern* (to desire), *Handeln* (to act).[1] Although Herbart affirms[2] that character is the embodiment of the will, he does not include the will as a separate function among the subjective aspects of character training. He is in this quite logical, for he had denied the existence in the mind of independent faculties and had likewise rejected the 'transcendental' freedom of the will. 'There is no such thing as an independent faculty of will.'[3] The will, for him, is not something apart from desire; 'action generated out of desire is will'.[4] The teacher's task is accordingly to assist the pupil to acquire the right desires, for when opportunity presents itself and the pupil realises that he can attain his end, action follows: 'will is desire combined with the assurance of the attainment of what is desired'.[5] This definition accords almost precisely with that given by a modern psychologist like Stout who defines volition as 'a desire qualified and defined by the judgment that so far as in us lies we shall bring about the attainment of the desired end because we desire it'.[6] The conviction that the desire is capable of fulfilment is based on the success attending previous efforts in similar circumstances, for 'from success springs the confidence of will whereby desire ripens into decision'.[7]

Volition has ultimately its roots in the circle of thought, not indeed in the details one knows, but certainly in the

---

[1] Herbart presents as alternatives to these verbs a series of adjectives, just as to the nouns signifying the four formal steps he offers as alternatives a series of verbs. The scheme with translations of the terms is as follows:

Klarheit (clearness) — *zeigen* (cognise)

Association (association) — *verknüpfen* (integrate)

System (system) — *lehren* (verify)

Methode (method) — *philosophieren* (generalise)

Merken (scan) — *anschaulich* (apprehensible)

Erwarten (expect) — *continuierlich* (mediating)

Fordern (desire) — *erhebend* (evocative)

Handeln (act) — *in die Wirklichkeit eingreifend* (objectifying)

[2] *The Science of Education*, p. 200.   [3] *Umriss*, § 58.
[4] *The Science of Education*, p. 212.   [5] *Lehrbuch*, § 223. Cf. § 107.
[6] *Manual of Psychology*, p. 711.   [7] *Umriss*, § 152.

combinations and total effect of the acquired presentations.[1] Herbart further explains : The circle of thought
comprises the contents that by stages can mount from
interest to desire, and desire through its realisation in
action constitutes volition. The whole inner activity,
indeed, has its abode in the circle of thought.[2] As
instruction forms the circle of thought it plays a part
both in intellectual and in moral training : 'It will be
seen that when the task of setting forth the whole of
virtue is reviewed in its completeness the main things are
accomplished by instruction.'[3] And the test of a perfect
instruction, Herbart concludes,[4] 'is exactly this — that
the store of knowledge and concepts which it has raised
by clearness, association, system and method to the
highest flexibility of thought is, by virtue of the complete
interpenetration of all its parts, at the same time capable
as an organisation of interests of compelling the will with
its utmost energy. Because this is wanting culture is
often the grave of character.'[5]

Educators previous to the time of Herbart had made
the training of character the end of education while
others had recognised the importance of instruction, but
it was left to Herbart to connect instruction with character training through interest and to provide techniques
based on psychological considerations for the attainment
of both. He made the proper selection of the content of
instruction and the right method of presenting the
selected content moral duties incumbent on the teacher,
and contributing factors to the achievement of the aim
which he had envisaged.

[1] *Umriss*, § 58.   [2] *The Science of Education*, p. 213.
[3] *Replik gegen Jackmanns Recension*.
[4] *The Science of Education*, p. 226 note.
[5] Although it contradicts his general position that 'Knowledge is one
thing, virtue is another' (*Discourses on University Education* (Dublin, 1852),
Discourse VI) Newman expresses Herbart's view in referring to 'that moral
persuasiveness which attends on tried and sustained convictions' (*Discourse I*, Introductory).

CHAPTER XI

FROEBEL[1]

WITH as much justification as Herbart, Froebel might have claimed that his educational principles were nothing apart from his philosophy;[2] in fact, when von Raumer issued his rescript in 1851 prohibiting the establishment of kindergartens in Prussia as dangerous to society — with their 'three-year-old demagogues', as a comic paper of the day commented — he did so on the ground that the principle consisted in laying at the foundation of the education of children a highly intricate theory.[3]

The philosophy which Froebel inherited, and by which through his attendance at the University of Jena[4] he could not but be influenced, was the idealism initiated by Kant and developed by Fichte, Schelling and Hegel. A short excursus into this philosophy is requisite to obtain the proper orientation for an adequate appreciation of

[1] 1782–1852. For life, see *Autobiography of Friedrich Froebel*, translated by E. Michaelis and H. K. Moore (London: Swan Sonnenschein, 1886); *Reminiscences of Friedrich Froebel*, by Baroness B. von Marenholz-Bülow, translated by Mrs Horace Mann (Boston: Lee & Shepherd, 1895); *Friedrich Froebel and English Education*, edited by Evelyn Laurence (University of London Press, 1952).

[2] In a letter written at Dresden, 20th January 1839, he says: 'You, my dear wife, could have told this man that, as this system of education, as he said, is clear and palpable to the youngest child, it also contains in itself all philosophy.' Friedrich Froebel, *Letters on the Kindergarten*, translated by E. Michaelis and H. K. Moore (London: Swan Sonnenschein, 1891).

[3] *Reminiscences*, pp. 199–200.

[4] Cf. *Autobiography*, p. 29: 'I studied nothing purely theoretical except mathematics; and of philosophical teaching and thought I learnt only so much as the intercourse of university life brought with it; but it was precisely through this intercourse that I received in various ways a many-sided intellectual impulse.'

Froebel's doctrines although at the outset it must be premised that, by reason of his irregular training, Froebel neither adopted nor developed a consistent philosophic attitude. He continued without ceasing, as he himself explains in a letter to Krause,[1] 'to systematise, symbolise, idealise, realise and recognise identities and analogies amongst all facts and phenomena, all problems, expressions and formulae; and in this way, life with all varied phenomena and activities became more and more free from contradictions, more harmonious, simple and clear, and more recognisable as a part of the life universal'.

The task which Kant set himself was to determine the conditions which made knowledge or experience possible. Locke had assumed that experience was a mere reflection of nature in the form of unrelated impressions, but Hume had demonstrated that this position when logically developed ended in scepticism. The other alternative was that nature must conform to our method of conceiving it. The world of science is found to be arranged in space and time, and its phenomena are connected in a causal series; this arrangement and determination, Kant maintains, results from the fact that the mind is so constituted that it is only thus that experience is possible for it. The world apprehended by the forms of space and time and conceived in accordance with the categories of substance, cause, etc., Kant terms the phenomenal world. He leaves open the possibility of another form of experience by postulating the existence of the noumenal world, a world which cannot be known through perception and understanding, but which might be experienced by an intuitive intelligence.

When we attempt to apply the forms of perception and the categories of the understanding beyond the sphere of the phenomenal world, that is, beyond the range of science, we find that such application gives rise to antinomies or

[1] *Autobiography*, p. 107.

conflicting conclusions apparently logically deduced. We can prove, for example, both that the world had a beginning, and that it had no beginning; that it had a First Cause, and that it had no First Cause; that the soul is a simple substance, and that it is not so. The conclusion which Kant draws from the antinomies is that the conceptions of cause, substance, etc., are valid only within the phenomenal sphere; it is their application beyond this sphere that creates the antinomies; causality is, for example, limited to the scientific world; in another form of experience or in another sphere, for example, the moral, freedom may be possible.

Kant in his *Critique of Pure Reason* thus restricts the application of the conceptions of space, time, substance, cause, etc., to the scientific realm, reserving nevertheless the possibility of the existence of another realm where freedom would be possible, and the immortality of the soul and the existence of God would not be self-contradictory conceptions. Opposed to the phenomenal world he sets the noumenal world, noumena being regarded as mere limiting conceptions implying the possibility of a form of experience other than the material and scientific.

In the *Critique of Practical Reason* Kant maintains that the noumena which in the first *Critique* were merely possible objects in a non-scientific world have positive significance and content. We find in the ethical sphere the conception of duty, a positive conception which in its nature implies freedom. Thus for Kant there are two spheres in which man lives, the phenomenal or scientific world governed by the conception of cause, and the noumenal or ethical world characterised by freedom. Kant fails to relate these two spheres satisfactorily to each other, but to him is due the credit of demonstrating that either alone is incomplete. He made materialism and naturalism as adequate philosophical explanations untenable, and by establishing the priority of the ethical life and the reality of the spiritual realm laid the foundation of modern idealism. The educational corollary of Kant's doctrine[1] is that in opposition to, but not incompatible with, a mechanical concatenation of external phenomena stands the free inner synthetic or creative activity of mind.[2]

The task set to his successors was to resolve the dualism inherent in Kant's system. His naturalistic and realistic interpreters, on the one hand, relying mainly on the first *Critique*, insisted on the connectedness and completeness of the phenomenal world, and resolved the realities of the noumenal or intelligible world — God, freedom and immortality — into mere serviceable illusions. Fichte, on the other hand, relying on the supremacy of the practical (moral) reason, emphasised the noumenal character of the intelligible world to such an extent as to reduce the phenomenal world to a mere appearance or illusion. The free activity of reason or self-consciousness could not, in Fichte's view, be conditioned by anything alien to itself. He consequently assumed that the object which consciousness demanded as a necessary condition of its own existence and progressive realisation was not a mere sensuous element externally 'given', but a product of the self-estranging process of consciousness itself.

While Schelling's standpoint was at the outset practically identical with that of Fichte, in his later writings he sought to correct the overstatement of Fichte which tended to reduce nature to a nonentity, by insisting that the Absolute manifests itself equally in nature and in spirit, and that the intelligence could find itself in nature as well as in itself. That Froebel was influenced by Schelling is

[1] Of Kant, even more than of Locke, it can be said that his philosophy was more influential than his education. Fichte has remarked (*The Educational Theory of J. G. Fichte*, by G. H. Turnbull, (University of Liverpool Press, 1926), pp. 8–9, 16), that Kant had no influence on Pestalozzi's development. That may be so, and any similarity in their views may be explained by the fact that both were disciples of Rousseau.

[2] Froebel in his *Autobiography* (p. 93) states that even in military exercises 'I could see freedom beneath their recognised necessity'!

beyond doubt, for in his *Autobiography*[1] he admits that he was acquainted with Schelling's work *On the World Soul*, stating 'what I read in that book moved me profoundly, and I thought I understood it'. In this work 'Schelling', it is said,[2] 'seeks mainly for a principle which shall reduce the whole of nature to unity. This principle must not be sought in any transcendental, supernatural region, whether called God or Fate, but in nature itself. A principle such as is sought Schelling seemed to find in a conception of matter as a unity of opposite forces, and hence he naturally attempted to reduce all the varied phenomena of nature to the single principle of a force that always manifests itself in opposite directions. Accordingly nature must no longer be divided up into separate groups of phenomena, with a special kind of force for each — mechanical, chemical, electrical, vital — but in all must be seen the same force in various forms, the same unity in duality. . . . In making the idea of force the supreme principle of nature Schelling has manifestly stripped that conception of its purely mechanical connotation, and thus it becomes practically identical with the idea of nature as an eternal process or manifestation of self-activity.' Schelling takes the aesthetic view of nature according to which reality is regarded as a living whole, as the expression throughout of spirit, the highest reach of thought, and the final attitude of speculation; Froebel likewise employs aesthetic metaphor to explain the relation of the world to God. Thus he states:[3] 'The relation of nature to God may be truly and clearly perceived and recognised by man in the study and elucidation of the innermost spiritual relation of a genuine human work of art to the artist.'

In Hegel[4] the idealism of Kant finds its consummation

[1] P. 40.

[2] J. Watson, *Schelling's Transcendental Idealism* (Chicago: S. C. Griggs & Co., 1882), pp. 95–96.   [3] *The Education of Man*, p. 153.

[4] 1770–1831. J. N. Findlay, *Hegel: A Re-examination* (London: George Allen & Unwin Ltd, 1958).

and completest expression. Instead of two realms — a natural and a spiritual — as with Kant, there is, for Hegel, only one form of existence, the spiritual, and it comprises the natural. The ultimate source of all being and of all knowing is Mind or the Absolute. It is analogous to Plato's 'Idea of the Good', and it is significant that in introducing the couplet — 'the real is the rational and the rational is real' — Hegel refers to Plato.[1] 'The Absolute', he explains,[2] 'is Mind (Spirit) — this is the supreme definition of the Absolute. To find this definition and to grasp its meaning and burthen is, we may say, the ultimate purpose of all education and all philosophy.'[3]

The dedication of Froebel's *The Education of Man*[4] — '*Ihm*', — might refer to Hegel's Absolute, while the opening paragraph expresses in vague terminology the Hegelian standpoint: 'The whole world — the All, the Universe — is a single great organism in which an eternal Uniformity manifests itself. This principle of uniformity expresses itself as much in external nature as in spirit. Life is the union of the spiritual with the material. Without mind or spirit matter is lifeless; it remains formless, it is mere chaos. Only through the entrance of the spiritual into the material does the cosmos originate. Spirit manifests itself in order. Every creature, every object is matter informed by spirit. . . . God is the presupposition, the condition of their existence. Without God they would not exist. God is the one ground of all

[1] *Hegel's Philosophy of Right*, translated by S. W. Dyde (London: George Bell & Sons, 1896), author's Preface, p. xxvii.

[2] *Hegel's Philosophy of Mind*, by W. Wallace (Oxford University Press, 1894), p. 7.

[3] Ibid., p. 11: 'The sphere of education is the individuals only; and its aim is to bring the universal mind to exist in them.' For Hegel's views on education see F. L. Luqueer, *Hegel as Educator* (London: Macmillan & Co., 1896).

[4] F. Froebel, *The Education of Man*, translated by W. N. Hailman (New York: D. Appleton & Co., 1909).

things. God is the all-comprehending, the all-sustaining. God is the essential nature, the meaning of the world.'

As the truth for Hegel is the whole, Mind or the Absolute cannot be contained within any fragmentary form of existence, and the effort to realise itself more and more adequately by successive stages follows a definite pattern, the dialectical movement. For Plato, as we have seen, dialectic was a search after the true and the real; the mediaevalists, unmindful of Plato's warning that dialectic was not a suitable study for the young, included it in the *trivium*, the earlier of the scholastic disciplines, with the result, as Plato predicted, that it degenerated into an exercise of solving intellectual riddles; it became a method of disputation instead of a method of discovery.[1] The Hegelian dialectic is a movement of thought of a unique type.[2] The impasse which results when categories applicable in one sphere are indiscriminately applied in other spheres, illustrated by Kant's antinomies, Hegel regarded as characteristic not only of Kant's Ideas of Reason but even of all thought. 'Collisions, in fact, belong to the nature of thought, the nature of consciousness and its dialectic.'[3] A transition into its opposite is

[1] Bertrand Russell in *History of Western Philosophy* (London: Allen & Unwin, 1946), p. 456, enumerates the defects of the scholastic dialectic: indifference to facts and science, belief in reasoning in matters which only observation can decide, and an undue emphasis on verbal distinctions and subtleties.   [2] Cf. Findlay, op. cit., pp. 68–71.

[3] *The Philosophy of Right*, § 211, addition.

Karl Marx adopted the Hegelian dialectic but applied it in the economic field, hence the dialectical materialism of modern communism. The dialectical method supports a revolutionary view of human progress, one extreme inviting another. It was abandoned by later idealists in favour of evolutionary development under the influence of Darwin's *The Origin of Species* (1859).

The dialectical method has apparently an attraction for some modern writers on education who would not care to be aligned with Hegel or Karl Marx. Cf. Sir Richard Livingstone, *Education for a World Adrift* (Cambridge University Press, 1943), p. 118; Basil A. Fletcher, *Education and Crisis* (University of London Press, 1946).

Other conceptions of development of which education has availed itself are the 'cyclical' and 'recapitulation'.

the result of extending a conception beyond its legitimate sphere. This 'law of opposites' Froebel freely exploited. 'Everything and every being comes to be known only as it is connected with the opposite of its kind, and as its unity, its agreement with its opposite, is discovered.'[1] Opposites have nevertheless significance only within a more inclusive unity; there can be no opposition between something in this room and something in next week. Hence the triadic structure of the Hegelian dialectic: the 'thesis'; this necessarily calls forth its opposite, 'the antithesis'; and the reconciliation of thesis and antithesis in a more comprehensive concept, the 'synthesis'. Froebel exemplifies this dialectical movement in his various writings: the child is a child of nature, a human child and a child of God.[2] Morality mediates between religion and practical efficiency.[3] The selection of objects constituting the second 'gift' is determined by the same sequence of triads. 'The sphere and the cube are pure opposites. They stand to each other in the relation of unity and plurality, but especially of movement and rest, of round and straight. The law of connection demands for these two objects of play a connecting one, which is the cylinder. It combines unity complete in itself in the round surface, and plurality in the two straight ones.'[4]

When the close analogy between his law of opposites with their reconciliation in a higher unity and the dialectical movement of thought in Hegel's philosophy was indicated by a visitor to his Kindergarten at Liebenstein in 1851, Froebel, while not disclaiming acquaintance with Hegel's principle, is reported[5] to have replied that

[1] *The Education of Man*, p. 42.

[2] *The Pedagogics of the Kindergarten*, translated by Josephine Jarvis (London: Edward Arnold & Co., 1900), p. 11.

[3] *The Education of Man*, ch. i.

[4] *Education by Development*, the second part of the *Pedagogics of the Kindergarten*, translated by Josephine Jarvis (New York: D. Appleton & Co., 1905), p. 204. Cf. p. 286. [5] *Reminiscences*, p. 225.

he did not know how Hegel had formulated and applied this law, as he had had no time for the study of the latter's system. This may well have been the case, since the idea of antithesis and their reconciliation in a higher synthesis is not peculiar to Hegel but is common to Fichte and Schelling.

With Krause, a philosopher almost unknown to English students of philosophy, Froebel was acquainted and maintained a correspondence. To one of Froebel's letters to Krause[1] we owe a knowledge of many of the autobiographical details of Froebel's life; that Krause's writings and his acquaintance with Froebel had an influence upon the latter, is acknowledged by Baroness B. von Marenholz-Bülow[2] in her *Reminiscences of Friedrich Froebel*, who explains that Krause's writings even lent expression to Froebel's views, in formulating which the latter experienced much difficulty. For Krause, 'this gentlest and humanest thinker of the nineteenth century',[3] everything exists in God. The world is not, however, God Himself, but it is only in and through God. Reason and nature are the two highest hemispheres of the world as they exist in God, bright and powerful as God's actual image and likeness. Nature is as holy, as worthy, as divine as reason. The life of reason is not lawless caprice nor the life of nature dead necessity; in both are recognised divine freedom and beauty. A parallelism obtains between the power and works of nature and of reason. This parallelism is necsesary and abiding, because both nature and reason exhibit the same essential being of the Deity. Man is the living unity of the two, and the inmost and most glorious part of that harmony of reason and nature which is established by God.

The further movement of Krause's thought may be inferred from Baroness von Marenholz-Bülow's statement

[1] 24th March 1828. See *Autobiography*, pp. 104–26.

[2] *Reminiscences*, p. 247.

[3] K. C. F. Krause, *The Ideal of Humanity and Universal Federation*, translated by W. Hastie (Edinburgh: T. & T. Clark, 1900), translator's Preface.

of his relation to Froebel. 'The theory in which Froebel and Krause agreed especially', she says,[1] 'is the idea of the analogy existing between organic development in nature and organic development in the spiritual world, and according to which the historical development of mankind had proceeded, obeying the same laws as those of nature and its organisms. The same logic of the one all-penetrating Divine reason rules in both, unconscious in the one (nature), conscious to itself in the other (mind). Therefore are the opposites ruling everywhere, not absolute, but relative, and always find connection or solution in the process of life.'

In direct contrast to Locke and Herbart, who assume that the mind is built up out of presentations, Froebel maintains that the mind unfolds from within according to a pre-determined pattern. 'All the child is ever to be and become, lies, however slightly indicated, in the child, and can be attained only through development from within outward.'[2] The pattern followed is that known as pre-formation according to which the germ contains in miniature the fully developed plant or animal, point for point. Thus in *The Pedagogics of the Kindergarten* he says : 'The tree germ bears within itself the nature of the whole tree'; 'the development and formation of the whole future life of each being is contained in the beginning of its existence'.[3] The development of the individual also parallels the course of development of the race. 'In the development of the inner life of the individual man the history of the spiritual development of the race is repeated.' It is also a continuous process. 'It is highly important',[4] Froebel affirms,[5] 'that man's development

[1] *Reminiscences*, p. 248.   [2] *The Education of Man*, p. 68.
[3] Pp. 5, 6. This is a biological formulation of predetermined development, the psychological equivalent of which is maturation ; for criticism of predetermined development see J. McV. Hunt, *Intelligence and Experience* (New York: The Ronald Press, 1961).
[4] *The Education of Man*, p. 160. Cf. pp. 40–41.   [5] Ibid., p. 27.

should proceed continuously from one point, and that this continuous progress be seen and ever guarded. Sharp limits and definite subdivisions within the continuous series of the years of development, withdrawing from attention the permanent continuity, the living connection, the inner living essence, are therefore highly pernicious, and even destructive in their influence.'

All creatures have one function only — to express the spiritual, the Divine, that slumbers in them. The aim of education accordingly consists solely in so treating man as to awaken in him his spiritual nature. 'Surely the nature of man is in itself good', Froebel declares.[1] This view of the innate goodness of the child Froebel doubtless acquired from Rousseau, with its corollary for the early stages of development — negative education. Were man's inner and divine nature not marred by untoward external influences, the ideal education would be passive, non-interfering. 'Indeed, in its very essence education should have these characteristics; for the undisturbed operation of the Divine Unity is necessarily good — cannot be otherwise than good.'[2]

This ideal condition of affairs but seldom obtains. 'Nature', Froebel admits,[3] 'rarely shows us that unmarred original state, especially in man; but it is for this reason only the more necessary to assume its existence in every human being until the opposite has been clearly shown; otherwise that unmarred original state where it might exist contrary to our expectation, might be easily impaired.' When, however, it is clearly established that the original nature of the individual has been marred,[4] then Froebel does not hesitate to prescribe categorical, mandatory education in its full severity.

As Kant's imperative was categorical, and his moral law was valid only for a free being who voluntarily imposed it on himself, so for Froebel 'in its inner essence the

[1] P. 120.   [2] Pp. 7–8.   [3] P. 9.   [4] P. 10.

living thought, the eternal spiritual ideal, ought to be and is categorical and mandatory in its manifestations. . . . The ideal becomes mandatory only where it supposes that the person addressed enters into the reason of the requirement with serene, childlike faith, or with clear, manly insight. It is true, in word or example, the ideal is mandatory in all these cases, but always only with reference to the spirit and inner life, never with reference to outer form.'[1]

As freedom is obedience to a law which is in conformity with our highest nature and as such is self-imposed, or, as Hegel puts it, as 'freedom is the truth of necessity', so for Froebel[2] 'in good education, in genuine instruction, in true training, necessity should call forth freedom; law, self-determination; external compulsion, inner free-will; external hate, inner love. Where hatred brings forth hatred; law, dishonesty and crime; compulsion, slavery; necessity, servitude; where oppression destroys and debases; where severity and harshness give rise to stubbornness and deceit — all education is abortive. In order to avoid the latter and to secure the former, all prescription should be adapted to the pupil's nature and needs, and enlist his cooperation. This is the case when education in instruction and training, in spite of its necessarily categorical character, bears in all details and ramifications the irrefutable and irresistible impress that the one who makes the demand is himself strictly unavoidably subject to an eternally ruling law, to an unavoidable eternal necessity, and that, therefore, all despotism is banished.'

While Froebel emphasises the principle of continuity in development, this does not deter him from recognising well-marked stages in development and agreeing with Rousseau that each stage should be fully exploited before advance is made to the succeeding stage, otherwise diffi-

[1] *The Education of Man*, p. 13.   [2] Ibid., p. 13.

culties will be created which it will be impossible later to rectify. The stages recognised by Froebel, namely, infancy, childhood, boyhood, youth, corresponded to Rousseau's divisions in the *Émile*. For Rousseau the activity characteristic of infancy is habit; for Froebel it is sensory development. Froebel's account of sensory development is highly artificial, the result of an attempt to impose on it the dialectical form. Childhood, the second stage, is distinguished from infancy by the appearance of language; it is then the child begins to represent the internal outwardly. Actual education now begins, attention and watchful care being less directed to the body than to the mind.[1] Speech training should now be begun. Each object should be given its appropriate name, and each word should be uttered clearly and distinctly. Pestalozzi was criticised by Fichte for regarding the name as an attribute of *Anschauung*, but on pedagogical grounds Froebel supports Pestalozzi, maintaining that to the child a name is still one with the thing,[2] and that the name creates the thing for the child.[3] He adds in *The Pedagogics of the Kindergarten*[4] that the name defines the object by connecting it with something familiar. The pre-eminent activity of the childhood stage of development is nevertheless play, and it is in treating of childhood in *The Education of Man* that Froebel enters a plea for the place of play in education.

Play is the characteristic activity of childhood : it is, says Froebel,[5] 'the highest phase of child-development — of human development at this period ; for it is self-active representation of the inner — representation of the inner

---

[1] P. 50. [2] P. 54. [3] P. 91. [4] P. 176.

[5] P. 55. Cf. Montaigne, *Essays*, Bk I, ch. 22 : We must take note that the games of children are not games in their eyes ; and we must regard these are their most serious actions.'

Also Locke, *Thoughts*, § 130 : 'All the plays and diversions of childhood should be directed towards good and useful habits, or else they will introduce ill ones.'

from inner necessity and impulse. Play is the purest, most spiritual activity of man at this stage, and, at the same time, typical of human life as a whole — of the inner hidden natural life in man and all things. It gives, therefore, joy, freedom, contentment, inner and outer rest, peace with the world. It holds the source of all that is good.'

To have educative value the play of the child must not be a purposeless activity; his play impulses must be directed and controlled by the employment of definite material necessitating an orderly sequence in the feelings engendered and in the activities exercised. 'Without rational, conscious guidance', Froebel is reported to have said,[1] 'childish activity degenerates into aimless play instead of preparing for those tasks of life for which it is destined. . . . In the Kindergarten the children are guided to bring out their plays in such a manner as really to reach the aim desired by nature, that is, to serve for their development. . . . Human education needs a guide which I think I have found in a general law of development that rules both in nature and in the intellectual world. Without law-abiding guidance there is no free development.'[2]

It was on the transition to adolescence that Rousseau inverted his procedure, experience henceforth to be acquired at second-hand, not first-hand. At a stage earlier than Rousseau, namely, at the transition from childhood to boyhood, Froebel proposes a similar inversion. Whereas the period of childhood is characterised as predominantly that of life for the sake of living, for making the internal external, the period of boyhood is predominantly the period for learning, for making the external internal.[3]

[1] *Reminiscences*, pp. 67–68.

[2] For the distinction between playing at teaching and teaching by play see Herbert Read, *Education Through Art* (London: Faber & Faber, 1943), p. 219; also J. Dewey, *Democracy and Education* (New York: The Macmillan Co., 1916), p. 230.

[3] *The Education of Man*, p. 94.

Here we have an illustration of Froebel's law of opposites. Education is no longer to be determined by endowment; it is to be environmentally determined. It is no longer to be child-centred; it is henceforth to be curriculum-centred. Actually it is both endowment and environmentally determined from the outset, and in *The Pedagogics of the Kindergarten*[1] Froebel virtually admits this through his recognition of a third or synthesising stage. 'Another fundamental idea is that all knowledge and comprehension of life are connected with making the internal external, the external internal, and with perceiving the harmony and accord of both.'

While play is the characteristic activity of childhood, work is that of boyhood. Interest in the process gives place to interest in the product. 'What formerly the child did for the sake of the activity, the boy now does for the sake of the result or product of his activity.'[2] 'If activity brought joy to the child, work now gives delight to the boy.'[3] Whereas during the previous period of childhood the aim of play consisted simply in activity as such, the aim lies now in a definite, conscious purpose.[4] The contrast is forced. Work is regarded as directed and purposive, whereas, in disregard of his previous statements on play, play is now simply an 'activity as such'. The distinction is likewise invalid. The more extended range of the pupil's environment has provided him with new patterns of activity in the shape of vocational occupations to be imitated; for the boy these are another form of play, not work in the sense of his parents' work. The pupil's activities at the boyhood stage are self-selected,

[1] Ibid., p. 174.   [2] P. 99.
[3] P. 102.   [4] P. 112.

Cf., however, J. McV. Hunt, *Intelligence and Experience*, p. 176. 'When the child instead of playfully using a chip of wood to represent a boat in his play, makes something approximating a boat by hollowing out the wood and putting on a sail, he is moving from the realm of playful assimilation towards that of imitation and work.'

their products have no economic significance, and their features are characteristic of play. In childhood the pupil imitates domestic activities, in boyhood neighbourhood occupations. This supports the conclusion that his development is determined, as indicated above, by the widening range of environment rather than by a sudden transition from inner experience to outer. There is, however, for Froebel a unity transcending the opposition between play and work, for both he regards as means to the individual's self-realisation. 'Man works', he affirms,[1] 'only that his spiritual divine essence may assume outward form, and that thus he may be enabled to recognise his own spiritual, divine nature and the innermost being of God.'[2]

The activities in which the boy engages have all the characteristics of projects — practical problems involving co-operative effort and affording intellectual and moral training. 'If in his former activity (in childhood) he emulated phases of domestic life, in his present activity (in boyhood) he shares the work of the house — lifting, pulling, carrying, digging, splitting.'[3] Even building a hut is instanced, and this justifies the claim of an American writer that Froebel, particularly in his *Education of Man*, has given the world no mean anticipation of Dewey's own school.[4]

The other main feature of boyhood education is instruction. It too serves to mark the transition from making the internal external to making the external internal. 'Instruction is conducted not so much in accordance with the nature of man as in accordance with the fixed, definite, clear *laws* in the nature of things,

[1] *The Education of Man*, p. 32.

[2] For the fallacies in the sharp opposition of play and work see J. Dewey, *How We Think* (London: D. C. Heath & Co., 1909), pp. 213–14.

[3] *The Education of Man*, pp. 101, 106, 113

[4] *The Philosophy of John Dewey*, edited by Paul Schlipp (Evanston: Northwestern University Press, 1939), p. 453.

and more particularly the laws to which man and things are equally subject. It is conducted in accordance with fixed and definite conditions lying *outside* the human being.'[1]

Although Rousseau had dispensed with a predetermined curriculum, in sketching Émile's development he incidentally indicates his attitude to the teaching of various subjects. Froebel in describing his pupil's life and education from the developmental standpoint likewise proposes various educational occupations and expounds his attitude to these. In addition he provides a more independent and systematic treatment of the subjects of the curriculum than did Rousseau. The subjects, it must be premised, are not to be regarded as ends in themselves; they are merely instrumental to the full realisation of the pupil's personality.

Froebel was an early advocate of the inclusion of manual instruction in the school curriculum. Manual work is a necessary condition of the realisation of the pupil's personality; through it he comes to himself. 'Every child, boy, and youth, whatever his condition or position in life, should devote daily at least one or two hours to some serious activity in the production of some definite external piece of work. . . . Children — mankind, indeed — are at present too much and too variously concerned with aimless and purposeless pursuits, and too little with work. Children and parents consider the activity of actual work so much to their disadvantage, and so unimportant for their future conditions of life, that educational institutions should make it one of their most constant endeavours to dispel this delusion. The domestic and scholastic education of our time leads children to indolence and laziness; a vast amount of human power thereby remains undeveloped and is lost.'[2]

[1] *The Education of Man*, pp. 94–95.
[2] Ibid., pp. 34–35. Cf. pp. 236–7.

In addition to manual instruction Froebel also recommends the introduction of such subjects as drawing, nature study and school gardening. He insists, like Herbart, on an all-round development as the aim of education, and as the main divisions of an educational curriculum he enumerates (a) religion and religious instruction, (b) natural science and mathematics, (c) language, (d) art and objects of art, remarking[1] that human education requires the knowledge and appreciation of religion, nature and language ; and with reference to instruction in art he states the aim :[2] 'Its intention will not be to make each pupil an artist in some one or all of the arts, but to secure to each human being full and all-sided development.'

Froebel did not complete *The Education of Man* by treating of adolescence but devoted the later part of his life to founding the Kindergarten[3] on which his fame mainly rests. Froebel considered 'childhood as the most important stage of the total development of man and humanity',[4] and in his *Reminiscences*[5] he gives his reason : 'The earliest age is the most important one for education, because the beginning decides the manner of progress and the end. If national order is to be recognised in later years as a benefit, childhood must first be accustomed to law and order, and therein find means of freedom'. For this stage of childhood he devised his gifts, the first being the soft ball, the second the sphere, the cube and the cylinder.

Not only does Froebel in his gifts anthropomorphise

---

[1] *The Education of Man*, p. 210.   [2] Ibid., p. 228.
[3] The name 'Kindergarten' came to Froebel one spring day in 1840 as with some friends he was proceeding from Keilhau to Blankenburg when from a hill he saw the valley of the Rinne, a tributary of the Saale, stretching out before him like a great garden and exclaimed, 'I have found it. Kindergarten shall the name be.' J. Prüfer, *Friedrich Fröbel: sein Leben und Schaffen* (Leipzig, 1927), p. 92. Prüfer also argues that it was not till 1843 that the institution of the Kindergarten, as we now know it, was founded, the date usually given — 1840 — being '*durchaus unrichtig*'. P. 89.
[4] *The Pedagogics of the Kindergarten*, p. 95.   [5] P. 143.

playthings and assume that children will be able to appreciate the symbolism involved,[1] but he also believes that the quasi-philosophic conceptions which underlie the games will impress themselves on the child's mind and determine his attitude to life. So obsessed is Froebel with his philosophical formulae that his psychological insight cannot save him from such absurdities as assuming that the child when dealing with the second gift, that is, during the second half of the first year of his life, has some dim perception of the nature and destiny of man.[2] In his account of the same gift he affirms :[3] man himself 'in play, even as a child, by play should perceive within and without how from unity proceed manifoldness, plurality, and totality, and how plurality and manifoldness finally are found again in and resolve themselves into unity and should find this out in life'. In reviewing the first gifts he observes :[4] 'In and by means of the ball (as an object resting in itself, easily movable, especially elastic, bright, and warm) the child perceives his life, his power, his activity, and that of his senses, at the first stage of his consciousness, in their unity, and thus exercises them. . . . The ball is therefore to the child a representative or a means of perception of a single effect caused by a single power. The sphere is to the child the representative of every isolated simple unity ; the child gets a hint in the sphere of the manifoldness as still abiding in unity. The cube is to the child the representative of each continually developing manifold body. The child has an intimation in it of the unity which lies at the foundation of all manifoldness, and from which the latter proceeds. In sphere and cube, considered in comparison with each other, is presented in outward view to the child the

[1] For criticism of Froebel's use of symbolism see W. H. Kilpatrick, *Froebel's Kindergarten Principles Critically Examined* (New York : The Macmillan Co., 1916).
[2] *The Pedagogics of the Kindergarten*, p. 92.
[3] Ibid., p. 98.   [4] P. 105.

resemblance between opposites which is so important for his whole future life, and which he perceives everywhere around himself, and multifariously within himself.'

By his methodological arrangement of the gifts and occupations[1] Froebel nevertheless founded a new type of educational institution, and although his system too readily lent itself to formalism with later generations of teachers who had not the spirit of the master, it ameliorated the lot of countless children. On the ground of its excessive symbolism his theory is open to criticism. Although, as Dewey says,[2] his love of abstract symbolism often got the better of his sympathetic insight, 'Froebel's recognition of the significance of the native capacities of children, his loving attention to them, and his influence in inducing others to study them, represent perhaps the most effective single force in modern educational theory in effecting widespread acknowledgment of the idea of growth.'

[1] Cf. *The Pedagogics of the Kindergarten*, pp. 233–4: 'A want of classification is the bane of all combination plays for children which have till now been known to me, and the said plays lose by this their formative influence for spirit and mind, as well as their applicability for life.'

[2] *Democracy and Education*, pp. 67–68.

CHAPTER XII

MONTESSORI[1]

FROEBEL died in 1852, Montessori in 1952. The intervening century brought about a complete change in the social background of education, Froebel's Kindergarten being founded at Blankenburg — charmingly situated at the entrance to the Schwarza Tal, one of the most picturesque and beautifully wooded valleys of Thuringia, Montessori's House of Childhood in the slums of a European capital. The contrast determined their respective standpoints. In an ideal rural environment Froebel centred attention mainly on the endowment and development of the child. Montessori on the other hand shifts the centre of gravity of her system to the environment. Thus in *The Secret of Childhood* she affirms:[2] 'Our own method of education is characterised by the central importance that we attribute to the question of environment; . . . it is well-known how our pedagogy considers the environment so important as to make it the central point of the whole system.'

To remove the social evils of the poorest quarters of Rome, the Association of Good Building was formed, its plan being to acquire tenements, remodel them, put them into a productive condition and administer them in the interests of the occupier.[3] The care of the reconstructed

[1] 1870–1952. E. M. Standing, *Maria Montessori: her Life and Work* (London: Hollis & Carter, 1957).

[2] M. Montessori, *The Secret of Childhood*, translated and edited by Barbara B. Carter (London: Longmans, Green & Co., 1936), pp. 69, 137.

[3] M. Montessori, *The Montessori Method*, translated by Anne E. George (London: William Heinemann, 1912), p. 56.

tenements was given to the tenants, and they did not abuse their trust. Difficulties nevertheless arose in regard to young children under school age. Left to themselves during the day, and unable to appreciate the motives which led their parents to respect the property, such children spent their time defacing the buildings. To cure this evil it occurred to the Director General of the Roman Association for Good Building 'to gather together in a large room all the little ones between the ages of three and seven belonging to the families living in the tenement. The play and the work of these children were to be carried on under the guidance of a teacher who should have her own apartment in the tenement house.'[1] Thus came to be instituted the House of Childhood — the school within the tenement. The expenses of the new institution were met, in accordance with the general self-supporting principle of the reconstruction scheme, by the sum that the Association would otherwise have been forced to expend upon redecoration and repairs.

Towards the end of 1906[2] the Director General of the Roman Association of Good Building entrusted to Montessori the organisation of the infant schools in the model tenements in Rome. The method adopted by her was determined by her training and previous experience. Montessori, having graduated in Medicine, was for a time in charge of the training of mentally defective children. Her success with these was remarkable. She taught a number of such children to read and write so efficiently that they were able to be presented for examination with normal children of the same age, and this pheno-menal result was attributed to the fact that her pupils had been taught by an improved method. She there-fore conjectured that if the methods employed with

[1] P. 43. All references in this chapter not otherwise indicated are to *The Montessori Method*.
[2] The first House of Childhood was opened on 6th January 1907.

defective children were applied in the training of
normal children, they would yield even more surprising
results.[1]

To be successful these methods should obviously be
applied with children at a mental level corresponding
somewhat to the stage of development of deficients, that
is, they should be employed in the training of infants;
at this period of life the child has not acquired the co-
ordination of muscular movements necessary to enable
him to perform deftly the ordinary acts of life, his sensory
organs are not fully developed, his emotional life is still
unstable and his volitional powers irresolute. The significance of the pedagogical experiment for which the
institution of the House of Childhood afforded the
facilities lies in this, Montessori explains:[2] 'It represents
the results of a series of trials made in the education
of young children, with methods already used with
deficients.'

Such an application to normal children of the methods
found successful with deficients was contemplated by the
earliest workers engaged in the education of the feeble-
minded. Thus, at the laying of the foundation stone of
the first American schools for defectives in 1854, the Rev.
Samuel J. May, basing his argument on the theological
or metaphysical doctrine that evil is never an end in
itself but always a means to some higher good, ventured to
declare with an emphasis somewhat enhanced, he admits,
by a lurking distrust of the prediction, that the time would
come when access would be found to the idiotic brain,
the light of intelligence admitted into its dark chambers
and the whole race be benefited by some new discovery
on the nature of mind.[3] This hope had been anticipated

[1] Cf. M. Montessori, *The Advanced Montessori Method*, translated by
Florence Simmonds and Lily Hutchinson (London: William Heinemann,
1917), vol. i, ch. 3. [2] P. 45.

[3] E. Séguin, *Idiocy: and its Treatment by the Physiological Method* (Columbia
University Teachers College Educational Reprints), pp. 10–11.

by Séguin in his treatise on Idiocy published in 1846 :[1]
'If it were possible that in endeavouring to solve the
simple question of the education of idiots we had found
terms precise enough that it were only necessary to
generalise them to obtain a formula applicable to universal
education, then, not only would we in our humble sphere
have rendered some little service, but we would besides
have prepared the elements for a method of physiological
education for mankind. Nothing would remain but to
write it.'[2]

Before proceeding to elaborate the principles underlying the Montessori method we should perhaps recall
the fact that the child under school age usually acquires
unaided an education which, if somewhat unsystematic
in character, is nevertheless not inconsiderable in amount.
When such early education is consciously controlled and
systematically directed, the results may be remarkable.

By discovering the main characteristics of the training
of defective children we shall have the key to the Montessori method. The first principle is to train the pupil to
be independent of others in respect of the ordinary
practices of life ; it appears also to necessitate approach
to the child mind at a lower level than can be adopted
with normal children, an appeal to the senses rather than
to the intellect. With physically defective children it
implies training one sense to function vicariously for
another ; for example, with deaf children, teaching words
not by hearing the sounds but by feeling the vibrations
of the larynx of the speaker. The ultimate reference is
to the sense of touch, which is regarded as fundamental
and primordial. The Montessori system accordingly
becomes an 'education by touch'. Montessori maintains

---

[1] *Idiocy*, p. 24. Cf. H. Holman, *Séguin and his Physiological Method* (London :
Sir Isaac Pitman, 1914).

[2] Cf. *Advanced Montessori Method*, vol. i, p. 81. 'The long, occult experiment — suggested to me by Itard and Séguin — is, in fact, my initial contribution to education.'

that the sense of touch is fundamental, that it undergoes great development during the early years of life, and that, if neglected at this age, it loses its susceptibility to future training.

Séguin, of whom Montessori claims to be a disciple, had designated his treatment of the feeble-minded as the physiological method. Recognising the advance which Montessori has made, and her adaptation to the training of normal children of a procedure specially devised for deficient children, we may characterise her method as the psychological method. Pestalozzi had sought to psychologise education but, as in his day there existed no psychology of the school child, he ended by mechanising instruction, and the methods which were successful with him failed with teachers of a later age.

The psychological method in education implies that the educative process is adapted to the stage of mental development of the child, and to his interests, and is not wholly subordinated to the necessities of a curriculum or to the teacher's scheme of work. 'By education', says Montessori,[1] 'must be understood the active help given to the normal expansion of the life of the child.' The 'psychological moment' in the educative process comes when consciousness of a need arises in the child's experience. 'It is necessary then', in the Montessori method, 'to offer those exercises which correspond to the need of development felt by an organism, and if the child's age has carried him past a certain need, it is never possible to obtain, in its fulness, a development which missed its proper moment;'[2] and, if a child fails to perform a task or to appreciate the truth of a principle, the teacher must not make him conscious of his error by repeating the lesson; she must assume that the task has been presented prematurely, and, before again presenting the stimulus, await the manifestation of the symptoms which indicate

[1] P. 104.   [2] P. 358.

that the need exists. The duration of a process is determined not by the exigencies of an authorised time-table, but by the interval which the child finds requisite to exhaust his interest. Thus in a Montessori school we may find a pupil working unremittingly at a self-imposed task for several days on end.

A further consequence of the adoption of the psychological standpoint is that there are in the Montessori system no prizes. The pupil's sense of mastery is his highest reward: 'His own self-development is his true and almost his only pleasure.'[1] Such correction as is admitted in the Montessori system comes from the material, not from the teacher. 'From the "Children's Houses" the old-time teacher who wore herself out maintaining discipline of immobility and wasting her breath in loud and continual discourse, has disappeared, and the didactic material which contains within itself the control of errors is substituted, making auto-education possible to each child.'[2] This is the principle of Rousseau and of Spencer, not, however, as by them confined to moral misdemeanours, that the child should meet with no obstacles other than physical; it is an intellectual 'discipline by consequences'.

The psychological method implies the perfect freedom of the child, the freedom which consists in absolute obedience to the laws of the development of his own nature. 'The method of observation (that is, the psychological method) is established upon one fundamental base — the liberty of the pupils in their spontaneous manifestations.'[3] This liberty necessitates independence of action on the part of the child: 'Whoever visits a well kept school is struck by the discipline of the children. There are forty little beings from three to seven years old, each one intent on his own work; one is going through one of the exercises for the senses, one is doing an arithmetical

[1] P. 356.   [2] P. 371.   [3] P. 80.

exercise, one is handling the letters, one is drawing, one is fastening and unfastening the pieces of cloth on one of the wooden frames, still another is dusting. Some are seated at the tables, some on rugs on the floor.'[1] To many this scene would suggest licence, not liberty; but, as Herbart explained:[2] 'When the environment is so planned that childish activity is directed along the lines of the useful and expends itself thus, the result is the most effective form of discipline (*Regierung*).'

As instruction should be adapted to the stage of development of the pupil, Montessori advocates that the environment should likewise be so adjusted: 'Give the child an environment in which everything is constituted in proportion to himself and let him live therein. Then there will develop within the child that "active life" which has caused so many to marvel because they see in it not only a simple exercise performed with pleasure but also the revelation of a spiritual life.'[3] Such an environment not only makes the liberty of the child possible but it is also necessary 'that the environment should contain the means of auto-education'.[4] 'He who speaks of liberty in the schools, ought at the same time to exhibit objects — approximating to a scientific apparatus which will make such liberty possible.'[5]

Passing from a consideration of the principles to the practices of the method, we find that they fall into three classes: (*i*) the exercises of practical life; (*ii*) the exercises in sensory training; and (*iii*) the didactic exercises.

The main task in the training of feeble-minded children is to teach them to take care of themselves. This is likewise the first phase in the training given in the House of Childhood. It is a training in liberty; for freedom, according to Montessori, does not consist in having others

[1] P. 346.   [2] *Allgemeine Pädagogik*, Bk I, ch. 1, § 2.
[3] *The Advanced Montessori Method*, vol. i, pp. 19–20.
[4] Ibid., vol. i, p. 72.   [5] Ibid.

at one's command to perform the ordinary services, but in being able to do these for oneself, in being independent of others. Thus in the House of Childhood the pupils learn how to wash their hands, using little wash-stands with small pitchers and basins, how to clean their nails, brush their teeth and so on. Exercises are also arranged to train the child in the movements necessary in dressing and undressing. The apparatus for these exercises consists of wooden frames, mounted with two pieces of cloth or leather, which are fastened by means of buttons and buttonholes, hooks and eyes, eyelets and lacings or automatic fasteners. After some practice in fastening and unloosening the pieces of cloth with the various types of fasteners, the child finds that he has acquired a dexterity which enables him to dress and undress himself; and, not content with the satisfaction derived from such independence, his consciousness of the possession of a new power excites in him a desire to assist in dressing the whole family.[1] All the furniture in the House of Childhood, tables, chairs, etc. — for there are no fixed desks — are of such a size and construction that the pupils can handle them easily; they learn to move them deftly and without noise, and are thus afforded a training in motor adjustment.

Montessori has also devised certain formal gymnastic exercises to develop in the child coordinated movements. She disapproves of the child practising the ordinary gymnastic exercises arranged for the adult. 'We are wrong', she maintains,[2] 'if we consider little children from their physical point of view as little men. They have, instead, characteristics and proportions that are entirely special to their age.' A new set of exercises must consequently be devised, and, in accordance with the general Montessori principles, this has been accomplished

[1] Josephine Tozier, *An Educational Wonder-Worker: the Methods of Maria Montessori* (New York: The House of Childhood Inc., 1912).
[2] Pp. 139–40.

by observing the spontaneous movements of the child. One piece of apparatus, namely, the little round stair, may be instanced.[1] A wooden spiral stairway enclosed on one side by a balustrade on which the children can rest their hands, the other side being left open, enables the children to habituate themselves to ascending and descending stairs without holding on, and teaches them to move up and down with movements that are poised and self-controlled. The steps are very low and shallow, and the children can thereby learn movements which they cannot execute properly in climbing ordinary stairways in their homes, in which the proportions are suited to adults. The general result of the new exercises is to give the pupils of the House of Childhood a gracefulness of carriage which distinguishes them from other children.

For the methods and the apparatus of her scheme of sensory training Montessori was largely indebted to the apparatus and tests employed by the experimental psychologist.[2] The standpoints of experimental psychology and of sensory training are nevertheless different. Experimental psychology measures the sensory capacities; it does not attempt to improve these, whereas Montessori is not interested in measuring the capacities but in furthering their development. In the application of tests by psychologists, especially when the investigation extends over a long period, practice-effects frequently disclose themselves. These practice-effects are to the psychologist disturbing factors which he must estimate and eliminate, but it is just these practice-effects that sensory education strives to secure.[3]

[1] Cf. p. 143.

[2] Cf. *The Advanced Montessori Method*, vol. i, p. 44. 'The technique of our lessons is governed by experimental psychology.'

[3] Ibid., vol. i, p. 73. 'This does not penetrate into the ancient ambit of pedagogy as a science that *measures* the personality, as the experimental psychology introduced into schools has hitherto done, but as a science that *transforms* the personality.'

K 2

The psychological techniques for determining sensory acuity and sensory discrimination had been applied by Montessori in training the feeble-minded. In applying them to normal children she found that they required modification. With deficient children the exercises had to be restricted to stimuli which were strongly contrasted; normal children can, however, proceed to finely graded series. Normal children manifest great pleasure in repeating exercises which they have successfully accomplished; deficient children when they succeed once are satisfied, and show no inclination to repeat the task. The deficient child when he makes mistakes has to be corrected; the normal child prefers to correct his own mistakes. The differences are summed up by Montessori in the statement that the didactic material which, used with deficients, makes education possible, used with normal children, provokes auto-education.[1]

'To make the process one of self-education,' Montessori explains in *The Advanced Montessori Method*,[2] 'it is not enough that the stimulus should call forth activity, it must also direct it. The child should not only persist for a long time in an exercise; he must persist without making mistakes. All the physical or intrinsic qualities of the objects should be determined, not only by the immediate reaction of attention they provoke in the child, but also by their possession of this fundamental characteristic, the control of error, that is to say, the power of evoking the effective collaboration of the highest activities (comparison, judgment).'

In sensory training Montessori, like Rousseau, believes in isolating the senses whenever that is possible. This procedure, it will readily be inferred, is suggested by the education of physically deficient children. Blind people, it is popularly assumed, acquire a very fine discriminative ability in the sphere of touch. We are not surprised then

[1] P. 169.   [2] Vol. i, p. 75.

to find that in the training of their tactual sense, the pupils of the Montessori schools are blindfolded, a feature of the training which seems to add zest to their efforts. The auditory exercises are given in an environment not only of silence, but even of darkness.

The material used in the sensory training recalls the apparatus of the psychological laboratory. For perception of size, series of wooden cylinders varying in height only, in diameter only or in both dimensions at once, are employed, likewise blocks varying regularly in size, and rods of regularly graded lengths; for perception of form, geometrical insets in metal, in wood or the shapes of the insets drawn on paper; for discrimination in weight, tablets of wood similar in size but differing in weight; for touch, a highly polished surface and a sandpaper surface; for sense of temperature, small metal bowls with caps; for auditory acuity, cylindrical sound boxes containing different substances; for the colour sense, graded series of coloured wools.

The procedure adopted may be illustrated from the method followed in the training in colour discrimination. Montessori accepts from Séguin the division of the lesson into three stages or steps: (i) the association of the sensory percept with the name. For example, the child is shown two colours, red and blue. When the red is presented, the teacher says simply, 'This is red'; when the blue, 'This is blue'. (ii) The second period or step involves recognition of the object when the name is given. Thus the teacher says to the child, 'Give me the red', 'Give me the blue'. (iii) The third step involves recalling the name corresponding with the object. Thus the child is asked, the object being shown, 'What is this?' and he responds, 'Red' or 'Blue'. Recall, as ordinary experience abundantly exemplifies, is more difficult than recognition.

This procedure follows the methods employed for testing

the colour-vision of children; but, as indicated above, instead of using the techniques for testing, Montessori employs them for training the sensory activities of her pupils.

Similar methods are adopted in developing the child's tactual acuity, and in training him to discriminate differences in temperature and in weight. In these exercises the child is blindfolded or is enjoined to keep his eyes closed during the tests; he is encouraged to do so by being told that he will thus be able to feel the differences better.

To the three periods or steps in a lesson recommended by Séguin, Montessori has in certain sensory modalities added a preparatory series of exercises which represents the real sense education or auto-education, and by which the pupil acquires an extraordinary ability in differentiating finely graded stimuli. For the colour sense these exercises require the sorting and grading of sixty-four cards of various coloured wools, and are preparatory to the naming step or period in the lessons on sense training.

The exercises which are directed to the development of form play such an important part in the Montessori system as to entitle them to separate treatment. The first exercise is to sort into heaps bricks and cubes such as are employed by Froebel. Young children come to recognise the forms of these merely by grasping them; they do not require to trace the contour. This exercise may be varied by the use of different materials, as for example, by the use of coins, and so expert do the children become that they can distinguish between small forms which differ but little from one another, such as corn, wheat and rice.[1]

The real training in the perception of form begins, however, when the child passes to the exercises of placing wooden shapes in spaces made to receive them, or in superimposing such shapes on outlines of similar form.

[1] P. 190.

Geometric insets of various designs, the initial ones strongly contrasted, the later ones merely dissimilar forms of the same figure, as for example, the triangle, are mixed up and have to be sorted out by the children and fitted into the frames made to receive them. The frames furnish the control necessary to test the accuracy of the work. Ordinary solids, for example, cubes, spheres, prisms, are not employed as is usually the case in the teaching of form, but, instead, insets representing solid objects with one of the dimensions greatly reduced and with the two dimensions determining the form of the plane surface made most evident; they differ in this respect from the Froebelian gifts, the reason being that the choice of material in the Montessori method is determined purely from the pedagogical standpoint, and that the objects most commonly met with in practical life, table tops, doors, window frames, etc., are of this form.

In learning to fit the geometric insets into the spaces provided for them the child employs not only the visual sense but also the tactual and muscular senses; he is taught to run the index finger of the right hand round the contour of the form and to repeat this with the contour of the frame into which the inset fits. It is frequently observed that children who cannot recognise a shape by looking at it, do so by touching it. The association of the muscular-tactual sense with that of vision, Montessori maintains, 'aids in a most remarkable way the perception of the forms and fixes them in memory'.

From the exercises with the solid insets in which the control is absolute, the child passes to exercises in the purely visual perception of form. The wooden insets have to be superimposed on figures cut out of blue paper and mounted on cards. In a further series of exercises the figures are represented by an outline of blue paper, which for the child represents the path which he has so often followed with his finger. Finally, he is required to superimpose the wooden pieces on figures whose outlines are represented merely by a line. He thus passes from the concrete to what is relatively abstract, from solid objects to plane figures represented merely by lines and perceived only visually.

Through such exercises the forms of the various figures, circles, ellipses, triangles, rectangles, etc., come to be known, and when the need for them becomes urgent the names of the figures are given. As no analysis of the forms is undertaken, no mention made of sides and angles, it may legitimately be contended that at this stage the teaching of geometry is not being attempted.[1]

The methods adopted in training the perception of form, involving as they do the extensive employment of tactual and motor imagery, prepare the way for the teaching of writing and other didactic processes. Before considering the didactic exercises it may be opportune to estimate the value of sensory training in the education of the child. Montessori maintains that if we multiply the sensations and develop the capacity of appreciating fine differences in stimuli we refine the sensibility and multiply man's pleasures.[2] Such a claim would be difficult to substantiate. To the practical exercises in the Montessori system no objection can be taken, for in addition to affording sensory training they are of direct value in enabling the child to meet the social situations which arise in everyday life. Nor can objection be urged against such exercises in sensory training as subserve the didactic processes of writing, etc.; but one may question the value of a specific training of the sensory powers for their own sake. While lack of certain forms of sensory training may prejudicially affect an individual's advancement in specific occupations and professions, high intellectual attainments may be compatible with serious sensory

[1] P. 236. For the teaching of geometry see *The Montessori Method*, p. 243; also *The Advanced Montessori Method*, vol. ii, pt iv.   [2] P. 221.

deficiency, as the well-known case of Helen Keller illustrates. It is also doubtful whether the results of a sensory training in a specific sphere can be transferred even to other sensory spheres; the assumption that they do transfer involves the doctrine of formal training or transfer of training. It has likewise to be added that the development of certain senses might not be socially advantageous; and in this connection we need only instance the sense of smell which Montessori significantly ignores. What Montessori designates sensory training should have been termed perceptual training, involving as it does judgment and comparison. This would have obviated some of the criticisms levelled against the early versions of the system.

It was by the success attending the application of the didactic processes of writing, reading and numbers, that popular interest was aroused in the Montessori method; but at the inception of the system it was not intended that such exercises should be included, and the results were incidental.

In the Montessori system the teaching of writing precedes the teaching of reading. Montessori maintains[1] that in normal children the muscular sense is most easily developed in infancy, and this makes the acquisition of writing exceedingly easy for children. It is not so with reading, which requires a much longer course of instruction and which calls for a higher level of intellectual development, since it treats of the interpretation of signs, and of the modulation of the voice in the accentuation of syllables, in order that the word may be understood. The former is a purely mental task; whereas in writing to dictation the child translates sounds into material signs and performs certain movements, the latter process being easy and usually affording pleasure to the child.

To her predecessors Montessori owes little in regard to the teaching of writing except by way of warning. The

[1] Pp. 226–7.

apparatus used by Séguin with deficient children was found inconvenient, and of his method Montessori remarks : 'We have Séguin teaching geometry in order to teach a child to write.'[1]

In accordance with her general principle Montessori adopts in respect to writing what we have termed the psychological standpoint. 'Let us observe an individual who is writing and let us seek to analyse the acts he performs', she proposes; and again : 'It goes without saying that we should examine the individual who writes, not the writing; the subject, not the object.'

The procedure followed in the teaching of writing emerged from the experience of teaching a feeble-minded girl to sew. Montessori discovered that weaving kindergarten mats enabled this child to acquire such control over the movements of the hand that she could execute sewing which she had previously been unable to perform. The general principle which she deduced from this was that 'preparatory movements could be carried on, and reduced to a mechanism, by means of repeated exercises, not in the work itself, but in that which prepares for it. Pupils could then come to the real work, able to perform it without ever having directly set their hands to it before.'[2]

Writing, according to the Montessori view, is not a mere copying of headlines, but significant writing, the writing of words which express ideas. In writing are involved two diverse types of movement, the movement by which the forms of letters are reproduced and that by which the instrument of writing is manipulated; in addition to these movements there is also necessary for the writing of words to dictation the phonetic analysis of spoken words into their elementary sounds. Preparatory exercises for each of these elements must, in accordance with the general principle enunciated above, be devised

[1] P. 256.   [2] P. 261.

and practised independently before writing is actually commenced.

As the children had already learned to know the forms of the geometric insets by running their fingers round the contours, so, to teach the forms of the letters, it occurred to Montessori to get the pupils to trace with the finger the shapes of the letters cut out in sandpaper and pasted on cards, the roughness of the sandpaper providing a control for the accuracy of the movements. The children, indeed, as soon as they have acquired facility in this tracing of the forms of the letters, take great pleasure in repeating the movement with closed eyes. Thus the forms of the letter are not learned and impressed on the minds of the pupils by visual analysis and retained by visual imagery, but by tactual and motor experiences and grapho-motor imagery.

The phonetic sounds of the letters are taught at the same time as the tracing of the forms, the steps in the lesson following the three-stage procedure already illustrated. The audio-motor imagery helps to reinforce the grapho-motor and to facilitate the retention of the forms of the letters. The children are also practised in analysing the spoken word into its sounds and in reconstructing the word with sandpaper letters. The way is thus prepared for reading.

The control of the pen is also attacked indirectly. Recourse is had for this training to the geometric insets, of which mention has already been made. Taking one of the metal frames into which the inset fits, the child draws on a sheet of paper with a coloured crayon around the contour of the empty frame. Within the figure which results he places the metal inset, and with a crayon of a different colour traces the outline of the inset. Thus are reproduced in different colours upon the paper the two figures. With another crayon of his own selection, held as the pen is held in writing, the pupil fills in the figures which he has outlined. In making the upward and downward strokes he is taught not to pass outside the contour. Variety is lent to the task by the choice of different coloured crayons and by the use of different insets, the employment of the latter also training him to make upward and downward strokes of various lengths. Gradually the lines tend less and less to go outside the enclosing boundary until at last they are perfectly contained within it, and both the centre and the frame are filled in with close and uniform strokes. The child is now master of the writing instrument; the muscular mechanism necessary to its manipulation is established.

The moment arrives when the partial processes are perfected, when the three prerequisites to writing are at the pupil's command, that is, when he has acquired control of the writing instrument, when he can reproduce the forms of the letters moving his fingers in the air, and when the composition of words out of the isolated sounds of letters can be effected mentally. At this point the imitative tendency in the child arouses in him the impulse to write, and a pupil who has given no previous indication of having developed ability in this direction begins straightway to write. The spontaneous emergence of this writing activity is recorded by the directress much after the fashion that the appearance of the first snowdrop or primrose would be recorded by a botanist. The children, not perceiving the connection between the preparation and the combined achievement, are possessed by the delusion that, having now grown to the proper size, they know how to write.[1]

In her first efforts Montessori brought several of her pupils at the same time to the completion of the preparatory training; thereupon what might be termed a pedagogical Pentecost possessed the school. The scene is thus described by Montessori :[2] 'One beautiful December day when the sun shone and the air was like spring, I

1 P. 288.   2 Pp. 287–8, 289.

went up to the roof with the children. They were playing freely about, and a number of them were gathered about me. I was sitting near a chimney, and said to a little five-year-old boy who sat beside me, "Draw me a picture of this chimney," giving him as I spoke a piece of chalk. He got down obediently and made a rough sketch of the chimney on the tiles which formed the floor of this roof terrace. As is my custom, with little children, I encouraged him, praising his work. The child looked at me, smiled, remained for a moment as if on the point of bursting into some joyous act and then cried out, "I can write! I can write!" and kneeling down again he wrote on the pavement the word "hand". Then full of enthusiasm he wrote also "chimney", "roof". As he wrote he continued to cry out, "I can write! I know how to write!" His cries of joy brought the other children, who formed a circle about him, looking down at his work in stupefied amazement. Two or three of them said to me, trembling with excitement, "Give me the chalk. I can write too." And indeed they began to write various words: mama, hand, John, chimney, Ada . . .

'After the first word, the children, with a species of frenzied joy, continued to write everywhere. . . . In these first days we walked upon a carpet of written signs. Daily accounts showed us that the same thing was going on at home, and some of the mothers, in order to save their pavements, and even the crusts of their loaves upon which they found words written, made their children presents of paper and pencil. One of these children brought to me one day a little note-book entirely filled with writing, and the mother told me that the child had written all day long and all evening, and had gone to sleep in his bed with the paper and pencil in his hand.'

Montessori reports[1] that the average time that elapses between the first trial of the preparatory exercises and the

[1] P. 294.

first written word is, for children of four years, from a month to a month and a half. With children of five years the period is much shorter, being about a month. The pupils are generally expert after three months.

The teaching of reading is prepared for in the Montessori system by the procedure adopted in the teaching of writing. Included in the exercises preparatory to writing is word-building with sandpaper script characters representing the sound of the spoken word. Reading demands the inverse process, that is, the reproduction of the sounds from the symbols and the fusion of these sounds into words. There is also necessary for the correct enunciation of the word the proper accentuation of the syllables, and this comes only with recognition of the meaning. Montessori consequently refuses to give the name 'reading' to anything less than this. Just as, in her system, writing is something more than mere copying pot-hooks and head-lines, so reading is not a mere 'barking at print' but the recognition of the meanings represented by the visual characters. 'What I understand by reading,' she says, 'is the interpretation of an idea from the written signs'; and again : 'Until the child reads a transmission of ideas from the written words he does not read.'[1]

The didactic material for the lessons in reading consists of slips of paper or of cards upon which are written in clear large script, words and phrases.

The lessons begin with the reading of names of objects which are known or which are present. There is no question of restricting the selection of words to those that are easy, for the child already knows how to read the sounds which compose any word. The procedure is as follows : The child is given a card on which a name is written in script. He translates the writing slowly into sounds, and if the interpretation is exact the directress restricts herself to saying 'Faster'. The child reads more

[1] P. 296. Cf. *The Advanced Montessori Method*, vol. ii, ch. xv.

quickly the second time, but still often without understanding. The teacher repeats, 'Faster, faster'. The child reads 'faster' each time, repeating the same concatenation of sounds; finally the word emerges in consciousness. When the child has pronounced the word, he places the card under the object whose name it bears, and the exercise is finished. It is a lesson which proceeds very rapidly since it is only presented to a child who is already prepared through writing.[1]

Sentences describing actions or expressing commands are likewise written on slips of paper, and the children select these and carry out the requests contained in them. It is to be noted that the child does not read the sentences aloud.[2] The aim of reading is to teach the child to discover ideas in symbols, hence the reading should be silent and not vocal. 'Reading aloud,' according to the Montessori analysis, 'implies the exercise of two mechanical forms of language — articulate and graphic — and is a complex task. The child, therefore, who begins to read by interpreting thought should read mentally.' 'Truly,' claims Montessori,[3] 'we have buried the tedious and stupid A B C primer side by side with the useless copybooks!'

The success of this method of teaching reading may be judged from the following incident related by Montessori,[4] which also indicates that the system was in its application in Italy not confined to the children of the poor. 'A four-year-old boy, educated in a private house, surprised us in the following way. The child's father was a Deputy, and received many letters. He knew that his son had for two months been taught by means of exercises apt to facilitate the learning of reading and writing, but he had paid slight attention to it, and, indeed, put little faith in the method.

---

[1] The child passes from the reading of script to the reading of print without guidance (*The Montessori Method*, p. 301), a point which has been noted by other experimenters in the teaching of reading.

[2] P. 301.   [3] P. 298.   [4] Pp. 301–2.

One day, as he sat reading, with the boy playing near, a servant entered, and placed upon the table a large number of letters that had just arrived. The little boy turned his attention to these, and holding up each letter read aloud the address. To his father this seemed a veritable miracle.'

As to the average time required for learning to read, it appears that the period intervening between the commencement of the writing process and the appearance of the ability to read is about a fortnight. Facility in reading is, however, arrived at much more slowly than in writing. Normal children trained according to the Montessori method begin to write at four years of age and at five know how to read.

The Italians start these processes with an undoubted advantage as their language is practically phonetic. The irregular system of representation of the English language handicaps teachers who seek to apply the method in English-speaking countries ; nevertheless 'individual English children who have been taught by the Montessori system have learned to read and write as rapidly as the Italian children in the Montessori schools.'[1] Tozier tells of a little boy, aged only three and a half years, who, without realising that he had done anything more than play, could read and write both in English and in Italian.[2]

Montessori's treatment of the teaching of number has not received the same general approval as her method of teaching writing and reading. This is, however, not surprising, for teachers have generally assumed that the concept of number in the child's mind originates in counting, whereas the Montessori procedure is based on a comparison of lengths, and is a long way on the road to the structural arithmetic proposed by Stern.[3]

---

[1] E. Holmes, *The Montessori System of Education*, p. 16.

[2] J. Tozier, *An Educational Wonder-Worker*, p. 13.

[3] Catherine Stern, *Children Discover Arithmetic: An Introduction to Structural Arithmetic* (New York : Harper & Brothers, 1949).

That the Montessori exercises are not inconsistent with the Gestalt

The device of which greatest use is made in the teaching of number in the Montessori system is the 'long stair', a set of ten rods, the first being one metre in length, the last one decimetre, the intermediate rods diminishing in length by decimetres. The rods are divided into decimetre parts, the spaces on the rods being painted alternately red and blue. When arranged in order they form what is called the 'long stair'. They are utilised in the sensory exercises for training the children in discrimination of length. In these exercises the rods are mixed up, and the teacher grades them in order of length, calling the child's attention to the fact that the stair thus constructed is uniform in colour at one end. The child is then permitted to build it for himself.

After the child has had practice in arranging the rods in order of length he is required to count the red and the blue divisions, beginning with the shortest rod, thus : one ; one, two ; one, two, three ; always going back to one in the counting of each rod and starting from the same end. He is then required to name the various rods from the shortest to the longest, according to the total number of divisions each contains, at the same time touching the rods on the side on which 'the stair' ascends. The rods may then be called 'piece number one', 'piece number two', and so on, and finally they may be spoken of in the lessons as one, two, three.

The graphic signs for the numbers are cut in sand-paper, and by the three-period lesson arrangement previously illustrated the pupil is taught to associate the names of the numbers with their graphic forms. The graphic signs are then related to the quantity represented.

Addition may then be attacked, and is taught by suggesting to the child to put the shorter rods together in such a way as to form tens ; 1 is added to 9, 2 to 8 and so on.

psychology has been shown by the writer in his *History of Infant Education* (University of London Press, 1933), pp. 78–80.

Subtraction, multiplication and division can also be introduced by means of the same didactic material, and later on the child is allowed to express graphically his operations with the rods.

The means and methods of dealing with the larger denominations of number and the higher arithmetical processes are dealt with in *The Advanced Montessori Method*,[1] as is also the teaching of drawing, music, grammar and prosody.

The system was originally criticised for its neglect of literary training and the training of the imagination. Unfortunately the critics identified these two imputed defects. In defence of Montessori, or in explanation, it may be said that she accepts the recapitulation principle in education : 'The child follows the natural way of development of the human race. In short, such education makes the evolution of the individual harmonise with that of humanity.'[2] To one who accepts this doctrine it would be open to contend that just as in the early development of mankind practical activities must have figured more largely than the literary, so the early education of the child should be more realistic than humanistic. In *The Advanced Montessori Method*,[3] however, Montessori rejects the recapitulation principle dismissing it as 'a materialistic idea now discredited'.

While Montessori is probably in error in regarding imagination as a substitute for the real and not an independent line of activity related to the real as play is to work, those who would employ fairy tales to train the imagination are in deeper error ; for not only does their position imply the faculty psychology and the doctrine of formal discipline, but the training which they desiderate is of the free or uncontrolled imagination, whereas the imagination that is of value is of the controlled and constructive

---

[1] *The Advanced Montessori Method*, Pt III.
[2] P. 160.   [3] Vol. i, p. 255.

type — the creative imagination of science[1] and of art based on truth.[2] The proper defence of fairy tales is that they form part of the literary heritage of a people and as such ought to be known.[3]

The Montessori method necessitates the employment of teachers who are possessed of a training in child-psychology and in its application to young children. On this Montessori repeatedly insists: 'The broader the teacher's scientific culture and practice in experimental psychology, the sooner will come for her the marvel of unfolding life, and her interest in it.'[4] 'The more fully the teacher is acquainted with the methods of experimental psychology, the better will she understand how to give a lesson.'[5] The training of the teacher should enable her to know when to intervene in the child's activities, and, what is more important, when to refrain from intervening. 'In the manner of this intervention lies the personal art of the educator.'[6]

As the function of the teacher in the Montessori system is different from that of the teacher in the ordinary school system, being confined mainly to observing the mental development and to directing the psychic activity of the child, Montessori has substituted for the title 'teacher' the term 'directress'; 'instead of facility of speech she has to acquire the power of silence; instead of teaching she has to observe; instead of the proud dignity of one who claims to be infallible she assumes the vesture of humility.'[7]

[1] Cf. Herbart, *Textbook of Psychology*, p. 73 — 'Quite as much imagination belongs to original scientific thinking as to poetic creation, and it is very doubtful whether Newton or Shakespeare possessed the more imagination.'

[2] Vol. i, pp. 241–55. See also whole ch. ix.

[3] In *The Advanced Montessori Method*, vol. ii, p. 191, the readings used are said to be numerous and of great variety, and include: 'fairy tales, short stories, anecdotes, novels, historical episodes.' For the child's preference for facts over fiction see, however, vol. ii, p. 195.

[4] P. 89.   [5] P. 107.   [6] P. 176. Cf. p. 224.

[7] *The Advanced Montessori Method*, vol. i, p. 128. See same work, vol. i, 'The Preparation of the Teacher'.

Montessori would probably have rested her fame on the introduction into early education of the special devices for sensory training. The significance of these she may have overrated. The permanent elements of her method are more likely to be the practical activities and the exercises subsidiary to the didactic processes. But the most significant feature of the system is the individualisation of instruction. Although this is characteristic of most recent advances in educational practice, Sir John Adams[1] considered himself justified in attributing to Montessori the credit of sounding the knell of class teaching.

[1] *Modern Developments in Educational Practice* (University of London Press, 1922), ch. vi.

CHAPTER XIII

DEWEY[1]

WE have to return to Pestalozzi to find an educationist who so dominated the educational stage as John Dewey did throughout the first half of the twentieth century, and he played this part by virtue of the fact that in him were concentrated in a special degree the progressive tendencies of his age and country. Writing of the democratic way of life and the significance in it of intelligence, Dewey explained that he did not invent this faith but acquired it from his surroundings, and the same explanation might be offered for the other features of his philosophic and educational outlook.

Dewey was a great educationist because he was a great philosopher; no one since the sophists has so intimately identified philosophy and education as Dewey has done. In fact, he himself declared that the most penetrating definition of philosophy which can be given is that it is the theory of education in its most general phases.[2] His philosophy, as might be expected of one who forthright rejected any situation, and condemned any institution, that was static, underwent constant revision. He was fully conscious of this trait and confesses :[3] 'I seem to be

[1] 1859–1952. A biography of John Dewey edited by his daughter is prefixed to *The Philosophy of John Dewey*, edited by Paul Arthur Schlipp, being vol. i of The Library of Living Philosophers (Evanston and Chicago : Northwestern University, 1939). *John Dewey: Master Educator*, edited by W. W. Brickman and S. Lehrer (New York : Society for the Advancement of Education, 1959).

[2] *Democracy and Education* (New York : The Macmillan Co., 1916), p. 386.

[3] *Contemporary American Philosophy*, vol. ii, edited by C. P. Adams and W. P. Montague (London : George Allen & Unwin Ltd. New York : The Macmillan Co., 1930). John Dewey — 'From Absolutism to Experimentalism', p. 22.

unstable, chameleon-like, yielding one after another to many diverse and even incompatible influences; struggling to assimilate something from each and yet striving to carry it forward in a way that is logically consistent with what has been learned from its predecessors.'

At the outset of his career, under the influence of his teacher of philosophy and later colleague at Michigan University, Professor George S. Morris, Dewey accepted the Hegelian standpoint in philosophy.[1] With the introduction, however, of the Darwinian conception of evolution — in the very year Dewey was born, idealists were faced with the alternative of replacing the Hegelian dialectic by the evolutionary view of development or of abandoning idealism completely. British Hegelians to whom Dewey admitted he owed much, adopted the former alternative maintaining resolutely the supremacy of spirit as the essential feature of idealism. Dewey on the other hand gradually abandoned idealism in favour of Darwinian naturalism with the concepts of adaptation and the struggle for existence; the tail started to wag the dog. At this stage Dewey was inclined to designate his philosophic position 'experimental idealism'.[2]

Hegelianism nevertheless left 'a permanent deposit' in Dewey's thinking. Hegel's synthesis of opposites — of subject and object, spirit and matter, the divine and the human — had a special attraction for him, and throughout his later writings we find him constantly contesting all dualisms.

Dewey was next to fall under the influence of William James (1842–1910) and pragmatism.[3] While pragmatism has always been the popular philosophy of the common

[1] Cf. Morton G. White, *The Origin of Dewey's Instrumentalism* (New York: Columbia University Press, 1943).

[2] In *The Study of Ethics: A Syllabus* (1894). See White, p. 83, also p. 111.

[3] Cf. *Contemporary American Philosophy*, vol. ii, p. 22: 'Upon the whole, the forces that have influenced me have come from persons and from situations more than from books.'

man in England, it became a recognised doctrine in
American schools of philosophy. It was initiated by
C. S. Peirce (1839–1914) as a logical method whereby
from its practical effects we could ascertain the meaning
of an abstract conception, but it was generalised and
popularised by William James in the form that the test of
the truth of an idea is to be found in the consequences of
the acts to which the idea leads.[1]   It was not so much
the pragmatic strain in James's philosophy that attracted
Dewey as the return to the biological conception of the
psyche which he discerned in James's psychology; that he
found most stimulating — 'the most distinctive factors in
his [James's] general philosophic view, pluralism, novelty,
freedom, individuality, are all connected with his feeling
for the qualities and traits of that which lives.   Many
philosophers have had much to say about the idea of
organism; but they have taken it structurally and hence
statically.   It was reserved for James to think of life in
terms of action.'[2]

In any activity which is in process of evolution we can
define the end only in terms of the means and account
for the means only by reference to the end.   Dewey not
content with recognising the relativity of ends to means,
subordinated the ends to the means, and even abolished
the distinction between them.   The end, for him, was
merely a series of acts viewed at a remote stage, and the
means are merely the series viewed at an earlier one; the
end is a name for a series of acts taken collectively, means
a name for the same series taken distributively.[3]   The
result of thus disposing of ends is to render life meaningless; an aimless life is accordingly something to be com-

[1] Cf. W. B. Gallie, *Peirce and Pragmatism* (Penguin Books, 1952). James
K. Feibleman, *An Introduction to Peirce's Philosophy* (London: George Allen
& Unwin, 1960).

[2] *Contemporary American Philosophy*, vol. ii, p. 24.

[3] *Human Nature and Conduct* (London: George Allen & Unwin Ltd.,
1922), pp. 34, 36.

mended rather than condemned; education, as it only too often unfortunately is, becomes an endless round — activity for activity's sake, like the cat chasing its own tail, and the whole process tends ultimately to disintegrate. Human ends are rather projections in imagination of a better state than the present; they determine the selection and organisation of the means and economise effort; they control the whole process. It is just the presence of this imaginative foresight in man, his capacity to create ideal ends that distinguishes human action and conduct from the behaviour of animals, unawareness of the end or outcome of the process being characteristic of instinctive activity. But Dewey, although he does not, as many naturalists do, revert in philosophy to instinct as the ultimate principle of explanation of man's behaviour, nevertheless insists on the continuity of animal and human life; the same principles of explanation are common to both; he recognises no difference between the protozoon and the creature who has been made a little lower than the angels; he refuses to acknowledge another dimension of experience in man than that assigned to animals; culture, art, morality and religion are all explicable on biological principles; there exists for him no 'realm of ends'. Everything is provisional; nothing ultimate. Knowledge is always a means, never an end in itself; it is purely instrumental, hence the title of Dewey's philosophy — Instrumentalism.[1]

An organism so long as it lives is subject to change and even after death to disintegration. Change accordingly becomes one of Dewey's most fruitful categories. In

[1] Cf. *The Quest for Certainty* (New York: Minton, Balch & Co., 1929), p. 295: 'It [knowing] marks a transitional redirection and rearrangement of the real. It is intermediate and instrumental.' And p. 298: 'Knowledge is instrumental. But the purport of our whole discussion has been in praise of tools, instrumentalities, means, putting them on a level equal in value to ends and consequences, since without them, the latter are merely accidental, sporadic and unstable.'

pre-Socratic days Heraclitus propounded the doctrine of
the flux of things; matter was unceasingly undergoing
transmutation; all life was involved in continual decom-
position and renewal.[1] In protest Socrates sought in the
definition something stable which would render discussion
possible, and Plato found in the 'idea' the permanent
element that made things what they are.

For Dewey there are no fixed beliefs; the quest for
certainty on which philosophers and men of science have
been engaged ever since the time of Socrates is an illusion
diverting man's attention and abilities from the possible
and practical realities within his comprehension — it is
dismissed as a 'compensatory perversion'.[2] Idealism, on
the other hand, contends that spiritual values are in-
destructible. It acknowledges 'the eternal realities which
do not change and the beauties that do not fade'.[3] The
great achievements of history are credited to men who
have faith in some fundamental principle. It is of such
Fichte wrote :[4] 'These men, and all others of like mind in
the history of the world won the victory because eternity
inspired them, and this inspiration always does, and
always must, defeat him who is not so inspired.' Mankind too in its long history down the ages has here and
there succeeded in hitting the right trail. There are
spheres in which the procedures that man has adopted
are never likely to be abandoned; although the methods
may be modified and expanded, the pursuit will continue
in the same direction; we do not anticipate change out of
all recognition. A. N. Whitehead in *The Aims of Education* declares[5] that the process [of science] is a search for

[1] Cf. T. Gomperz, *Greek Thinkers*, English translation, vol. i, ch. 1
(London : John Murray, 1901).
[2] *The Quest for Certainty*, p. 229.
[3] R. H. S. Crossman, *Plato To-day* (London : George Allen & Unwin
Ltd, 1937), p. 225.
[4] *Addresses to the German Nation*, English translation, p. 122.
[5] P. 228.

permanence, uniformity and simplicity of logical relation. In *Science and the Modern World* he elaborates :[1] Apart from recurrences, knowledge would be impossible, for nothing could be referred to our past experience. Also apart from some regularity of recurrences measurement would be impossible. But there is a complementary fact — nothing ever recurs in exact detail. Men expected the sun to rise, but the wind bloweth where it listeth. There are thus two principles inherent in the very nature of things, the spirit of change and the spirit of conservation. There can be nothing real without both.

Dewey himself cannot remain faithful to the principle of change. In *How We Think*[2] he refers to 'securely established facts and principles', and recognises that if thinking is to be possible at all 'the standard of reference must remain the same to be of any use. The concept signifies that a meaning has been stabilized, and remains the same in different contexts.' In *Freedom and Culture*,[3] referring to Jefferson's speeches and letters Dewey explains that it is the *ends* of democracy, the rights of *man* — not of men in the plural — which are unchangeable. And his disciple W. H. Kilpatrick in spite of devoting a section to the 'Philosophy of Change' in *Education for a Changing Civilisation* concedes :[4] 'Consider chemistry. It changes, but the tested results remain reliable.'

An exclusive dependence on change would render reference to the past useless, and planning ahead futile ; one could only wait till the necessity should arise. Participation in, rather than preparation for, life became the watchword of education. It led to the incredible extravagances of some progressive schools which did not believe in teaching facts because facts are constantly

---

[1] Cambridge University Press, 1926, pp. 6, 40, 250.
[2] London : D. C. Heath & Co., 1909, pp. 95, 151.
[3] London : George Allen & Unwin Ltd, 1940, p. 157.
[4] New York : The Macmillan Co., 1926, p. 12.

changing and regarded the teaching of geography as use-less because maps alter so rapidly. It would justify the student who, to his tutor's query why he was not working for an examination, replied that he wanted to come fresh to it!

The issue of permanence or progress in education was raised by Kant in his *Lectures on Education*: 'Children', he says,[1] 'ought to be educated, not for the present, but for a possibly improved condition of man in the future.' Plato having established his ideal state would allow no innovations; his ideal was permanence. Herbert Spencer,[2] on the other hand, rejects government control as conservative and regards education as a progressive force in society. 'All institutions have an instinct of self-preservation growing out of the selfishness of those con-nected with them. Being dependent for their vitality upon the continuance of existing arrangements, they naturally uphold these. Their roots are in the past and the present, never in the future. Change threatens, modifies them, eventually destroys them; hence to change they are uniformly opposed. On the other hand, educa-tion, properly so-called, is closely associated with change — is its pioneer — is the never-sleeping agent of revolu-tion — is always fitting men for higher things, and *unfitting* them for things as they are. Therefore, between constitu-tions whose very existence depends upon man continuing what he is, and true education, which is one of the instruments for making him something other than he is, there must always be enmity.' Both permanence and progress are essential, and Dewey by his emphasis on change has challenged the mediaevalism that would shackle education to the past.

In addition to the naturalistic bias, Dewey derived

---

[1] English translation, p. 14.
[2] *Social Statics: or the Conditions essential to Human Happiness* (London: John Chapman, 1851), p. 341.

L

from James the doctrine of pragmatism but not without qualification. Dewey, in fact, accuses James of a paradoxical habit of merely turning things upside down — instead of the thought being father to the deed, the deed is father to the thought. By contrast Dewey affirms that the essence of pragmatic instrumentalism is to conceive of both knowledge and practice as means of making good — excellencies of all kinds — secure in experienced existence, and he explains :[1] 'It does not imply that action is higher and better than knowledge, and practice inherently superior to thought. Constant and effective interaction of knowledge and practice is something quite different from an exaltation of activity, for its own sake. Action when directed by knowledge, is method and means, not an end. The aim and end is the securer, freer and more widely shared embodiment of values in experience by means of that active control of objects which knowledge alone makes possible.'

Notwithstanding this disclaimer there are numerous statements throughout Dewey's writings which are scarcely, if at all, distinguishable from the pronouncements of James. Thus in *Democracy and Education*[2] dealing with the development of the experimental method he says : 'It means that we have no right to call anything knowledge except where our activity has actually produced certain physical changes in things, which agree with and confirm the conception entertained.' In *Human Nature and Conduct* he maintains[3] that the act comes before the thought, and that a motive does not exist prior to an act and produce it. In *The Quest for Certainty* he declares that the experimental procedure is one that installs doing at the heart of knowing, that the validity of the object of thought depends upon the consequences of the operations which define the object of thought ; and he repeats

---

[1] *The Quest for Certainty*, p. 37 note.
[2] P. 393.   [3] Pp. 30, 120.

— the test of ideas, of thinking generally, is found in the consequences of the acts to which the ideas lead.[1]

An objection urged against hedonism in ethics is that we cannot tell beforehand how much pleasure a given course of action will yield. So with pragmatism; we cannot tell till the deed is done what the consequences may be and whether the idea on which we acted is right. We can be wise only after the event. As Whitehead says:[2] 'If we wait for the necessities of action before we commence to arrange our ideas, in peace we shall have lost our trade, and in war we shall have lost the battle.' Dewey himself in another connection concedes[3] that the final outcome can never be foreseen: 'The point is the intervention of an indefinite number of indefinitely ramifying conditions between what a person does and the consequences of his actions, including even the consequences which return upon him. The intervals in time and space are so extensive that the larger number of factors that decide the final outcome cannot be foreseen. Even when they can be anticipated, the results are produced by factors over which the average person has hardly any more control than he has over those which produce earthquakes.'[4]

[1] *The Quest for Certainty*, pp. 36, 129, 136. Cf. p. 166: 'thought is a mode of directed overt action'; p. 167: 'knowing is itself a kind of action'; p. 207: knowing 'a form of doing'; p. 245: knowing 'an existential overt action'.

[2] *The Aims of Education*, p. 155.   [3] *Freedom and Culture*, p. 58.

[4] The fallacy of both hedonism and pragmatism was succinctly formulated in another connection by Lord Justice Donovan when, on delivering judgment in the Soblen case, he said: 'otherwise the quality of an act would be determined by its consequences, which was obviously untrue, because cause and effect were not the same thing.' — *The Times* Law Report, 31st August 1962.

John Milton, *Prose Works*, vol. i, *The Second Defence of the People of England*, p. 276. 'On the nature of success I will say a few words. Success neither proves a cause to be good, nor indicates it to be bad; and we demand that our cause should not be judged by the event, but the event by the cause.' Also, 'Whether it is lawful to rise against a tyrant', Milton (vol. ii, p. 23) answers: 'that the vulgar judge of it according to the event, and the learned according to the purpose of them that do it.'

Anticipating such a self-contradictory dogma, John Ruskin in *Unto This Last* has robustly formulated the idealist position, 'No man ever knew, or can know, what will be the ultimate result to himself, or to others, of any given line of conduct. But every man may know, and most of us do know, what is a just and unjust act. And all of us may know also, that the consequences of justice will be ultimately the best possible, both to others and ourselves, though we can neither say what is best, or how it is likely to come to pass.' If we accept Dewey's statements that the test of truth lies in the consequences to which it leads, and that we can never know what these consequences are, we are convicted of pure scepticism.

The pragmatists' exaltation of practice over theory, of experimental inquiry over speculation, of action over contemplation is historically untenable. Ideas are more powerful and lasting than actions the influence of which is limited to a particular time and place. Ideas have the capacity of perpetual self-reproduction which Plato's *Symposium* declared was the characteristic of immortality. Apart from the teaching of the great religious leaders, ideas have changed the course of the world's history; we need only instance Rousseau's *Social Contract* and the French Revolution or Karl Marx's *Das Kapital* and modern communism. Dewey's view[1] that practice inspires theory, that educational practices and direct experience in the field originate and determine educational ends and theories is contradicted by the history of education; almost all the great educators have been philosophers and have not been renowned for their skill in practical teaching — in fact, some of them take an impish delight in confessing their failure as practitioners.

Some mental activities cannot be said to have any practical consequences, for example, the pursuit of a

[1] *Sources of a Science of Education* (New York: H. Liveright, 1929), pp. 55-60.

subject for its own sake which is just its cultural value, the appreciation of a work of art or the enjoyment of a symphony. These are not instrumental; they are autotelic or, to use Dewey's term, 'consummatory'; they have intrinsic worth; they are ends in themselves. In a democratic society the individual too has to be treated as an end in himself. Dewey tries to evade this conclusion by designating certain excursions into higher mathematics as 'playing with concepts', but play itself is just another autotelic experience.

Pragmatism, laying stress on consequences, ignores or disparages motives. Thus Dewey says :[1] 'We call a biting dog ugly, but we don't look for his motive in biting. . . . It is absurd to ask what induces a man to activity generally speaking. He is an active being and that is all there is to be said on the score.' Yet courts of law in judging whether the accused committed a murder do not hesitate to consider the motive of the crime.

Tried by every practical test — its own criterion, pragmatism fails to account for the facts; as it has been said, it is not a philosophy, but a way of trying to do without philosophy. Its value in education might be expressed in the words of Francis Bacon :[2] 'But this is that which will dignify and exalt knowledge; if contemplation and action may be more nearly and straitly conjoined than they have been.'

Pragmatism is reflected in Dewey's curriculum, if in his educational philosophy we dare speak of a curriculum. In *The Dewey School*[3] the main hypothesis was that life itself, especially these occupations and associations which serve man's chief needs, should furnish the ground experience for the education of the child. Herbert Spencer in

[1] *Human Nature and Conduct*, p. 119.
[2] *Philosophical Works* (London: Routledge, 1905). *Of the Advancement of Learning*, p. 60.
[3] By K. C. Mayhew and A. C. Edwards (New York: D. Appleton – Century Co., 1936), p. vi.

Education: Intellectual, Physical and Moral,[1] answering his own question 'What knowledge is of most worth?', adopted the same principle, and anticipating by a century certain modern writers, oriented education from the scientific standpoint, claiming that a curriculum based on science would satisfy all the requirements of a liberal education.[2] He classified the activities which constitute human life in order of importance as follows: the biological, the social and political and the cultural, adding that accomplishments, the fine arts, *belles-lettres* as they occupy the leisure part of life, should be subordinate to that instruction and discipline on which civilisation rests. Modern curriculum makers would classify these activities in the order of frequency, a criterion which Dewey rightly rejects, claiming that while the principle contributes at most to the more efficient practices in some subjects, it does not give any help in larger questions of curriculum reconstruction and methods.[3]

Dewey, however, unlike Spencer and modern curriculum makers, maintains that it is impossible to classify human activities for educational purposes. We cannot establish a hierarchy of values among studies, he affirms:[4]

[1] The original article appeared in *The Westminster Review*, July and October 1859.

[2] Cf. *The Authoritarian Attempt to capture Education* (New York: King's Crown Press, 1945). 'The Arts of Liberation', Irwin Edman, p. 29. 'Science is popularly often conceived to be a palace of mechanical wonders or a chamber of mechanical horrors. But the fruits of science are spiritual and educative as well, and these are only beginning to be realised or broached in modern study and teachings. They have scarcely affected the imagination of the general educated public, or even the basic forms and assumptions of thought of scientists themselves. The very method of scientific inquiry is a moral lesson in objectivity, disinterestedness and detachment. Its careful, patient procedure is a lesson in devotion and responsibility, respect for the facts as they are found to be, and faith in the infinite resources which understanding might make of nature for human uses. There is a whole making of a whole religion in the landscape of experience as inquiry discloses it, and the prospects for mankind that that landscape suggests.'

[3] *The Sources of a Science of Education*, pp. 65–66.

[4] *Democracy and Education*, p. 281.

'It is futile to attempt to arrange them in an order beginning with one having least worth and going on to that of maximum value. In so far as any study has a unique and irreplaceable function in experience, in so far as it marks a characteristic enrichment of life, its worth is intrinsic and incomparable . . . the only ultimate value which can be set up is just the process of living itself.' This view that there are no ultimate ends to which the concrete satisfactions of experience are subordinate dispenses with a predetermined curriculum, the result being thus stated by the President of Yale University : 'To-day the young American comprehends the intellectual tradition of which he is a part and in which he must live only by accident.' 'The crucial error', he adds, 'is that of holding that nothing is any more important than anything else, that there can be no order of goods and no order in the intellectual realm.   There is nothing central and nothing peripheral, nothing primary and nothing secondary, nothing basic and nothing superficial.[1]

Dewey himself had earlier scented this danger, for in an article entitled 'How Much Freedom in the New Schools'[2] he issued the warning that it is the absence of intellectual control through significant subject-matter which stimulates the deplorable egotism, cockiness, impertinence and disregard for the rights of others apparently considered by some persons to be the inevitable accompaniment, if not the essence, of freedom, and he challenged the progressive schools to furnish a new type of subject-matter. 'And this subject-matter can be provided in a way which will obtain ordered and consecutive development of experience only by means of the thoughtful selection and organisation of material by those having the broadest experience — those who treat impulses and

[1] Quoted by Jacques Maritain in *Education at the Cross Roads* (Yale University Press, 1943), p. 55.   [2] *The New Republic*, 9th July 1930.

inchoate desires and plans as potentialities of growth and not as finalities.'

In spite of his contention that we cannot classify human activities for educational purposes Dewey does indicate an order of preference; the curriculum, he says,[1] echoing Spencer, must be planned with reference to placing essentials first and refinements second. And his answer to the questions — what are the essentials? what are men's chief needs? — is biased by his pragmatic philosophy: 'Men's fundamental common concerns center about food, shelter, clothing, household furnishings, and the appliances connected with production, exchange and consumption. Representing both the necessities of life and the adornments with which the necessities have been clothed, they tap instincts at a deep level; they are saturated with facts and principles having a social quality.' While Spencer with his insistence on pure science and individualism is typical of the nineteenth century, Dewey with his insistence on applied science and industrial arts and on the social factor is representative of the twentieth century. Both nevertheless tend to underrate the importance in man's life of the spiritual values, on which T. Percy Nunn[2] insisted in defining the essentials of life: 'Among the strains or currents in a national tradition the highest value belongs to those that are richest in the creative element. These are themselves traditions of activity, practical, intellectual, aesthetic, moral with a high degree of individuality and continuity, and they mark out the main lines in the development of the human spirit. Consider what man has made of poetry, and what poetry has made of him; what a noble world he has created out of the sounds of vibrating reeds, strings and brass; think of the expansion of soul he has gained through architecture and the arts of which it is the

[1] *Democracy and Education*, p. 223.
[2] British Association Address to Section L (Educational Science), 1923.

mother and queen; of the achievements of his thought, disciplined into the methods of mathematics, the sciences and philosophy. Do we not rightly measure the quality of a civilisation by its activities in such directions as these? and if so, must not such activities be typically represented in every education which offers the means to anything, and can properly be called fullness of life?' Dewey evidently plumps for food and furniture, Nunn for poetry and philosophy — an illustration of the age-long conflict in human thought between the materialistic and the idealistic views of life.

Not content with maintaining that consequences are the ultimate test and criterion of meaning and validity, Dewey complemented the pragmatic principle by emphasising origins, claiming that thinking arises out of practical needs, that only through action is knowledge acquired and progress made possible. He was, in fact, more interested in the means or instrumentality of attaining knowledge than in testing its validity. The method whereby this is attained is the experimental. 'That western civilisation is increasingly industrial in character is commonplace; it should be an equally familiar fact that this industrialization is the direct fruit of the growth of the experimental method of knowing.'[1] So impressed is Dewey with its efficacy that he is led to assume that it is the only method of knowing. Thus in *How We Think*[2] he maintains that from the scientific side, it is demonstrated that effective and integral thinking is possible only where the experimental method in some form is used. This contention has suggested the alternative title to his philosophy, namely, Experimentalism.

On both counts Dewey's thesis is inadequate. While necessity is the mother of invention, pure intellectual curiosity likewise stimulates the extension of knowledge.

[1] *The Quest for Certainty*, p. 79.   [2] P. 188.

Aristotle in his *Metaphysics*[1] affirmed that philosophy originated in wonder, but all that we need do to discount Dewey's assumption is to examine the instances of operational thinking cited by Dewey himself in *How We Think*.[2] Two of the three originate in theoretical curiosity not in practical needs, namely 'A Case of Reflection upon an Observation', the significance of a long white pole bearing a gilded ball at its tip which projects nearly horizontally from the upper deck of ferryboats; and the cause of bubbles appearing on the outside of the mouth of tumblers and going inside when the tumblers are washed in hot soapsuds and then placed mouth downwards on a plate. The third instance 'A Case of Practical Deliberation', namely, to decide which of several routes to take to enable him to keep an appointment does arise out of practical needs. The ratio of the theoretical to the practical is evidently not in Dewey's favour.

Not only does thinking not originate solely in practical needs, but productive thinking does not exclusively depend upon the experimental method. In the resolution of Dewey's practical perplexity regarding keeping his appointment there is no evidence of overt action or of operational thinking; it is a case of reflection involving deductive inference based on previous experience. The problem of the use of the pole on the ferryboats is a purely theoretical one, originating, as we have said, in intellectual curiosity; it, too, is solved without resort to any overt action or any form of experiment; possible explanations are canvassed in imagination — 'I then tried to imagine all possible purposes of such a pole', until a satisfactory solution is reached. The second example — the movement of the bubbles from the outside of the tumblers to the inside, approximates more closely to a scientific induction necessitating experiment, but the solution involves 'a knowledge of securely established physical facts and

[1] Bk II.   [2] Pp. 91–94.

principles',[1] the origin of which may not have been experimentally acquired.

There are, as Whitehead has said,[2] two kinds of logic — one of which, however, Dewey ignores — the logic of discovery and the logic of the discovered. 'The logic of discovery consists in the weighing of probabilities, in discarding details deemed to be irrelevant, in divining the general rules according to which events occur, and in testing hypotheses by devising suitable experiments. This is inductive logic. The logic of the discovered is the deduction of the special events which, under certain circumstances, would happen in obedience to the assumed laws of nature. Thus when the laws are discovered or assumed, their utilisation entirely depends on deductive logic. Without deductive logic science would be entirely useless. It is merely a barren game to ascend from the particular to the general, unless afterwards we can reverse the process and descend from the general to the particular, ascending and descending like the angels of Jacob's ladder. When Newton had divined the law of gravitation he at once proceeded to calculate the earth's attraction on an apple at its surface and on the moon. We may note in passing that inductive logic would be impossible without deductive logic. Thus Newton's calculations were an essential step in his inductive verification of the great law.'

The history of science does not support Dewey. Advances in the mathematical sciences have come about mainly by deduction: 'Humanity has waited centuries for the revelation of certain properties of the circle and the ellipse which we know were nevertheless implicitly contained in the definition of these curves, since we can deduce them from it by syllogisms and with the help of a small number of postulates and of axioms recognised as valid at all times. But for the circle and the ellipse we

[1] *How We Think*, p. 95.   [2] *The Aims of Education*, p. 80.

use no experiments. Of what avail could they be since it is a question of purely rational deduction.'[1] In view of the difficulty of applying experiment in astronomy Dewey shifts his position and explains[2] that the progress of inquiry is synonymous with advance in the invention and construction of physical instruments for producing, registering and measuring changes. Physics is the field where experiment has been pre-eminently successful, but even here progress is not exclusively dependent on experiment, some scientific principles having been arrived at by deductive reasoning.[3] And Whitehead adds :[4] 'The paradox is now fully established that the utmost abstractions are the true weapons with which to control our thought of concrete fact.' While in the biological sciences the scope of experiment is being considerably extended, the great change of outlook in biology in the nineteenth century — Darwin's doctrine of evolution — was not achieved by experiment but by observation and deduction. In psychology the most significant advance since the time of Aristotle — Freud's disclosure of the 'Unconscious' — was not the result of experiment but of clinical observation.[5] In the social sciences the complexity of the factors makes experiment difficult, and leads Dewey to confess :[6] 'What purports to be experiment in the social field is very different from experiment in natural science ; it is rather a process of trial and error accompanied with some degree of hope and a great deal of talk.'

Although the verdict on Dewey's appeal on behalf of experiment as the essential feature of all productive thinking is 'Not Proven', this should not detract from the

[1] E. Meyerson, *Identity and Reality*. English translation (New York, The Macmillan Co., 1930), p. 396.   [2] *The Quest for Certainty*, p. 84.

[3] Meyerson, p. 398: 'The principle of kinetic theories . . . must be attributed to a deduction.'   [4] *Science and the Modern World*, p. 41.

[5] Cf. also *Twentieth Century Psychology* (New York: The Philosophical Library, 1946). D. B. Klein, 'Psychology's Progress and the Armchair Taboo'.   [6] *Freedom and Culture*, p. 65.

credit of insisting that in the acquisition of knowledge acquaintance with the process is essential to the full understanding of the result to which it leads.[1] The virtue of the heuristic method[2] lay in this rather than in following the order of the original discoveries. The experimental method that Dewey proposes is a definitely planned procedure; it is not, as he warns his too ardent disciples,[3] 'just messing around nor doing a little of this and a little of that in the hope that things will improve'. The stages of the method are those of any logical induction — formulation of problem, suggestion of hypothesis, testing hypothesis, formulation of principle — but expressed by Dewey as follows :[4] 'They are first that the pupil have a genuine situation of experience — that there be a continuous activity in which he is interested for its own sake; secondly, that a genuine problem develop within this situation as a stimulus to thought; third, that he possess the information and make the observations needed to deal with it; fourth, that suggested solutions occur to him which he shall be responsible for in an orderly way; fifth, that he have opportunity and occasion to test his ideas by application, to make their meaning clear and to discover for himself their validity.'[5]

The two aspects of thinking — that thinking arises out of practical needs and the testing of results by their practical consequences — are combined in the project method.[6] The method is a natural corollary to his teaching, although Dewey repeatedly warns us of its

[1] Cf. *Democracy and Education*, p. 204, where claims advanced for it are: directness, open-mindedness, single-mindedness, responsibility.

[2] H. E. Armstrong, *The Teaching of Scientific Method* (New York: The Macmillan Co., 1925), 'The Heuristic Method'.

[3] *Problems of Men* (New York: The Philosophical Library, 1946), pp. 137–8.   [4] *Democracy and Education*, p. 192.

[5] Cf. Max Wertheimer, *Productive Thinking* (New York and London: Harper & Brothers, 1943), pp. 190–1.

[6] Dewey was not the originator of the term. Personal letter to present author, 9th February 1933. 'The term project was not original with me.'

limitations. Thus in *Democracy and Education* he mentions that projects may be too ambitious and beyond the pupil's capacity to accomplish : 'It is quite true that children tend to exaggerate their powers of execution, and to select projects that are beyond them' ;[1] and in *The Way Out of Educational Confusion*[2] he indicates the opposite defect that projects may be too trivial to be educative.

In view of the title of Dewey's main educational work *Democracy and Education*, we cannot conclude our review without reference to his political doctrines. He himself was brought up in 'a classless society',[3] and any form of authoritarianism was foreign to his nature. He accepted Aristotle's principle[4] that 'that which most contributes to the permanence of constitutions is the adaptation of education to the form of government', hence a democratic state should have a democratic form of education. Much has yet to be done to make education really democratic even in countries professedly democratic, and to augment these efforts fresh inspiration can be derived from Dewey's writings.

There were times nevertheless when, in the absence of absolute and universal moral standards and denied any support from historical precedents, he was inclined by reason of his faith in experimentation to sponsor any revolutionary effort no matter what the outcome, but ultimately he returned to the democratic way of life ; we had hoped also that as the deficiencies of naturalism and pragmatism declared themselves he might return to an idealism that was yet dynamic and inclusive of all that was valuable in both these schools.

In education we cannot but be grateful to Dewey for his great services in challenging the old 'static cold-storage ideal of knowledge'[5] and in bringing education

---

[1] P. 231.   [2] Harvard University Press, 1931, p. 31.
[3] See biography prefixed to Schlipp's *The Philosophy of John Dewey*.
[4] *Politics*, v, §§9, 11.   [5] *Democracy and Education*, p. 186.

more into accord with the actualities of present-day life. The general principle underlying the developments in his philosophy and his applications of these in education appears to be that both philosophy and education should reflect the main currents of contemporary thought and incorporate the techniques that have so signally contributed to modern industrial and social progress.

INDEX OF TOPICS AND TITLES

(in text only)

329

INDEX OF NAMES

(in text only)

THE END

PRINTED BY R. & R. CLARK, LTD., EDINBURGH

LIBRARY
SOUTH BEND CAMPUS
INDIANA UNIVERSITY